Role of Women in Maratha Politics

(1620-1752 A.D.)

Role of Women in Maratha Politics

(1620-1752 A.D.)

DR. (MISS) SUSHILA VAIDYA

Foreword

BABASAHEB PURANDARE

SHARADA

Sharada Publishing House

Delhi-110035

2000

First Published : 2000

ISBN : 81-85616-67-1

Published by :
B.L. Bansal
SHARADA PUBLISHING HOUSE
(Publishers on India's Past & Present)
40, Anand Nagar, Inderlok,
Delhi - 110035. Tel. : 5117390

Laser Typesetting by :
Sri Balaji Computers
4615/13, Tri Nagar, Delhi-35
Ph. : 7108270

Printed at :
Santosh Offset
Delhi-110 035

DEDICATED TO OUR DEAR BROTHER

LATE SHRI TARKESHWAR S. VAIDYA

WHO SMILINGLY GAVE HIS TODAY FOR OUR TOMORROW

SUSHILA VAIDYA

Foreword

The number of women who excelled by their great work in the political history of Maharashtra is very small. We find that there were only five of them who contributed in a very large measure by their great achievements. They were Jijabai, Tarabai, Umabai Dabhade, Ahalyabai Holkar and Laxmibai, the queen of Jhansi. Even those few others whose contribution was comparatively less, have left such an indelible impression that their memory cannot be erased.

Dr. Ku. Sushila Vaidya has very painstakingly gathered information about these able women from the historical documents and other materials. Dr. Sushila Vaidya has left no paper unread to collect this information about the period from 1620 to 1752 A.D. For this purpose she had transplanted herself to Maharashtra from Jabalpur in Madhya Pradesh to which she originally belongs. She zealously studied originally documents in various languages such as Persian, Marathi, English, Sanskrit, Deccani Urdu, *etc.* She also derived great benefit from the great stalwarts of history such as Late Dr. R.P. Tripathi, Dr. Datto Vaman Potdar, Dr. G.H. Khare, and N.K. Joshi. All her persistent efforts have borne a delicious fruit in the form of this book.

It is indeed a difficult task to prepare a systematic account of the abilities and achievements of Jijabai, mother of Shivaji Maharaj, and her two daughters-in-law, Tarabai and Yesubai, but Dr. Sushila Vaidya has studied each document with relevant references in great detail and depth. It has resulted in this excellent political biographies of these three Royal Maratha Women. Dr. Sushila Vaidya's perseverance and writing skill are worthy of great appreciation.

Similarly, she has written in highly informative manner about the political lives of Radhabai Peshwa, Umabai Dabhade, Sakwarbai Bhonsle and others. The Marathas, though poorly equipped with only their horses could establish their strong rein over areas from Kaveri to the Attack (North-West frontier) only because their valour was backed by the strong power of their inspiring, intelligent and capable wives. Every generation must take note of the effective and dynamic power of the women. That is why, I strongly feel that Dr. Sushila Vaidya's book should be translated in every Indian language. This book deserves an active and respectful support by every Indian University. Presently, the movement for women's liberation is very active all over India and if that movement has to succeed, literature similar to Dr. Sushila Vaidya's book must make a deep impression on the mind of every woman also every man, so great is the value and importance of this book.

BABASAHEB PURANDARE
Shree Shivrajya Shaka-320
Falgun Shudha 12
Dec. 24 March 1994
26, Parwati Purandare Wade
Pune 411009

Shri Balawantrao Moreshwarao Purandare
***alias* Babasaheb Purandare**

1. A student in Marathi History.
2. A drama writer and authority in Marathi History.
3. So far delivered about 11,000 lectures on the life and teaching of Chhatrapati Shivaji Maharaj.
4. A Author of 30 books.
5. About Rs. 1,25,00,000/- donated so far from the realisation from various lectures.
6. Toured in Europe and America on account of lectures.

Preface

The present book dedicated to our respected elder brother Late Shri Tarkeshwar S. Vaidya, is based on my thesis, "Role of Women in Maratha Politics (1644-1752 A.D.)", submitted for Ph.D. Degree of the University of Sagar, Saugar, Madhya Pradesh, under the guidance of eminent historian (Late) Professor Dr. R.P. Tripathi, M.A., D.Sc. LL.D., Ex-Vice Chancellor of the University of Sagar (M.P.), India.

The subject presents an analytical study of the characteristic of the Maratha women — their activities concerned with the problems of state-craft, their victories and failures, the handicaps and limitations under which these women had to rally the available resources in men and material in the face of heavy odds of the Muslim and Moghul interferences and their determination to subjugate the southern powers which they could never achieve even by the most astute of Moghul Emperor, Aurangzeb who had the vigour, tenacity and a will to devour Deccan for which he tried incessantly for about twenty-five years of his life without success, circumstantially, this had brought in the decline of the Moghul Power in north as well.

The galaxy of such women nine outstanding personalities have been included, seven of them belonged to the Bhonsle family who were directly connected with the rulers of the Maratha Confederacy. They were-*Jijabai* (1620-74 A.D.); *Soyarabai* (1674-80); *Yesubai* (1689-1719 A.D.); *Tarabai* (1700-52 A.D.); *Sakwarbai*, *Sagunabai* and *Virubai* the queens and mistress of King Shahu respectively. They bore prominence because of their activities concerned with the royalty and the problem of succession.

There were others also who participated in and influenced the Maratha politics, prominent amongst them were two, namely

Radhabai (1700-52 A.D.); wife of Balaji Vishwanath and mother of Peshwa Bajirao; and *Umabai Dabhade* (1728-52 A.D.) wife of Khanderao Dabhade, Senapati of Shahu. Their role stands on different footing, while Radhabai's activities has drawn scant attention of the historians, no methodical study of the role of Umabai Dabhade has been undertaken so far. Hence, an attempt has been made to evaluate their historical worth and material for this has been drawn from sources like, "Purandara Daftar," and "Senapati Dabhade Daftar."

The most redeeming feature of Maratha women was their service to the cause of their family and the state which may be called exemplary but no attempt has been made to present a total picture of their activities in the Maratha political panorama during this period (1620-1752 A.D.).

As for the sources, an attempt has been made to examine and utilize all the available material both original and secondary in Sanskrit, Marathi, English, Kanarese and Persian—their translation referred to in the chapter Introduction (*Sources and their Evaluation*). These sources are listed in the Bibliography, appended at the end of this study.

I am indebted to Dr. Professor R.P. Tripathi from whose towering personality emanated inspiration for his students and I was lucky to avail of it for his valuable and sympathetic guidance. Though a hard task master, he never failed to put my wagons on the rails whenever I felt confused or beaten. To merely say that I am indebted to him is hardly enough to gauge my gratefulness to him. My special thanks are due to Professor G.S. Sardesai, one of the authorities in Maratha History for the blessings and faith he had put in me that I would complete this work. Besides, I am thankful to Dr. M.M.D.V. Potdar for the encouragement which brought forth the confidence in me to carry on the work enthusiastically. At the same time I cannot forget the assistance and co-operation from Dr. G.H. Khare and Babasaheb B.M. Purandare, Poona, for enabling me to shift out the relevant and reliable material from the vast multitude of published and unpublished papers or accounts, concerning the period of study at "Bharat Itihas Sanshodhak Mandal, Poona." Besides the suggestions of Dr. S.N. Sen, Calcutta (W.B.) to *"Think and Think,"* provided an incentive to me to go ahead with the work for which I am thankful to him. Nearer home, a special and sincere thanks is extended to Prof. (Retd.) Dr. K.N. Sinha, Head of the Mediaeval and Modern History Deptt., for going through the manuscript critically and in detail. I also thank Prof. (Retd.) Dr. R.K. Sharma, Head of the Deptt. of Ancient Indian History both of Rani Durgavati Vishwavidyalaya, Jabalpur for their valuable suggestions and co-operation to get the book published in the present form.

Last but not the least, I am thankful to the scholars and authors of different books original and secondary which I referred to in the course of this study. I also thank the library authorities of Bharat Itihas Sanshodhak Mandal, and Maharaja Chhatrapati Pratishthan, Poona who were always willing to furnish to me the requisite materials at their disposal. I thank the library authorities of National Library, Calcutta and National Archives, Bhopal for their co-operation. At the same time, I cannot forget the devotion of my people at home and friends who were always helpful to me in various ways to complete this study.

February 1999 **SUSHILA VAIDYA**

468, Kamla Nehru Nagar (Smarak)
Garha Road, Jabalpur (M.P.)

Abbreviations

ERS	: English Records on Shivaji
FBS	: Foreign Biographics of Shivaji
S.P.D.	: Selections from Peshwa-Daftar
P.D.	: Purandare-Daftar
Khand	: Marathavancha-Itihasanchi-Sadhane by V.K. Rajwade
H.I.H.	: History of India as told by its own Historians
SANGRAHA	: Shiv-Kaleen-Patra-Sar-Sangraha
BARODA STATE RECORDS	: Historical Selection from Baroda State Record.
LIFE OF SHIVAJI	: Shrimant Chhatrapati Sambhaji Maharaj Ani Rajaram Yanche Charita
HAKIKAT	: Kavya-Itihas Sangraha-Senapaṭi Dabhade wa Gaekwad Yanche Hakikat
LIFE OF BRAHMENDRA SWAMI	: Shree Mahapurush Brahmendra Swami Dhawadshikar Charitra wa Patra Vyawahar
ORMES	: Historical Fragments of the Moratoes and of the English Concern in Hindustan from the year MDCLIX.

Contents

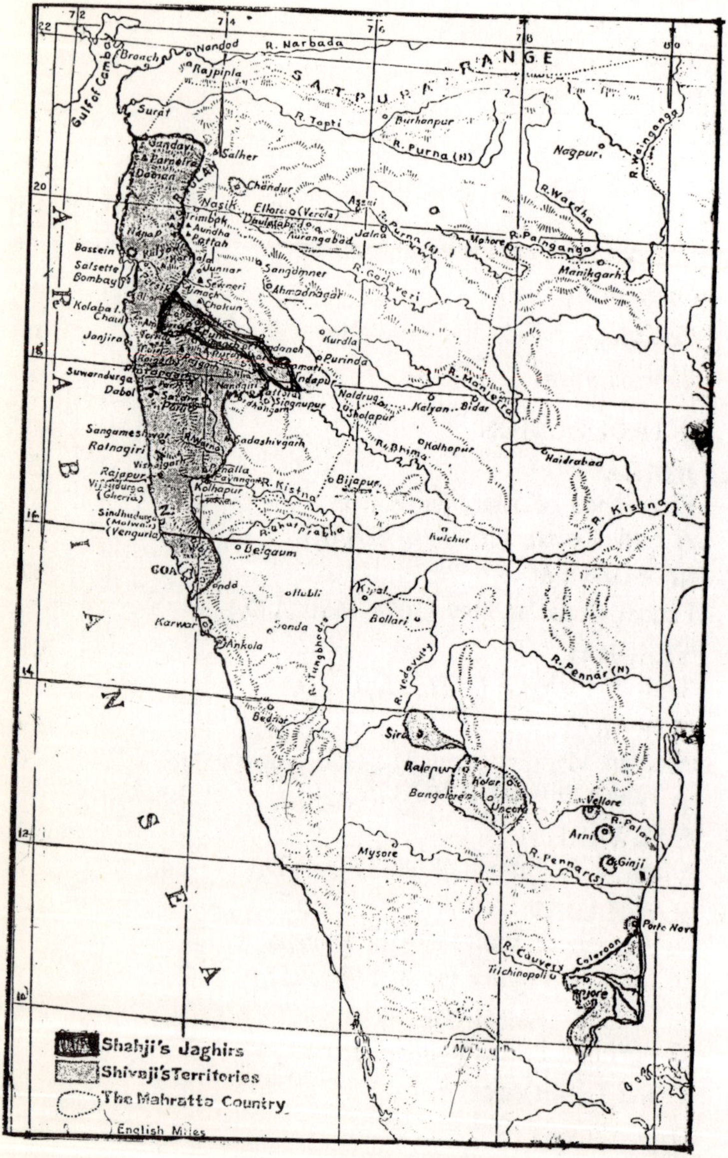

R. Narbada
SATPURA RANGE
Gulf of Cambay
Broach
Nandod
Rajpipla
Surat
R. Tapti
Burhanpur
R. Purna (N)
Nagpur
R. Waingangā
Salher
Chandur
Nasik
Ellora
Daulatabad
Aurangabad
Jalna
R. Wardha
R. Painganga
Manikgarh
Bassein
Salsette
Bombay
Junnar
Sangamner
Ahmadnagar
R. Godaveri
Kolaba I.
Chaul
Janjira
Chakun
Kurdla
Purinda
Indapur
R. Manjera
Suwarnderga
Dabol
Naldrug
Sholapur
Kalyan
Bidar
Sangameshvar
Ratnagiri
Sadashivgarh
R. Bhima
Kolhapur
Haidrabad
Rajapur
Vijaidurga
(Gheria)
Panhalla
Kolhapur
R. Kistna
Bijapur
Sindhudurga
(Malwan)
(Vengurla)
R. Ghatprabha
Raichur
R. Kistna
Belgaum
GOA
Hubli
Bollari
Karwar
Sonda
Ankola
R. Tungbhadra
R. Pennar (N)
Bednor
Sira
Balapur
Kolar
Bangalore
Vellore
R. Palar
Arni
Ginji
Mysore
R. Pennar (S)
Porto Novo
R. Cauvery
Coleroon
Trichinopoli
Tanjore
A R A B I A N   S E A
Shahji's Jaghirs
Shivaji's Territories
The Mahratta Country
English Miles

Introduction

"Role of Women in Maratha Politics" (1620-1752 A.D.); needs critical evaluation, as they influenced the course of Maratha politics by emerging as centres of power by their own rights. They had acquired this position by facing, not only the political challenges but also the challenges posed by social and religious obscurantism from time to time. Sometimes, they succeeded and sometimes they failed. However, their success and failure both provide an insight into a critical study of Maratha polity and contemporary social and religious panorama.

The seventeenth century Maratha polity and society had been shaped by twin forces of Maratha Cultural renaissance and the desire to found a Hindu State on the ruins of the crumbling power of the Shia kingdoms of Ahmadnagar, Bijapur and Golkunda. An interesting feature of this phenomenon was that these kingdoms were being propped up both by the Muslims and Maratha Sardars. Hence, an attempt to carve out an independent State in opposition to these kingdoms was bound to arouse hostility of both the Muslims and Maratha Sardars who looked at the new rising centre of the Maratha power as a threat to their position in the court politics of their respective Shia kingdoms and their political existence with the result that many of the Maratha Sardars serving the Shia kingdoms were not the supporters of the new emerging Maratha State.

Under these circumstances, Jijabai and Shivaji, the founder of the "Independent Maratha State" had to look to new pastures for their sustenance, support and strength. This made the founder of the Maratha State not only to ally those Sardars who were amiable to this rising State but also to obtain support of the grass root level for this cause. Fresh ground was to be broken and new support base was to be created for which he turned towards the hardy people of Sahyadari Hills (Maval). Shivaji converted them into his ardent followers. This was all the more needed to give a firm foundation to the project of Jijabai, the guiding spirit for establishing a "Hindu State" with the aim of protecting the women and religion. This was no vision of a fundamentalist or of an obscurantist. She was opposed to any type of tyranny with the result that the Muslims living in "Swarajya" also enjoyed the same place of respect as was being enjoyed by the "Hindus". She was opposed to religious oppression but was not against the believers of any religion. Shivaji's "Hindu-Pad-Padshahi" never aimed to annihilate others, who were non-Hindus, but in fact "Hindu-Pad-Padshahi" was for all who lived within it. This concept is not the replacement of one tyranny by perpetuating another tyranny.

Jijabai initially started under severe handicap of having almost no known resources for founding such a state to carve out a place for her son Shivaji, under the Sun. Moreover, at that time both mother and son were victims of misfortune, as the person who should have shouldered their responsibility had to leave them and that person was Shivaji's father Shahji in 1636 A.D. However, adversity brought out the best in her personality and the spirit of dauntless struggle against adversity. Adversity taught the mother and the son nothing but endured defiance of it.

An important asset that proved handy both for the mother and the son was the nature of physical configuration of the land over which the new state was to be founded. This territory was almost divided into three regions of 'Konkan', 'Maval' and 'Desh'. The physical conditions had made the life of the people living in these regions hardy, adventurous and sea-faring. Later on, these qualities moulded them into formidable and tough fighting force under Shivaji. They were also deeply influenced by the devotional preachings of reformers such as saints Eknath, Tukaram, Swami Ramdass and others who were the precursor of the spirit of 'Renaissance' in the region preceeding the political revolution being brought out by the mother and the son. This spirit was reflected in "Powadas" i.e. War Songs which they often chanted loudly with open heart, while preceeding on military campaigns. Not only this, the other softer values of life were never absent from them. Their "Lavani" rhymes depicted the life of pleasantry, zest and enthusiasm which they sang even while living in their small dwellings, thatched huts with meagre food and no niceties of life.

Furthermore, this study also reveals the personality of those women, their actions to the State-Craft, their victories and failures, the handicaps and limitations under which they had to rally the available resources in men and material, in the face of heavy odds of the Muslim and Moghul interferences, and their determination to subjugate the southern powers, which they could never achieve even by the most astute of the Moghul Emperor Aurangzeb who had the vigour, tenacity and a will to devour 'Deccan', for which he incessantly fought for twenty-five years of his life without success. This attempt had in fact brought in the decline of the Moghul power in the north as well.

In the galaxy of such women, nine outstanding personalities have been included in this study. Six of them belonging to the Bhosle family who were directly connected with the rulers of the Maratha confederacy. They were - Jijabai (1620-1674 A.D.), Soyarabai (1674-80 A.D.), Yesubai (1689-1719 A.D.), Tarabai (1700-1752 A.D.), Sakwarbai, Sagunabai and Virubai (1707-49 A.D.), Radhabai (1700-1752 A.D.) wife of Peshwa Balaji Vishwanath and mother of the Peshwa Bajirao and Umabai Dabhade (1728-52 A.D.), wife of Shahu's Senapati Khanderao Dabhade of Gujarat. So far no independent study has been made about the role of these two women.

Hence, in this study, an attempt has been made to evaluate their historical worth.

Among these women, Jijabai, daughter of Lukhji Jadhavarao, Deshmukh of Sindkhed at Ahmadnagar, wife of Shahji Bhonsle and mother of Shivaji, holds a significant place for her contribution in the emergence of the Maratha power, and the establishment of

Maratha State, due to the perpetual fight among the Shia States of Ahmadnagar and Bijapur and the Moghul attack to subjugate them.

The sad plight of Jijabai after the "Elephant Episode," 1621 A.D. when her father left Nizamshahi and joined the Moghuls, can be imagined well. Further during the battle of "Bhatvadi" in 1624 A.D., the Moghuls and the Nizamshahi armies fought, in which her father and her husband stood for the two opposing powers – the Moghuls and the Nizamshah. The Moghuls were routed. It is to be observed, how in spite of this, neither the relation between Jijabai and Shahji, nor Shahji and the Nizamshah was affected.

Again in 1633 A.D., when Shivaji was merely three years old, Jijabai, had to flee from fort to fort and place to place in the endeavour of Shahji to uphold the cause of Murtiza Nizamshah-II, a puppet (Prince) at Bheemgad on whose name Shahji carried on the administration of Ahmadnagar. Once she apprehended that Shivaji would be captured, she sent him away to live in obscurity; instead got herself captured. It is to be seen how Jijabai could be released later on.

As usual, Moghul Emperor Shahjahan, realizing the ambition of Shahji, marched on to south with Mirza Raja Jaisingh and the Moghul general Shaistakhan on 4th Jan. 1636 A.D. It is to be observed, how Shahji fought desperately to save the prince. At the crucial moment, to save Shahji from utter defeat the Bijapur general Rustam-i-Zamankhan stood security for Shahji, made him sarlashkar with an offer of four lakhs rupees, and a Jagir in far south, to which Shahji had to accede, however he had to handover the prince to the Moghuls who was sent to Gwalior fort to reside. Shahji proceeded to south with his second wife Tukabai and her son Ekoji as well as Jijabai's eldest son Sambhaji.

Henceforth, Jijabai resided at Poona with Shivaji and Dadaji Konddeva. It has to be seen how instead of being alone she courageously withstood her emotional feelings in the most secular manner, yet she put her mind in the rehabilitation of Poona, then a marshy land at the confluence of rivers Mulla and Mutha full of dense forest and wild animals.

Jijabai's role has to be studied in the context of land improvement, distribution and her active participation in revenue supervision, and maintenance of religious institution by liberal grants and donations to temples, masjids and darghas, and even to Matanayakin, a muslim dancer who had received State grants from Shahji. It is to be seen how her humanitarian activities in the most secular manner brought in love, respect, reverence and support to her and her family, which was so necessary for the emergence of Maratha power then.

Jijabai's stay in the north, has been asserted as an issue of Separation between Shahji and Jijabai by the eminent historians. This has been examined, considering the sequence of events, their ambitions and personal relations vis-a-vis the conditions obtained in Deccan between 1636-1643 A.D., and 1661 A.D.

That Jijabai was quite keen to seek patrimonial estate for Shivaji has to be observed as to how her visit to Bangalore with Shivaji and Dadaji Konddeva could gain to her the authority to establish their sway in their region they had taken and its administration at Poona, yielding 40,000 hons (about one and a half lakh of rupees annually), by 1644-45 A.D. when they had returned to Poona from Bangalore.

Thus, it has to be observed how at one stroke, she secured an opportunity to win the confidence of the people of the estate of Poona, the main support of the nobles at the time. Similarly her visit to the ruined Vijayanagar Empire with Shivaji had the desired effect on his mind to aspire for the Maratha independent state can well be imagined. In all these works Dadaji Konddeva was with her, speaks of her farsight and endurance where-in 1645, she got seal of Shivaji bearing the words.

"प्रतिप्पचंद्र लेखेव । वर्धिष्णु विश्व वंदिता ।
शाहसूनोः शिवस्येषा । मुद्रामुदाय राजते ।"

Besides, her humanitarian work and construction of Lal-Mahal, a Tank at Ghrishneswar temple, Shahibag and town of Shivpur, establishing Bazaar or peths, spoke of her future plans and the way she aroused the feeling of respect and love for Shivaji, so necessary to achieve his aim.

Henceforth, the role of Jijabai has to be studied in context of campaigns, "Panhalla in 1660 A.D." and the treaty of Purandar in 1665 A.D. It is interesting to know how Shivaji entered into matrimonial alliances, more for political than personal reasons.

It may be noted that in 1660 A.D. during "Panhalle-Siege" the Moghul generals had cornered Shivaji at Panhalla, supported by Siddi Jauhar, the arch enemy of the Marathas, Bijapur general Fazl Khan, son of Afzal Khan, lateron, supported by Henry Revington, Chief of English factory at Rajapur and his assistant Gifford Mighaum, as well as a few members from Jijabai's family of Sindkhed. It is to be seen how during the siege, Jijabai was carrying on defence personally at Rajgad, it being an impregnable fort as well as having "treasure-hold" of the Marathas while Shivaji was at Panhalla. The battle was going on two fronts e.g. at Panhalla and at Rajgad. On one occasion, Panhalla siege assumed toughness. The Maratha Senapati Netaji Palkar and Siddi Hillal, rushed to Jijabai at Rajgad, apprised her of the desperate situation. Exasperated, she snubbed them for leaving Panhalla siege and 'Shivaji' in desperate condition. Resolutely, she asked them to look to the defence of Rajgad, while she would personally march to Panhalla and see that Siddi-Jauhar is not only defeated but killed, and whose chopped off head, she would bring from the battle field. This determined attitude of Jijabai had the desired effect on them and they left for Panhalla, assuring Jijabai to carry on the assault more vigorously. It should be borne in mind that Jijabai was not less than 60 years of age but this age factor could never stop her from determined action, and she continued to meet any challenge how-so-ever tough it was for the welfare of the estate. Thus once more the Marathas had won over the united challenge of the Moghuls, the Siddis, the Bijapur king and the English successfully. Henceforth, Shivaji hurridly reached Rajgad to Jijabai and she had the pleasure to see Shivaji safe.

This rebellious attitude of Shivaji could not be tolerated by the Moghul emperor Shahjehan who sent his generals Mirza Raja Jaisingh, Diler Khan, Shaistakhan to crush the growing power of the Marathas. Mirza Raja Jaisingh took his position at Purandar. There was tough fight between the Marathas and the Moghuls. The pressure was so heavy, that it was evident that the Marathas would not hold for long. Perceiving this, Shivaji sought an audience of Mirza Raja Jaisingh and offered to give him the whole of Deccan, if he worked for "Hindu-Pad Padshahi". After some time the Moghuls seige was raised to the great annoyance of Dilerkhan by the treaty of Purandar in 1665 A.D. According to this treaty Shivaji accepted to pay audience to the Moghul Emperor Aurangzeb with his son Sambhaji as well as agreed to handover twenty forts to him, after which Shivaji, leaving his principality to be managed by Jijabai as regent, started for march on 5th March 1665 A.D.

Jijabai's administration has to be esteemed in the words of Mirza Raja Jaisingh who commented, "Although Shivaji had to remain, absent for nearly six months, "Swarajya" was not reduced by an inch in spite of the enemies like Siddi-II of Janjira, Portuguese and Bijapur king." Besides, as if to maintain the tradition adopted by Shivaji not to allow any respite to the enemy, she sent Raoji Somnath to Talkonkan, to capture the fort of Rangna, another invulnerable fort.

Jijabai's role to welcome Shahji, Tukabai and other members of the family in 1661 A.D.; has to be studied in the context of their decision to make Rairi into Raigad, the future capital of Maratha state as Shahji had also brought 'Sanad' from the Bijapur king to assign to Shivaji to rule the territory which he had taken till then, on the promise that he (Shivaji) would not harass or carry on assaults on Bijapur territory to which Shivaji had agreed.

Thereafter, Shahji returned but in 1664 A.D., he died in an hunting expedition. It has to be seen how Jijabai was prevailed upon not to commit 'Sati' to which she had prepared herself, only after taking into consideration the welfare of Shivaji and the Maratha state as desired by the people.

The Pinnacle of Jijabai's success was the coronation of Shivaji on 11th June 1674 A.D. after which she died on 17th June a week after the memorable day, after serving Maratha state from 1621 to 1674 A.D. for about 45 years and left for her son Shivaji a sound financial exchequer the backbone of the welfare of any state.

Shivaji's queen, Soyarabai, has been held responsible for his "Karnatak Expedition", "Succession Issue" and "Poison-Episode". It is to be examined whether her influence on Shivaji or her supposed craving for two kingdoms as expressed by a few writers, could have prevailed on Shivaji to proceed on the hazardous journey to Karnatak or the allegation of her complicity in the "succession-issue", has to be taken into consideration, by the fact that Shivaji never declared his successor. It has to be seen whether the "Poison Episode" was a sheer figment of imagination and a deliberate concocted blemish on her character.

Yesubai, Sambhaji's queen had to deal with rather complex personalities and situations. Her role is to be studied in the background of Sambhaji's flight to the Moghul General Diler Khan on 13th December, 1678 A.D.; and the series of executions, after gaining the throne at Rajgad in 1680 A.D.; which brought in deep anxiety to Yesubai as to the future of Maratha State and kept the royal seal under her control which also shows that Sambhaji had faith in her. As known Sambhaji was captured by the Moghuls on 1st February 1689 A.D. and later on he was executed on 3rd March 1689 A.D., at Vadu, near Karegaon. It has to be examined how Yesubai, without giving way to despair, provided that matured thinking, which could maintain the internal solidarity among the Marathas as well as a will to meet the challenge of the Moghul

Emperor till Shahu was old enough to undertake the responsibilities of State Craft and Welfare. "Let Shahu be the king and Rajaram the Regent", could win for her the goodwill and confidence of Rajaram and the sardars as well as disappointed the Moghul Emperor who wanted to create dissension among the Marathas. Aurangzeb asked his general Itikad Khan to lay siege at Raigad, where Yesubai, Rajaram and other of the family inmates had taken shelter at this critical moment with Ramchandrapant Amatya, Sachiv Shankaraji Malhar and other eminent sardars. Marathas fought with zeal and determination but soon the futility of resistance with the limited resources compelled Yesubai to advise Rajaram to leave the fort with few Maratha Sardars and to reach Jinji fort and let the other Maratha Sardars counter-act the Moghul onslaughts. Hence, Rajaram escaped on 5th April, 1689 A.D.

It has to be studied how Yesubai proved to be alert, active and adopted a sustained policy and high morale that it could infuse courage among the Marathas, to fight on and on, while the Moghul general pressed the Marathas to surrender the fort. On suspicions that some one else would deliver the fort to the Moghuls, she after consonance of the Sardars surrendered the fort to the Moghul general Itikad Khan on 25th March 1689 A.D.; Yesubai, Shahu, Bhavanibai and others were taken captive with a few sardars. They were received cordially by the Emperor's establishment. Aurangzeb honoured them with awards, previleges and honour.

Henceforth, Yesubai remained a captive at the Moghul royal court for nearly thirty years from 1689 A.D. to 1719 A.D. It is to be studied, how during this period, she played what may be called a "Dual-role" by her communication to Rajaram, presumed to be through a few loyal sardars. Thus, she constantly stood the risk of being exposed to dangerous consequences especially under the most astute Moghul emperor Aurangzeb, but steered clear off all such possibilities, besides, she kept up the tradition of her family in an alien atmosphere and thus could serve the cause of Maratha State.

The role of Tarabai, in its different aspects covers the period of half a century of sustained struggle against odds from 1690 to 1752 A.D. Her career can be divided into three different stages. In the first stage she followed her husband to Jinji and came back with co-wives Rajasbai and Ambikabai to Vishalgad in 1699 A.D.

It has to be studied how during this period, she started taking interest in Rajaram's activities, by sending Maratha armies across Narmada to check Moghul advances into Deccan in 1699 A.D. Rajaram carried on ravages and plundered Moghul camp, so much so that once he reached very near to Yesubai but could not get them (Yesubai and Shahu) released.

In 1700 A.D., after the death of her husband Rajaram, Tarabai coronated her son Shivaji II, much against the suggestions of Ramchandra Pant and others. It has to be seen, whether the coronation of her son Shivaji II, a minor was due to her anxiety that the vacuum created by the death of Rajaram might result into internal dissensions or due to the realisation that in the circumstances prevalent then might give an opportunity even to the meanest of soldiers to rise to power and position by merit. In between the on-slaughts and skirmishes the Moghul emperor Aurangzeb died, on 20th Feb. in 1707 A.D. at Dohad and the Moghul entourage continued to march towards north alongwith Yesubai, Shahu and inmates of Shivaji's family with other Maratha Sardars.

The second stage deals with the causes of Shahu's return to south and Tarabai's declaration that he was an imposter, causes of which have been discussed to arrive at a correct appraisal. It has to be studied how and why she was imprisoned by Rajasbai, other wives of Rajaram in 1714 A.D. and Rajasbai's son Sambhaji II, was coronated at Kolhapur. Henceforth Tarabai remained at Kolhapur till the battle of Warna fought between Shahu and Sambhaji II in 1731 A.D. Tarabai preferred to remain at Satara where Shahu kept her as royal captive.

In the third stage, there is a quest for the successor to the

Satara throne. Tarabai got Ramraja declared as Shahu's successor in 1749 A.D.

It has to be examined, as to why Tarabai, after the "Sangola Pact" imprisoned Ramraja at the Satara fort and declared him to be an imposter. She fought against the Peshwa for nearly three years. Ultimately, she was defeated. The final reconciliation between her and the Peshwa Balaji Bajirao took place in September 1752 A.D. These events provide an opportunity to evaluate her role and its effect on the family as well as the Maratha State on different occasions.

It was evident that by the year 1745 A.D., the Maratha state and the palace experienced two distinct issues. The one was the "financial stringency" being felt in the palace and the other was the "succession issue" which gained impetus as Shahu started remaining ill and he had no issue.

Shahu's queens Sakwarbai and Sagunabai have been held responsible for bringing in the financial stringency leading to deterioration in the palace atmosphere as well as in the Maratha kingdom about 1745 A.D. It has to be examined whether the queens were responsible for this situation. It is to be noted that the financial stringency had been caused by the constant campaigns undertaken by the Peshwa Bajirao, Chimnajee Appa, the Peshwa Balaji Bajirao as well as a few other sardars from time to time.

The role of Virubai, mistress of Shahu has also been discussed, keeping in view the palace management, Satara Court Politics and the events taking place in Maratha kingdom, specially in context of the view expressed by Captàin Gorden from Bombay, who had communicated that "As we could not see Virubai, a woman of consequence, we sent her letters and presents. She gave a civil profession in return." Shahu lost her valuable services after her death in 1740 A.D.

With regard to their role in the "Succession Issue", there is no evidence to indicate that the queens were extraordinarily interested in any candidate in particular. Moreover there is no reliable reference to support the contention that the Peshwa Balaji Bajirao and Ramchandra Pant Amatya of Kolhapur had tried for the merger of Satara and Kolhapur Houses. Hence, it is to be studied whether the queens were victims of a few interested personalities who wanted to serve their selfish interests.

Radhabai had carefully guided her son Bajirao before he met Nizam-ul-Mulk in 1735 A.D. which illustrates her interest and insight in the affairs of the Maratha politics. Moreover, the significance of her northern journey has also to be studied to find out whether it was a religious tour or had political significance specially for the Maratha Rajput relations. Her singular tactful handling of the affairs saved Peshwas family from social disgrace on account of "Bajirao-Mastani" affair.

Umabai Dabhade is the most sagacious and impressive character who had scant regard for her perilous existence on account of her role in the Maratha politics, pliancy for manipulation and military adventures have brought her a distinguished place in the affairs of the Maratha kingdom. She suspected Bajirao of Treachery in killing her son Senapati Trimbakrao Dabhade and therefore her revengeful attitude towards the Peshwa never allowed him any peace of mind till his death in 1740 A.D. But it was her tragedy that she had to witness the decline of the House of Dabhades in the affairs of the Maratha State.

The following note on – "Sources and Their Evaluatioin" brings out the sources consulted by me for writing this work.

Sources and Their Evaluation

This study is mainly based on contemporary Marathi sources and other accounts. These secondary accounts were used because, at places, sufficient original material of evidentiary value, regarding the life and activities of women, included in this study, was not available. The raw material has been shifted into :

(1) Documentary Sources;

(2) Original Narratives, Charitra, Bakhars, Ballads and Persian sources;

(3) Foreign Sources; and

(4) Modern Works or Compilations.

As far as documentary sources are concerned, letters written by, and to, the kings, the Peshwas and other State Officials are found in numbers; but these written by, or to, women are few and often vague. However, relevant letters have been utilised and referred to.

Maratha history has an advantage. The letters concerning the activities of one person are often in one and the same volume. As such, the repetition of references from one and the same volume could not be avoided. The letters, thus referred to, have, in some places, been summarized while, in other places, detailed accounts from the letters are given and quoted.

Peshwa Daftar

The forty-five volumes of Peshwa Daftar are of importance so far as historical research is concerned. The documents, published in these volumes, are selected from the State Records, preserved in the Alienation Office at Poona. Among other pieces of information, these contain accounts of activities of persons concerned in different spheres such as State affairs, battles, treaties, etc. I have made extensive use of these volumes. The section, Shahu Daftar, contains information about events that took place in Shahu's court and such other affairs up to 1749 A.D. "Shahu Roznishi" contains extracts from the diary or Rozkird as it is included in the Peshwa Daftar. Similarly, the volume, Nana Roznishi, contains extracts from the diaries kept by Shahu and his successors and the Peshwas and therefore, are quite useful.

Purandare Daftar

The three printed volumes of Purandare Daftar consist of material from the records of Sardar Purandare of Saswar. The

Purandares served the Peshwa as their agents or Diwans. Often, they worked together. Therefore, the records published in these volumes are original, and provide first hand knowledge. These volumes contain a record of events that took place in Shahu's palace or in the Maratha kingdom. These have provided me with valuable, authentic information for the chapters dealing with Jijabai and Tarabai.

Marathyancha Itihasanchi Sadhane

During the period between 1898 and 1926 A.D., Shri V.K. Rajwade, who holds a unique place among the writers of Maratha history, brought out 22 volumes of his 'historical material', consisting of original letter and documents. The documents included in these volumes were written by persons who took part in day to day activities in Maratha Politics. As such, these provide a realistic idea of the period, which is obviously indispensable for this study. Besides, Shri Rajwade compiled three volumes of his translation and also contributed critical and other articles in ten to fifteen magazines and newspapers. Volume IV is an analysis and examination of the Maratha Bakhars in general. It provides a critical study of "Shivaji's life", which is very enlightening. This volume also evaluates different Bakhars of Maratha history. Documents from these volumes have been immensely used by me in Chapter I (Jijabai), Chapter IV (Tarabai), Chapter V (Sakwarbai, Sagunabai and Virubai) and Chapter VII (Umabai Dabhade).

Bawda Daftar

These are in two volumes and contain many letters from Bawda Jagir. From here Shri V.K. Rajwade secured some letters and published them in Volume VIII of Marathyancha Itihasanchi Sadhane. Therefore, these can be relied on as authentic.

Vaidya Daftar

The documents in the Vaidya Daftar pertain to the years 1743 to 1749 A.D., and are divided in seven parts, each part containing documents pertaining to one calendar year. Five volumes of the same material have also been published. The Vaidyas were essentially the bankers of and well connected with the affairs of the Maratha State during Shahu's reign. As such, they could leave full account of the events that took place during the last years of Shahu's reign, that is, from 1745 A.D. onwards. The letters provide an opportunity to find out whether the queens of Shahu, namely, Sakwarbai and Sagunabai, were responsible for the deteriorated financial condition of the State which the king, the queens, the Peshwas and the Sardars had to face from 1745 A.D. onwards.

Senapati Dabhade Daftar

The first volume contains one hundred and fifty letters. These letters are valuable source of information about the Dabhades. As known the Dabhades served Shivaji, Rajaram, Tarabai and Shahu. However, the letters mostly concern revenue papers and provide meagre information about Umabai Dabhade.

Aitihasik Patra Vyawahar

The volume contains letters concerning different events and activities of persons in the Maratha kingdom from 1699 to 1750 A.D. It is a valuable book of source material regarding the activities of Tarabai, Sakwarbai and Sagunabai.

Shiv Charitra Sahitya

The series have been published in 11 volumes and contain first grade source material. The letters published in these volumes have been collected from old historical families. These letters have been put to vigorous scrutiny before their publication. Therefore, these can be taken as thoroughly genuine and authentic. Some of these volumes have been summarized and published in Shiv Kaleen Patra Sar Sangraha and Sambhaji Kaleen Patra Sar Sangraha. Wherever, in these volumes, information relevant to this study could be found, I have made use of it.

Shiv Kaleen Patra Sar Sangraha, Vols. I, II & III & Sambhaji Kaleen Patra Sar Sagraha

Strictly speaking these volumes cannot be called original source books, but these are a useful calendar of all the available records of the periods of Shivaji and Sambhaji. These also contain summarised letters from a number of books which are not easily available now. A few of the volumes of Shiv-Charitra Sahitya have been included in these volumes also. I have used, and referred to, these volumes whenever I could not find original source material.

Sanada-Patre

It contains original source material. Unfortunately, it has not been properly edited and therefore, it diminishes its value as source material. Therefore, I have used it with caution.

Shri Sampradayachi Kagad Patre

The volume contains relevant and reliable letters on various matters. I could make use of only one such letter in Chapter III (Yesubai).

Besides, original narratives, Bakhars and Powadas (contemporary) written by different persons have been immensely used. These are the carefully recorded narratives of events as and when they occured. But, in most of the cases, the Bakhars and Powadas are not contemporary. These are late individual compilations, the authors of which had neither first-hand knowledge of the incidents concerned, nor had they any authentic documents to rely on. In some cases, statements from Bakhars were correct. In some other cases the statements were not borne out by contemporary authentic records. I have referred the relevant portions from Bakhars only when the information is corroborated by other authentic records and also when these were found absolutely indispensable in the absence of original sources and other documents.

Shiv-Bharat

It is an invaluable source book. Originally, this book was written in Sanskrit and later translated in Marathi. The author of the book was a contemporary of Shahji and Shivaji. Besides, the different accounts show that he was thoroughly aware of the events of his age. This fact is corroborated by the contemporary documentary evidence. The dates of Shivaji's birth and of Afzalkhan's death, as given in Shiv-Bharat, are corroborated by those given in Jedhe-Yanche-Shakawali. The two letters in Indian Historical Records Commission Proceedings Vol.XVI, p.45, indicate that Kavindra Parmanand had accompanied Shivaji in his northern journey in 1665 A.D. Kavindra Parmanand has mentioned, in detail, the role of Jijabai, the reasons for which she had to leave Bangalore and reside at Poona, Shivaji's education, Jijabai's effort to safeguard Raigad and retaliate the combined attacks of the Bijapur Sultan, the Moghuls and the Siddis of Janjira at Panhalla in 1660 A.D. The events described and information given in the book are corroborated by other historical authentic sources. The account given in the book has enabled me to evaluate Jijabai's role in Chapter I Jijabai-Emergence of Maratha Power–a new vision, 1620 to 1674 A.D.

Shiv Charitra Pradeep

The book is published by Shri D.V. Apte and S.M. Divekar. It is included in Buraskrut Mala of B.I.S. Mandal, Poona. It contains a collection of papers, contributed by several scholars of Maratha history and includes Jedhe Shakawali, Jedhe Kareena and other chronologies, a few original letters of Shivaji's times and a number of papers about the birth of Shivaji. It also gives an evaluation of Bakhars as a source material. As such it is immensely useful for this work and has been extensively referred to.

Anupuran

The Oriental Institute of Baroda has published a Sanskrit work, called "Parmanand Kavyam", in Gaekwad Oriental Series

No.CXX. A few chapters of this work are said to have been composed by Kavindra Parmanand, the well-known author of Shiv-Bharat. The other few verses are said to have been written by his own son Devdatta and his grandson Govind. According to the opinion of scholars, no chapters in the book have been really composed by the well-known poet Parmanand. It narrates the life of Shivaji during the last three years of his life that is, from 1677 to 1680 A.D. It provides information about Sambhaji's early activities, Soyarabai and the Expedition of Shivaji to Karnatak, Shivaji's death and the 'Manchkarohan' ceremony of Rajaram. The information has been found useful for Chapter II (Soyarabai) included herein.

Jedhe-Shakawali

It is another source of information, kept by the Jedhes, a Maratha family residing in the Rohida valley in the hilly part of Western Ghats. The documents were originally found by Late Lokmanya Tilak. These are printed in the IV Sammelan Vrutta of the B.I.S. Mandal, Poona, in 1916. Now it has also been published in Shiv Charitra Pradeep with some minor corrections. It is an accurate chronology. The authenticity of this work depends on Kanhoji Jedhe and his son who took part in a number of events with Shahji, Shivaji and Sambhaji. The events are stated in a chronological order along with the dates. The entries range from 1618 to 1697 A.D., a period of eighty years when most of the incidents described in this work took place. It is quite evident that the entries made by the Jedhes are full and often explanatory. Jedhe Kareena (narrative) is another document and provides information like Jedhe Shakawali.

Shri Maha-Purush-Brahmendraswami Dhawadshikar Charitra va Patravyawahar

As the name suggests, the book provides information about the life account of Brahmendraswami, a saint who first resided at Chiploon and then moved to Dhawadshi. The latter part contains original letters, a few of which are either sent by or addressed to Shahu, Sakwarbai, Sagunabai, Virubai, Radhabai, Bajirao, Chimnajee and to many other sardars. These letters are of great value to the students of the early Peshwa period. These are quite authentic as well.

Rajaram Charitam Athawa Jinji-ch-Pravas

It is a versified description of Rajaram's itinerary from Raigad to Jinji from 1689 A.D. onwards. As it is composed by a contemporary person, it can be relied on as an authentic record of different events and situations which Rajaram had to face at the critical hour for him and the Maratha kingdom. However, it supplies comparatively scanty information.

Ichchalkaranji Sansthan ch Itihas

The book provides account about the Ghorpade sardars of Ichchalkaranji and about others also who took part in various activities of the Jagir and the Maratha kingdom. It also contains letters which provide authentic information. As such it can be used as original source material.

Kavya Itihas Sangraha Patre wa Yadi

The book is immensely valuable for historical research purpose. It contains five hundred and one letters collected and published some seventy-five years ago. In its first and second editions, no dates were given to individual letters, but in the last edition, which I have used, all the letters have dates, of course, provisional and are arranged in a chronological order. Almost all the letters in the book appear to be genuine and authentic. However, the method of publishing the letters was not quite scientific, being a pioneer work of this type. The letters deal with different affairs of various sardars and Maratha kingdom. It also includes 'Kaifiyat' of Shahji Bhonsle, 'Hakikat' about the death of Afzalkhan, the account of Balaji Vishwanath, Bajirao and Balaji Bajirao, Shahu, Tarabai, Sakwarbai and Sagunabai and information about other events.

Among the bakhars, I have used Shiv Chatrapati che Charitra written by Sabhsad. He is one of the earliest biographers of Shivaji. He wrote the account in 1694 A.D. The account mainly confines itself to personality description of Shivaji and his activities, more of political nature than otherwise. The accounts given in this work are corroborated by other evidences and I have taken them to be authentic.

The other bakhar referred to by me is "Shrimant Chhatrapati Sambhaji Maharaj ani Rajaram Yanche Charitra". The narration is about the lives of Sambhaji and Rajaram, son of Shivaji written in 1810-13 by M.R. Chitnis. Thus, it is quite a late composition. It gives an elaborate description of political events and different persons concerned therewith. I cannot establish it to be reliable or authentic, yet I had to refer to it and rely on it in absence of contemporary account concerning Yesubai and Soyarabai, the subject-matter of this work. I have also gone through the following bakhars and used them only when found unavoidable though with caution. These are Nagpurkar Bhonsle Yanchi bakhar, Shahu Maharaj Yanchi bakhar, Peshwanchi bakhar, Shahu Maharaj Yanche Charitra and Senapati Dabhade wa Gaekwad Yanchi Hakikat. As the names of the bakhars suggest, they mainly contain accounts of the persons mentioned and their activities.

Marathyancha Kavyamaya Itihas : Vol. I. Aitihasik Powade

The volume contains 'ballads' or 'powadas', written to commemorate different events. These are to be sung in a rhythmic way. Such ballads have been included in the above book which is also a "Purashkrut" work by B.I.S. Mandal, Poona. The book is nicely annotated and given all the notes which makes the reader understand Historical references clearly. The ballad "Afzalkhan-Wadh" is composed by Shaheer Ajyandas. It depicts the role of Jijabai at the time of Shivaji's march to meet Afzalkhan. The account further corroborates with the account given by Sabhasad and Kavindra Parmanand. According to the author, the words नवगजी, सरजा, फिरंग बीरमाल, used in the ballad are only found in the documents of those times. Hence, the ballad can be relied on as an authentic one.

The other ballad is about "Sinhgad-Vijaya". It is composed by Shaheer Tulsidas and informs about Jijabai's interest and effort to take back Sinhgad fort from the occupation of the enemies. But M.M.D.V. Potdar has refuted the belief of its being an early composition, in an article published in Quarterly (Varsh 19, Ank 1, p.13), B.I.S. Mandal, Poona. He has proved it to be composed after many years when the events had taken place. Hence I have not referred to it.

As far as Hindi sources are concerned, nothing worthwhile, exists to be referred to 'Shiv Raj Bhushan' and 'Chhatraprakash' written by Shivaji's court poet, Bhushan, and Lalkavi respectively are not contemporary. Hence these cannot be relied on from historical point of view.

Muhammadan writers have also given their accounts in Persian about the events and the state affairs in the Moghul and the Maratha Kingdoms. "History of India as told by its own Historians" contains such accounts. This work has been edited by Prof. J. Dowson in several volumes, among which volumes VI, VII and VIII contain the relevant material concerned with this study, especially the account given by Khafi Khan in volume VII. It is a long narration of the reign of Aurangzeb. It can be said that it is authentic as far as the accounts of the Moghul Emperors and their activities and such other event are concerned but regarding the events in the Maratha kingdom and activities therein, the account does not appear to be always authentic. This might be due to the reason that by the time the information reached the writer, it deviated from its originality. Such accounts as could not be supported or corroborated by other reliable accounts have been given a secondary place by me.

Mathir-ul-Umara

Volumes I and II contain the biographies of the Muhammadan

and Hindu officers of the Timrid sovereigns of India from 1500 to about 1780 A.D. The biographies provide in detail, the activities of respective persons and as such, are useful for reference in historical research.

History of Dekkan

Ferishta wrote an account of "Moslem rule in Dekkan". He was a Persian historian. His work is uncritical and occasionally erroneous. However, he has preserved writings that might have been lost. He held high office at the court of Ibrahim Adil Shah of Bijapur. He has also compiled "History of the Delhi Emperors". His main work concluded with the fall of Ahmadnagar. His work can be used as source book after verification from other authentic sources.

Memoires of Jahangir, Vols. I & II

Tuzuk-i-Jahangir or the memoires of Jahangir provide a lively and graphic account of India of the early years of the 17th century. In the volumes, Jahangir wrote about himself and the events that took place in his life. The accounts can be relied on after careful shifting of exaggerated narration and expression. It also serves the purpose of records of his reign.

Maasir-i-Alamgiri

The volume contains an account of the reign of the Moghul Emperor Aurangzeb, by Saqi Mast'ad Khan, translated by Sir J. Sarkar. The narration has been put chronologically in an abridged form from 1657 to 1707 A.D., that is, till the death of Aurangzeb. It also refers to other incidents which took place in the Moghul Empire and the Maratha Kingdom. The relevant portions from this work have been utilised by me.

Besides, letters written by East India Company servants and other foreign travellers provide another source of historical research. These contain narrations more of political events and other affairs than of activities of women. However, they supply valuable information on historical events.

English Records on Shivaji

The volume contains extracts from letters sent by the servants of the East India Company or factories, who resided in the West coastal towns and the interior. It provides information regarding the events that took place in the kingdom of Bijapur, Golkunda and other parts of south India. The writers have tried their best to give as correct an account as possible. There is certainly an element of hearsay, exaggeration and falsification. Therefore, it must be used with caution.

Foreign Biographies of Shivaji

The volume contains long narrations about Shivaji activities, written by foreign travellers, Sosina-de-Guarda, Jean-de-Thevenot, Barthlemy Carre', Francois Martin and Francois Valentini, extracts from Dutch Records and the account of the visit of the embassies to the court of Shivaji. But the travellers, other than the English, appear to be inferior in providing exact account of the events that took place at the time of their residence in India. The material from these sources has been sparingly used by me as it contains less information on my subject of study.

Historical Fragments of the Moratoes and of the English Concern

This is a compilatory work, prepared with great labour, by Robert Orme (1720-1801 A.D.). It is not a contemporary account, yet it can be used as a source book because the author is said to have an access to personal information and such other material of the time. Hence it can be depended on to be authentic.

Historical Miscellany No. 31

The booklet contains seven chapters. Four from these are extracts from different original letters. The articles are, "The Marathas in Southern India, according to Jesuit Sources" by H. Heras, S.J., "A Brief Survey of Portuguese Sources of Maratha History" by Dr. S.N. Sen., "Life of Shivaji" by Prof. J. Sarkar, translated from the French writer Abbe Carre. The articles can be taken to be authentic as far as the letters are concerned. The Jesuits, being foreigner had often to rely on secondary sources. Besides, they were not well conversant with the manners and customs of the Indian people. Hence, the information provided by them should be used with caution.

Travels by Thevenot & Gareri

Both the travellers came to India in the 17th century. Jean-de-Thevenot has given "a fairly good pen-picture of the Moghul Emperor Aurangzeb." Gareri has, among other accounts written about Akbar (son of Aurangzeb), Sambhaji (son of Shivaji) and Akbar's flight to Persia, which are relevant to this study. The account cannot be relied upon without knowing the sources of information.

Storia-Do-Mogor

Another traveller in India during the 17th century was Niccolao Manucci. His life was full of adventures. He had entered the services of Mirza Raja Jaisingh. He has given a vivid account of the events that took place in the Moghul Empire as well as in the Maratha Kingdom. Much of the account appears to be exaggerated. Therefore, the material should be relied on only after corroboration from other authentic sources. His account of the conditions that prevailed in the Moghul camp during the march of the Moghul Emperor, Aurangzeb, against the Marathas from 1700 to 1707 A.D. is relevant to this study and has been referred to.

Selections from the Letters, Despatches and other State Papers

The publication consists of three Home Series volumes. Volume I contains Selections from Surat letters (1630-1700 A.D.), Selections from the Bombay Letters (1677-1700 A.D.) and Selections from the Surat Diaries (1660-1781 A.D.). Volumes II and III contain letters and narration of different events. However, a major part of these volumes is not relevant to this study. Hence they have been sparingly used.

Besides the above sources, compilatory or modern works have also been utilised and referred to. These are neither contemporary nor original, yet contain material which can be called authentic by virtue of its being based on reliable papers found by the authors concerned, otherwise I would not have referred to these works.

Potdar Commemoration Volume

It contains first grade articles written by eminent scholars. The letters, quoted in different articles as well as other information contained therein, can serve the purpose of documentary evidence on different topics. As such these are quite useful and are referred to by me.

Similarly, Sardesai Commemoration Volume is another attempt to furnish historical information on different topics, but it contains less documentary evidence than the first one.

Shivaji Nibandhawali

The volumes contain independent articles by scholars, based on reliable and authentic sources, after careful perusal. Volume I contains such chapters as "Shivaji from Tanjore Mss.", and "The Karnatak Expedition (from unpublished Dutch extracts from the Hague Colonial Archives). Volume II contains such chapters as "The Rise of the Maratha Power in the South", "Shivaji from Assamese Sources" and "The Preparation of the Ground for Shivaji's South Indian Expedition". Thus, the material found in these volumes, is closely relevant to this study and hence has been utilised and referred to by me.

Similarly useful is "Shivaji Charitra Nibandhawali", though it has been sparingly referred to by me.

Shiv Charitra Vrutta Sangraha

The three volumes, published by B.I.S. Mandal, Poona contain contemporary and useful material for historical research. Volume

I is devoted to Kannadi sources written on Aitihasik Kavya Champu Shailee. Volumes II and III are compiled by G.H. Khare. He gives a useful introduction to Persian dates and incidents. The extracts are translations from Persian narratives as Futuhat-i-Adilshahi, Alamgir-Nama, Munta-Khabu-L-Lubab and Maasir-i-Alamgiri. The information is useful to supplement description of events after corroboration from other contemporary records.

Selected Documents of Shahjehan's Reign and of Aurangzeb's Reign from 1659 to 1706

These deal mostly with chronology and other aspects of the administration and state affairs in the reign of the respective Moghul Emperors. As such the material is useful for reconstruction of narration of historical events.

Similarly, Historical Selections from Baroda State Records, Vol.I (1724-1768) and History of Gujarat by J.W. Watson, from Bombay Gazetteer 1297 to 1700 A.D. has been found immensely useful for Chapter VII, "Umabai Dabhade Contrifugal Power Politics (1725-1552 A.D.)".

The relevant material Ittivruttas (Ahwals or Annuals) and Quarterlies of B.I.S. Mandal, Poona, the volumes of Vividh Gyan Vistar and Ramdas-Ramdasi containing old original papers have been consulted and referred to. The volumes of the *Itihas Sangraha*, a defunct magazine, contain original letters and family narratives. These are collected from the descendants of the XVII Century families, the members of which happened to be participants in the politics of the century. Therefore, the material can be relied on as authentic. The records in the volumes are very useful for the reconstruction of history and therefore, rather indispensable for this work. The volumes of the *Modern Review* and the volumes of the *Journal of the Royal Asiatic Society* have been utilised and referred to. I have also immensely used the material from Indian Records Commission Proceedings and its volumes. The material, contained in these volumes, has been critically and thoroughly examined before being published. Therefore, I have taken them as authentic.

It will not be out of place to mention here that references from other sources could not be made use of because either they did not directly concern this study or it was difficult to establish the authenticity of certain information contained therein, e.g., V.S. Bendre's Unpublished Paper's in numerous volumes, at Poona and Late Dr. P.K. Gode's enlightening talk on Champabai. The latter was kind enough to show me certain extracts about Champabai, which are now included in his Studies in Indian Literary History Vol.II. In this connection I also went through an article "Chattrapati Sambhaji, Shambhudas Desai Ani Champa" written by B.R. Kulkarni published in "Nav Bharat" June, 1961 issue (Poona). It is difficult to establish that "Champabai" was married to Sambhaji, son of Shivaji.

I have also gone through the book "Chhatrapati Sambhaji Maharaj written by V.C. Bendre. It also contained account from the unpublished volumes at that time. I have referred from the book where I found the material reliable.

Similarly, "Karweer Riyasat" Karweer Chhatrapati Gharanyacha Itihas (1710-1883) pub. in 1968, also contain valuable information of the Chhatrapaties of Kolhapur. Besides, Tarabai-Kaleen-Kagad-Patre, Khand-I, II, III and "Tarabai Papers - A collection of Persian papers" published by Shivaji Vidyapeeth, Aitihasik Granth Mala pub. in 1978, and "Tarabai Papers" as well as "Maratha History Seminar Papers" pub. by Shivaji University, Kolhapur in 1971 provide valuable and original documents very useful for further research.

CHAPTER 1

JIJABAI

Emergence of Maratha Power – A New Vision (1621 - 1674 A.D.)

Jijabai initially started under the severe handicap of almost no known resources for founding a state but she was aware of the needs to do so and the challenge she was facing in doing so she had to carve out a place under the sun for her son Shivaji, at a time when both mother and son, Jijabai and Shivaji, had been the victim of misfortune, almost left to manage themselves by the person who should have shouldered their responsibility and that person was Shivaji's father, her husband Shahji. However, adversity brought out the best in her personality and that was the spirit of dauntless struggle against adversity. Adversity taught her nothing but endured defiance of it.

During the XVII and XVIII centuries the political situation in the trans-Narmada region commonly known as Deccan was volatile, the seeds of which were sown right from 1490 A.D., when the five Shia kingdoms of Ahmadnagar in which the paternal home of Jijabai was located at Sindkhed. The other states were Bijapur, Golkunda, Bedar and Berar which had emerged on the ruins of Bahmani kingdom. However, despite all the five being Shia kingdoms, they continued to be in ferment of political upheaval because the rulers of these kingdoms were for most of the time engaged internecine wars. They rarely displayed any sense of political unity and understanding, with the result that after the establishment of the Moghul Empire in northern India, the Moghuls turned their attention towards these rich and prosperous trans-Narmada kingdoms, finding them a good hunting ground where

Daulatabad Fort

the Maratha and Muslim sardars had emerged as prominent political factors.

In fact, the path of the Marathas to emerge as an important military force was paved by Malik Ambar, the Vizier of Nizamshah of Ahmadnagar who trained these hardy folks in the art of guerilla warfare as a component of Nizamshahi army to consider the menace of Moghul domination over the Deccan in general and his kingdom in particular. The Marathas served as "Shilledars"[1] and "bargis" of the various Shia kingdoms, the rulers who provided service to the able and ambitious Maratha sardars.

They were often awarded the titles of 'Raja', 'Naik' and 'Rao'. The state of Bijapur which extended from Neera to Tungabhadra rivers and Ahmadnagar, comprising of the whole of Maharashtra had in their army a large number of the Marathas, they being almost mercenary soldiers, served their masters without any distinction of religion, sect, language or national feelings. Among these sardars, the Moreys,[2] Naiks, Pawars, Ghatgeys, Shirkeys, Ghorpades and Jadhavrao held the best position and were connected with the affairs of the state in one or other ways.

Jijabai was the daughter of Lukhji Jadhavrao, the Deshmukh of Sindkhed, the noble in the Deccan at the time. He was the descendant[3] of the famous dynasty of Yadava kings of Devgiri and held a jagir under the Nizamshahi kingdom to support 10,000 horses during 1578 A.D. and most powerful general at the time having the title of "Das-Hazari" i.e. he could maintain 10,000 soldiers at his disposal. Thus, Jijabai fortunately belonged to that traditionally political minded woman who inherited all the qualities of her ancestors as they served the Nizamshah of Ahmadnagar.

Waghoji Naik, better known as Jagpalrao, was famous for his plundering activities.[4] Similarly Ghatgeys, Shirkeys were noted for their valour, the latter more for the revengeful attitude.[5] Mannes[6] and Ghorpades enjoyed the same place and position in the state.

Besides, there were the Bhonsles who by their valour and enterprising spirit made a career of their own, first in cooperation of the Jadhavas and later on independently.

Their authentic history begins from Babaji Bhonsle,[7] a grand son of Subhakrishna. He had two sons, Maloji and Vithoji. They were sturdy warriors, Patils[8] of Verul, Dewalgaon Raja, Hingne, Berdi, Junti, Wawi, Basendra and 'claimed Rajput' origin which has not been disproved.

According to 'Shiv-Bharat' it can be said that Maloji[9] was not in the service of either Nizamshah of Ahmadnagar or Adilshah of Bijapur, though afterwards he joined Nizamshahi services alongwith his brother Vithoji. Maloji and Vithoji served[10] Waghoji Naik the Chief of Phalton whose sister, Umabai,[11] was married to Maloji and as such, she became the first lady of the Bhonsle family. Maloji was ambitious and also religious. He rebuilt[12] the temple at Verul known as Ghrisheshwar, and a garden.[13] These activities helped him to enhance his position and gain in popularity.

During this period Burhan Nizamshah was ruling at Ahmadnagar, and Lukhji Jadhavrao was in his service. He marched with Nizamshah in his campaigns against Ibrahim Adilshah of Bijapur. Since Maloji had also earned a reputation as a soldier, Nizamshah called him in his own services.[14] Hereafter, Maloji resided at Daulatabad with his brother Vithoji. Soon Maloji was made[15] "Panj Hazari" and received the title of "Raje" alongwith the *jagirs* of Poona and Supa.

Maloji and Umabai had two[16] sons, Shahji and Sharifji, said to have been born through the blessings[17] of Saint Shah Sharifji. Nothing definite is known about the date[18] of birth of Shahji, though it can be said that he must not have been born later than 1600 A.D. Umabai appears to have resided at Verul, her home while Maloji and Vithoji went on military campaigns in support of Burhan Nizamshah, a puppet[19] in the hands of Malik Ambar and took part in the war waged against Ibrahim Adilshah, the two being the keen contestants of power in the Deccan.

In the campaigns, Maloji generally followed Lukhji Jadhavrao and proved[20] superior to all. He was enterprising, self-reliant, and strong-willed. Unfortunately for Umabai, Maloji lost[21] his wife in the battle of Indapur in 1605 A.D. Vithoji had often to remain away from home due to his manifold activities and as such Umabai naturally looked[22] after the interest of Shahji and Sharifji. Nizamshah bestowed[23] upon him Malojis *jagir* and the title of "Raje" together with other presents befitting the occasion. The available accounts show that he had started issuing[24] "Sanad" as early as 1606 A.D.

Lukhji Jadhavrao found in Shahji a suitable match for his daughter Jijabai and married[25] her to Shahji. It is said that Nizamshah graced[26] the occasion by his presence. Thus Jadhavs and Bhonsles were now related to each other through this matrimonial alliance. Later on as and when required, Shahji, Sharifji and eight sons of Vithoji accompanied Malik Ambar[27] in his campaigns. At this stage it was almost difficult for any Maratha Sardar to think of complete independence.

At a time when such momentous changes were taking place in the Deccan, Jahangir succeded[28] the Moghul Emperor Akbar on 24th October, 1605 A.D. He continued the Moghul policy of subjugating the Deccan states and repeatedly attacked the Nizamshahi kingdom of Ahmadnagar. Malik Ambar, the capable[29] Vizier, always tried to defend Ahmadnagar. However, Prince Parvez and Shahnawaz defeated[30] Malik Ambar at Roshangoan after a fierce battle in which Malik Ambar had to take shelter in the fort of Daulatabad but as soon as the Moghuls retired to North, Malik Ambar recaptured the territories the Moghuls had taken from him. This was followed by the march of Prince Khurram to the south alongwith Khan-i-Khanan Mahabat Khan and the other Moghul Generals.

The Moghul Emperor Jahangir personally marched[31] towards the south in 1616 A.D. and reached Mandu to be near the battlefield. Malik Ambar and Ibrahim Adilshah were again defeated and they made peace with the Moghuls by restoring all the Thanas to them which Malik Ambar had previously occupied. In spite of this peace Malik Ambar entered into negotiation for a joint campaign of Adilshah, Nizamshahi and Kutubshahi armies against the Moghuls who were always trying to subdue them. Their combined armies even ravaged[32] the territory of Khandesh and Berar. Once more Prince Khurram came to the South and drove Malik Ambar beyond the river Godawari. He again submitted[33] to the Prince in March 1621 A.D., who offered him mild terms because Prince Khurram was anxious to march towards the north as the succession[34] issue at the Moghul Court had gained importance. Other aspirants were Prince Shaharyar (son-in-law of Nurjehan) and Parwez.

Meanwhile a significant event known as "Elephant-Episode"[35] took place at Daulatabad. It so happened that during a large gathering at Nizamshahi Darbar, an elephant of Sardar Khandagle became violent. It crushed the soldiers and was beyond control. Dattaji, son of Lukhji Jadhavrao and others got enraged[36] and in their instigation, their soldiers attacked the infuriated animal with arrows, spikes and spears. The pitious cry of the wounded animal enraged Sambhaji and Khelogi, sons of Vithoji, who came to the assistance of Sardar Khandagle whose elephant was being killed.

Shahji supported his cousin Sambhaji forgetting his relations with Dattaji. In the melee, Dattaji was killed. Being enraged Lukhji Jadhavrao attacked[37] Sambhaji and Shahji. Shahji was badly[38] hurt and Sambhaji was killed. It was only the mediation of Nizamshah which could pacify the opponents. However, soon after the incident Lukhji Jadhavrao deserted[39] the Nizamshahi services and joined the Moghuls as he suspected that Nizamshah might conspire[40] to endanger his life. As such this "Elephant Episode" sowed the seeds of conflict between the families of Jadhavs and Bhonsles. At the same time this situation had put Jijabai on the horn of a terrible dilemma because now there was an open enemity between her father and the husband. The defaction of Lukhji Jadhavrao was a matter of great concern to

Nizamshah as Lukhji Jadhavrao was an experienced general of his army. It was ironical that what had been a loss of Nizamshah was a matter of rejoicing for Adilshah of Bijapur because the valour of Lukhji Jadhavrao on the battlefield had often turned tables against him in any struggle against Ahmadnagar.

The strange plight of Jijabai can be well imagined as now her father Lukhji Jadhavrao and her husband were serving the two contestants for the supremacy over the Deccan. They were the Moghuls and Nizamshah.

During such trying moments of agony and mental tormentation a bright ray of happiness appeared when she was blessed[41] with a son born to her in 1623 A.D. at Verul[42] who was named Sambhaji. Bakhars state that Nizamshah attended[43] the "Nam-Karan Sanskar". Thus, it is evident that Lukhji Jadhavrao going over to the Moghuls had not affected the relation between Jijabai and Shahji and the King. However, Shahji continued his excursion.

It may be interesting to note that Prince Khurram, one of the aspirants to the Moghul throne, had to march to the North in 1622 A.D., but the Moghul court politics compelled him to turn a rebel.[44] Apprehending a combined attack by Prince Khurram in league with Malik Ambar, Jahangir hurried[45] to the South. He sent his forces to help Ibrahim Adilshah of Bijapur to defeat Prince Khurram and Malik Ambar. Thus, Adilshah got the cherished opportunity to defeat the Nizam Shah and also to have Lukhji[46] Jadhavrao on his side as he was with the Moghul army with his sons Bahadur, Achal and other relations and the followers.

Nizamshah sent Malik Ambar to face the combined forces of the Moghuls. The Maratha Sardars Shahji, Sharifji, Khelkarna, Malhar Rao and others marched with Malik Ambar. There was a fierce battle between the combined forces of the Moghuls and Bijapur and Nizamshahi forces under Malik Ambar at Bhatwadi[47] in 1624 A.D. in which the Moghuls were routed. Moreover, this battle provided an opportunity to Shahji to show his mettle on the battlefield which even evoked the jealousy of Malik Ambar.

This brilliant performance of Shahji proved to be a land mark in the career of Shahji. It filled him with confidence but at the same time he also became conscious of the danger to his position in Ahmednagar court which might be caused due to the jealousy[48] of Malik Ambar. Under these circumstances he thought of seeking new pasture in himself which could also incidently bring him advantage of not being in a camp hostile to his father-in-law Lukhji Jadhavrao. This could also bring peace of mind to Jijabai, if her husband and father could perhance be in the same camp. This was now a certainty that some time or the other Shahji might be obliged to join Bijapur court, and with this in view he retired to his own *jagir* at Poona and Chakan.

However, an opportunity came up when Malik Ambar killed[49] Mulla Mohammad Lari, the Bijapur General and continued his ravages on Adilshahi territory. These adventures of Malik Ambar offered Shahji an opportunity to join[50] Adilshahi services. He received a welcome call from Morar[51] Jagdeo, a minister of Adilshah and was given the title of Sar-Lashkar.[52]

However, the journey of Shahji from his *jagir* of Poona and Chakan to Bijapur was full of thoughts and danger. The Moghuls with whom was Lukhji Jadhavrao, were determined to prevent him from reaching Bijapur and hence he started his journey to Bijapur from Poona with his wife Jijabai who was in advanced stage[53] of pregnancy, he was closely pursued by the Moghuls including[54] his father-in-law Lukhji Jadhavrao who was with them. The need of the hour for Shahji was to march rapidly to Bijapur for his safety but it was not possible to do so in company with Jijabai due to her advanced stage of pregnancy. Shahji hence decided to leave Jijabai behind and to proceed rapidly towards Bijapur. He was aware that even if Jijabai fell into the hands of Lukhji Jadhavrao, he would not be cruel to his daughter but if Shahji was captured, his pursuers would not spare him as now the two were in deadly hostile camps.

This calculation of Shahji proved correct. When Lukhji

Jadhavrao met Jijabai, he asked her to accompany[55] him to Shindkhed or Daulatabad but Jijabai declined to accept this offer of her father and decided to stay at Shivneri. Her mother Mahalsabai under these circumstances decided to live with her. This analysis of the events illustrates that the charges made against Shahji that he had deserted Jijabai at a critical stage of her health does not bear testimony of the facts.

However, at this juncture the scenario at Ahmadnagar, Bijapur and the Moghul court was fast changing. Malik Ambar died on 14th May, 1626 A.D. His son succeeded[56] him as Vizier but he could not[57] be as useful to the state as Malik Ambar was, with the result that the administration soon deteriorated.[58] Jahangir died on 20th October, 1627 A.D. Prince Khurram was at Junnar and marched towards the north and ascended[59] the Moghul throne on the 4th February, 1628 A.D. as Emperor Shahjahan.

During these days of political upheaval at three power centres, Shahji was not sitting idle at Bijapur. He utilised his time in strengthening and expanding Bijapur state. He annexed Keral (Andhra) and Karnatak in Bijapur Kingdom show of his valour by which Shahji was much appreciated[60] by the Adilshah but this also aroused jealousy[61] of senior Sardars of the Bijapur court. While Shahji was busy in his campaigns, Jijabai along with the

Shivnery (Gateway)

other members of her family was residing at Shivneri when Shahji visited his family on 26th November, 1629 A.D. Umabai the mother of Shahji issued[62] a grant to the Ghrishneshwar Temple on the 26th November 1629 A.D. Shahji and Jijabai married their son Sambhaji to Jayantibai,[63] daughter of Shrinivasrao, the keeper of the fort.

However, Lukhji Jadhavrao was still serving the Moghuls but since he was an old general of Nizamshahi Kingdom, he knew the secret[64] details regarding the strength and weaknesses of the strategic positions of the Nizamshahi force. Nizamshah was quite aware of this danger and hence he called Lukhji Jadhavrao on the pretext of holding some important consultation with him and got him murdered,[65] with two of his sons, Achal and Raghu on 29th July 1629 A.D. alongwith a few other relations. Those who survived escaped towards Sindkhed largely due to the skill, foresight and patience of Girjabai.[66] Thus ended[67] the life of Lukhji Jadhavrao at the ripe age of eighty years. However, this tragic situation sounded alarm bell for Shahji to take immediate steps for safeguarding his interest and he hurried towards Poona. He also sought protection[68] of the Moghul Emperor Shahjahan through the Moghul General Azamkhan. He was able to join the Moghuls in 1630 A.D.[69] whereby he was made a Panj-Hajari[70] and received a jewelled dagger, a flag, a drum, a horse and an elephant with a gift of two lakhs of rupees and other presents. Soon he proceeded[71] to take Junnar, the capital of Kutubshah and Sangamnir.

Jijabai was still at Shivneri. She gave birth[72] to her son Shivaji on the 19th February, 1630 A.D. Tukabai[73] the other wife of Shahji also gave birth to a son in 1631 A.D. who was named Ekoji.[74] Meanwhile Shahji found good opportunity to extend his territory. It was firstly, due to the departure[75] of Shahjehan for the North in 1631 A.D. and secondly, due to the murder of Moghul General Khan-i-Jehan Lodhi and Daryakhan because of their rebellious acts. Shahji took advantage of this confusion in the Moghul camp and started occupying Nizamshahi as well as some Adilshahi territory. Soon Shahji acquired[76] Champhargoda and the area around Poona. He was already in possession[77] of the area round about Poona, Nasik and Puntambe.

Shahji now broke[78] of all relations with the Moghuls. He collected a large force and established himself at Nizamshahi again. He also won over the support of Ibrahim Adilshah of Bijapur and occupied all the Nizamshahi territory extending from Poona and Chakan Balaghat, Junnar, Ahmadnagar, Sangamir, Trimbak, and Nasik. Now he had grown in power and even turned down the suggestion of the Moghul Commander Irradat Khan to join him. Shahji even installed[79] a Nizamshahi prince at Bheemgad in 1632 A.D. and began to carry on the administration of the kingdom in his name.

These activities of Shahji were unbearable for the Moghuls and the Moghul Emperor sent his general Mahabatkhan to subdue Shahji. Accordingly Mahabatkhan marched[80] to attack Daulatabad and captured it on 17th June 1633 A.D. But this did not dishearten Shahji who moved from fort to fort and from face to face in his effort to uphold[81] the cause of the Nizamshahi prince.[82]

It is held that Jijabai accompanied[83] Shahji from fort to fort and suffered hardships with him. It is also mentioned that once the Killedar of Trimbak Fort, Mhaldarkhan wanted to win Moghul favour by capturing Shivaji with the intention to hand him over to the Moghuls. Apprehending[84], Jijabai sent Shivaji to live in obscurity at Shivpur and thus foiled the designs of Mhaldarkhan who failed to get any clue of Shivaji but he could imprison Jijabai. One of her relatives, Jagdeo, who was in Moghul services paid ransom and got her released.[85]

These critical conditions made Shivaji apprehensive regarding the safety of his family and he entered into correspondence[86] with the Portuguese Governor at Chaul to provide shelter to his family members, but the same being refused, Shahji had to keep Jijabai and other family members at Puntambe.[87] After thus ensuring the safety of his family Shahji went to Mahuli and from there to Junnar[88] where he kept the puppet king Murtiza Nizamshah and carried on plunder in the environs of Daulatabad.

However, Shahjehan was not blind to this situation and realised the danger to the Moghul authority being passed by Shahji and hence he marched[89] on to Daulatabad on 4th Jan., 1636 A.D. with Mirza Raja Jaisingh, Shaistakhan and other young generals to conquer Golkunda, invade Bijapur and crush Shahji.

This Moghul onslaught was so severe that Ibrahim Adilshah of Bijapur had to submit before the Moghuls. This made Shahji to realise that now it would be impossible to him to uphold the cause of Nizamshahi prince. To save Shahji from utter defeat, Ramdaullah Khan Rustam-i-Jehan, the Bijapur General, mediated for him with the Moghuls and assuring that he would not indulge in any harmful activity against the Moghuls. He also agreed to confir a *jagir* of four lakhs to Shahji for handing him over the Nizamshahi prince to the Moghuls. The prince was sent to Gwalior Fort. Later Adilshah sent Shahji for the conquest of Karnatak but Shahji was unable to retain[90] his ancestral *jagir* at Poona. Thus ended the struggle between the Moghul Emperor and the combined forces of Adilshah and Nizamshah in 1636 A.D.

While embarking on his Karnatak expedition, Shahji took with him Tukabai and Ekoji. There he founded[91] a new capital for the southern *jagir* at Bangalore. Jijabai remained[92] with Shivaji and Dadaji Konddeva at Poona till the construction of Rajgad. At Poona a house named Lal-Mahal[93] and a town called Shivapur[94] were built by Dadaji Konddeva for Jijabai and Shivaji. A garden named Shahibag[95] was also laid out. Jijabai built[96] the Temple of Kaspa Ganpati in Poona in 1636-40 A.D. Not satisfied only with this, she issued a "Sanad"[97] for free distribution of food to needy and gave vatan for the maintenance of the temples at Alandi and Chinchwad (for Dewasthan). She also continued[98] the Vatan of Matanayakin, the dancer, who had received state grants from Shahji. The result of this liberal policy was that she won the reverance and confidence of not only the Hindus but of the Muslims as well in the region of Poona and Supa.

Despite being busy with the project to give a new face to Poona, both Jijabai and Dadaji Konddeva, did not fail to give due attention to the education[99] and training of Shivaji befitting for his future responsibilities. His education and training which included the art of warfare also.

After taking these primary steps to consolidate her position in the region of Poona and Chakan and organizing the affairs there, Jijabai undertook[100] a visit to Bangalore with Dadaji Konddeva to meet Shahji to make a regular provision for Shivaji worthy of "a first grade nobleman's son," as he could not be left to vegetate on a mere food allowance like an illegitimate son. Dr. Sarkar further[101] remarks that both the wives of Shahji quarrelled with each other for the cause of their respective sons. He states, "A man with knowledge of the world can easily imagine the stormy scene in the harem of Shahji, the rival wives faced each other and for their respective sons."

However, these short comments of Dr. Sarkar do not stand critical scrutiny as he has not mentioned the sources he has relied to make these comments. Moreover, it was known that Sambhaji was living with Shahji and he being the elder would have succeeded him and that at the same time enjoyment of certain rights and privileges were generally not denied to the younger brothers and step-brothers and therefore there was no cause for Jijabai to have rival feeling over this issue. Besides these, the allegation that Shahji himself called Jijabai and Shivaji to Bangalore because of a hint from Bijapur Sultan to put a check on the activities of Shivaji holds no grounds as Shivaji was no power then even generously compared to other petty Jagirdars of the time.

Jijabai since was a deeply religious lady, she converted her Bangalore visit into a pilgrimage as well and visited[102] many holy places. Shivaji also went to the ruined capital of Vijayanagar kingdom which inspired him with a vision to found a glorious Hindu kingdom as was once the "Vijayanagar Empire". After some time she decided to leave for Poona. However, here we again come across an evidence to show that Bangalore visit of Jijabai had not caused any ill feeling between her and Shahji because before Shivaji left for Poona, Shahji bestowed[103] on him the estate of Poona yielding 40,000 Huns (about a lakh and a half of rupees) annually. It was also decided that four persons would accompany them to Poona, and Shivaji would look after the welfare of the estate while Jijabai was to manage the public courts. Thus, Jijabai got an opportunity to win the confidence of the people and of the main support of the nobles at one stroke. Onwards, Jijabai resided at Poona with Shivaji away from her husband Shahji which has been asserted as an issue of separation between them and as such needs to be examined, considering the sequence of events and personal relations vis-a-vis the other obtaining conditions between 1630-36 and 1643 A.D.

The analysis of the facts regarding Bangalore visit of Jijabai also contradicts the view that there were strained relations between Jijabai and Shahji, due to second marriage of Shahji with Tukabai holding the view that the relation between Jijabai and Shahji were strained. Kincaid and Parasnis have stated[104], ".... and after his second marriage seems to have broken off all but formal relations of her husband". Sardesai writes[105] ...." when the second wife came to the house, the first one started living separately". Dr. Sarkar concludes[106] "her husband's neglect drove the mind of Jijabai and a sudden childish impulse and her father's..... have brought in a loveless marriage and he seems to have felt an increasing aversion to Jijabai". According to Patwardhan and Rawlinson[107] Shahji having disagreed with his wife on account of his hatred to her father, resolved on separation and accordingly sent her with the infant Shivaji to reside at Poona. Forest mentions[108], "Owing to the ill treatment which he had received from Jadhavrao Shahji made a resolution never to see Jijawai or his son Shivaji in consequence married another wife Tukabai, daughter of a man called Mohite." Ferishta states[109] "Shahji having disagreed with his wife on account of his hatred to her father resolved on separation and accordingly sent her, with the infant Shivaji to him who showed no affection to reside at Poona."

Despite this, it has already been mentioned that though Shahji had married Tukabai Mohite, sister of Baji Mohite, a prominent sardar of Bijapur, yet he had maintained his contact with Jijabai at Shivneri fort and visited her in 1630 A.D. Neither any event nor any account shows that they had any idea of separation then. She again lived with him at Mahuli in 1634-36 A.D. with Shivaji and Dadaji Konddeva. It was thus seen that for stretches of periods both of them did maintain their contacts and lived together.

Besides, Shahji's second marriage should neither have given her a chance nor desire for separation for there are examples when co-wives lived happily together contributing in their own ways towards the prosperity of the same family. Moreover, poligamy was never an unusual practice forbidden religiously or socially. Jijabai could have lived with Shahji at Bangalore if she so desired. No account indicates that she was ever prevented from living there. The more significant reason appears to be that Poona was their ancestral home and the revenue supervision at Poona required personal attention though it was being efficiently managed by Dadaji Konddeva.

Despite the reluctance of Shahji to go ahead to form a Maratha State, Jijabai was never in doubt about the need and justification for founding a Hindu-Pad-Padshahi and made small town like Poona perpetually ruined by different invaders from time to time to be the centre of her activities as such she had deep firm roots here. A course such as this was no easy task and required much labour and perserverance for its improvement but she was determined to do so. Kincaid and Parasnis write[110] "Ordinary persons would have given up the attempt in despair. But Jijabai and Dadaji Konddeva were not ordinary persons." This was the place where she had stayed with Shivaji and now she launched her scheme of its rehabilitation of Poona with active cooperation of Dadaji Konddeva. She knew that she had no easy task at her hand and hence, as the first step, she concentrated her attention on improving the agrarian system. On the one hand such an attempt was bound to win support of rural folk for her at grassroot level and on the other hand it was to lead to the improvement and better management of the state finances and tapping of new resources. This was bound to strengthen her authority. Since she was aware that grassroot problems were to be tackled first, she gave her first attention to the problem of land improvement and better collection of revenue. She was so firm in her determination that in 1646 A.D. she directed Dadaji Konddeva to revise his land distribution scheme instead of his scheme of land distribution[111] – "Nime Vatan" (to divide into two). She ordered that land be distributed by "Gotmukhi" (Jury) system.

Though Jijabai was keen to improve the lot of grassroot and ordinary agriculturists, but at the same time she was not willing to hurt the interest of the land-owning class. She was aware of the significant role in the agrarian and political structure. This is evident from her letter she wrote[112] in 1651-52 to the officers and Mokaddams of the village Beherwada, Pargana Poona about Ganogabji's land in which she declared, "that the land had been granted to him perpetually and therefore, it was to be continued[113] to him though her son Shivaji on .... wrote a letter (may be Ganogabji or the officers of Beherwada or both of them) had asked to discontinue the same temporarily but that the inam should be continued and no new letter regarding the grant of the land should be entertained". The letter indicates that she was firm in her views and was willing even to set aside the order of Shivaji, if needed, although she always kept him in the forefront.

This assertion of her authority by Jijabai sometimes created rather delicate positions for Dadaji Konddeva who was not merely a clerk. He too was a good administrator who had managed[114] the estate in the past years without any counsellor and had worked[115] in the past years as a Subedar and also as Kiledar of the fort Kondava and hence, it is to the credit of Jijabai that despite her firm assertion of authority in policy matter she adjusted with Dadaji Konddeva in day to day affairs of the estate.

Under these circumstances, at a time when Jijabai was busy

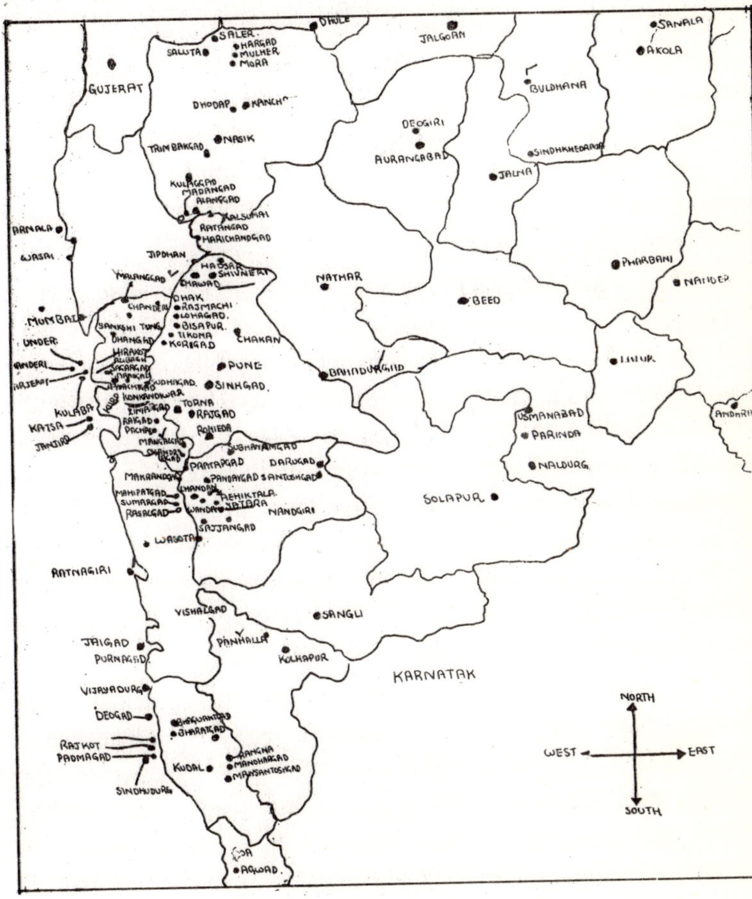

Sahyadari Forts.

in her manifold activities Shivaji began to plan the foundation of an independent kingdom. On his return from Bangalore he had already conquered twelve naval countries and aspired to extend his Jagir. Though Dadaji Konddeva had his own doubts[116] about the scheme of Shivaji still reliable accounts show that Dadaji had extended his full support to him as evident by the oath[117] they took together in the temple of Raireshwar at Bhor (District Poona) for founding an independent kingdom. In persuance of his scheme Shivaji issued[118] his seal in 1645 A.D. This also demonstrates his ambition to have the ever rising fame and prosperity for his kingdom.

They soon realised[119] the importance of forts and went on campaigns to gain new strategic positions and conquer new territories. The forts were to provide them protection against the onslaughts of the enemy. The Marathas could also successfully utilise these forts a strategic points from where the gurilla warfare could be launched which was preferable than open warfare and pitched battles. Hence, Shivaji captured the Torna fort and renamed it as Prachandgad. They also started building the fort of Rajgad with other smaller forts, so as to make the place more secure and safe for offensive as well as defensive actions. Jijabai and the inmates of the family mostly resided at Rajgad.

These activities of Shivaji attracted anxious attention of both Adilshah and Shahji. Shahji demanded an explanation from Dadaji Konddeva for the deeds of Shivaji who gave an evasive reply saying,[120] "I gave my humble advice to Shivaji Raje but to nothing that I said would he consent." However, the course of Shivaji met a serious setback when Dadaji Konddeva died[121] in 1647 A.D.

Under these circumstances Shahji also became a suspect[122] in the eyes of Adilshah. A charge against Shahji was that he had sent to Shivaji to administer the territories under his control and also sent[123] Kanhoji Jedhe and Dadji Krishna Lokhare to help Shivaji. Shahji felt unsafe and wrote to Kutub Shah of Golkunda to give him shelter but he declined[124] to do so. The relations between Shahji and Adilshah had became so bitter that when during siege of Jinji Mustaf Khan and Bajiraja imprisoned[125] Shahji by treachery and whose game was responsible for his captivity brought him under custody[126] at Bijapur. Adilshah threatened him with entombment.[127] Later on, he agreed to release[128] Shahji if Shivaji handed over the fort of Kondava and Sambhaji the city of Bangalore.

These developments placed Jijabai and Shivaji in a highly delicate and difficult situation. Jijabai was on the horns of a dilemma, whether to protect the interest of the son or to save the life of the husband but rose to the occasion and maintained cool temper and cautiously watched the situation, before responding to the demand made by Adilshah. She was aware that the moment was critical as Shivaji had become so excited that he wanted to go to the rescue of his father and fight[129] against Adilshah. According to the Bakhars, Shivaji was prevented from doing so by his wife Saibai who advised[130] that Shivaji should not go to Bijapur as his father was there as a prisoner at the mercy of Adilshah. Grant Duff also states[131] Saibai said, "You have a better chance of effecting Shahji's liberty by maintaining your present power than by trusting to the mercy of a government notoriously treachrous."

At this time Shahji made a diplomatic move and pleaded to the Adilshah that his son (Shivaji) was as much against him as he was against the king but this proved futile[132]. Shivaji entered into correspondence[133] with Moghul prince Murad to seek his intervention but finally Shivaji and Sambhaji handed[134] over the fort of Kondava and the city of Bangalore respectively to Adilshah and secured the release of Shahji to much relief of Jijabai and the Bangalore house of Shahji. The tension having thus subsided Shivaji resided at Rajgad till 16th May 1649 A.D. But at the same time he maintained a close vigil on the foreigners i.e., the English, the Dutch and the Portuguese who had established themselves by planting their factories lying on the Western Ghat at Rajapur, Vengurla and Chaul by 1648 A.D.

An opportunity for further territorial expansion soon came up when Niloji Nilkanthrao, an officer of Nizamshah and the Kiledar of the highly strategic fort of Purandar[135] died and a family dispute between his two sons arose for power. This was utilised by Shivaji who stormed the fort and captured it. During this campaign Jijabai also participated in it and stayed at Purandar for some time after the victory. Here she met[136] a learned priest, Gopal Bhatt Shridhar Bhatt, in 1653 A.D. and performed "sun-worship" etc., for the welfare and prosperity of her son. Afterwards she relied on him for performing all religious functions and penances. Her role during this campaign and thereafter illustrates her courage twined with religious beliefs.

Soon after Shivaji's attention was drawn towards Jaoli because of its strategic importance and defensive position, it was located amidst hilly and thickly wooded forest with evergreen trees. The narrow rugged and steep Crest of Sahyadari rising from nearly a thousand feet or more above sea level formed its western[137] wall. There were, besides countless gorges, foot-tracks leading from Jaoli to Kokan. It also provided the best means of safety against an enemy from south Western Ghats. It was under the charge of the Moreys who had received the grant of the village from the Bijapur king. As such for Shivaji, it was necessary to win over the Morey Sardars first, if he wanted to capture Jaoli.

Hence, it is said that Shivaji opened negotiations[138] with Chandrarao Morey of Jaoli and during these negotiations, Hanmant Rao Morey, the Diwan of Chandrarao was killed[139] while Chandrarao escaped[140] from Jaoli which facilitated the path of Shivaji to establish his sway over Jaoli. Jijabai was also equally interested[141] in the acquisition of Jaoli.

It was not that these activities of Shivaji and Jijabai were going unnoticed by Bijapur court and Sultan Mohammad Adilshah and on his death in 1656 A.D., his successor Ali Adil Shah II being minor, his regent mother Badi Begam,[142] was conscious of the challenge posed by the rising Maratha power.

Meanwhile Jijabai was concentrating her attention on the agrarian problems and progress of cultivation. She encouraged people to bring under cultivation the fallow tracts and live near such land and region. To offer them more facilities, she established Bazzars (Peths), denoted[143] land perpetually to those persons who were interested in cultivation and horticulture. She also bestowed[144] on Vinayak Bhatt Thakar the Vatan of Peth "Jijapur" to meet the general expenses of the temple. Jijabai and later Raja Jaisingh donated[145] Vatan (land) to Shri Moraya "Devasthan" (Poona) for the same purpose. This practice was continued by the Peshwas also.

Besides, Jijabai took effective steps to curb mutual quarrels and disputes among her officials. Once she scolded Deshkulkarni of Poona and wrote[146] to him, "You are having a quarrel with Mukund regarding his landed property. This cannot be justified. If you go on disputing, my son will not tolerate it. See that we no more hear of such quarrels." However, she was equally sympathetic towards the difficulties of her officials[147] and helped them to overcome the same by providing funds and other requirements.

She was always willing to remedy[148] any injustice to her people. Once Rangbhatt Kulkarni of four villages of Khode had absconded leaving his mother and wife during famine days. In his absence, Vinayak Bhatt Thakur gave protection to Kulkarni's mother and his wife. When Rangbhatt Kulkarni returned and claimed his rights to the land Vinayak Bhatt Thakar placed the matter before Jijabai who continued the inam (land) of four villages of Khode to Vinayak Bhatt Thakar. It is thus evident that she maintained the sanctity of the traditions and contracts and to avoid frictions and disturbances in the estate.

Meanwhile, Shivaji undertook various excursions and conquests. He ravaged Junnar and Ahmadnagar in 1657 A.D. He also completed the construction[149] of Pratapgad by 1658 A.D., in the village of Jaoli and raided South Konkan, Rajapur and seized territories belonging to the Siddis of Janjira. By 1658 A.D. he had established his sway over the northern and southern South Konkan, with the result that his ambition to found an independent kingdom had been partially realised. From now onwards he styled himself as "Raje".

At a time when Shivaji was busy in consolidating his position in Deccan, the Moghul policy at Delhi also attracted his attention. He was aware that his struggle would not confine merely against Bijapur and one day he might have to face the Moghul power. Hence, he closely watched the political developments at Delhi. This was the time when the Moghul Emperor Shahjehan fell ill in 1658 A.D. and a war of succession ensued[150] among his sons, Princes Dara Shikoh, Murad, Shahshuja and Aurangzeb. Aurangzeb was at Aurangabad. He started for the north on 23rd Jan., 1658 A.D. but before leaving the Deccan, he had warned[151] the Bijapur authorities to check Shivaji's growing strength who, according to him, was quite alert to use any opportunity for further expansion. Aurangzeb defeated[152] Dara Shikoh on 29 May, 1658 A.D. and deposed Shahjehan. He ascended[153] the Moghul throne on 22nd July 1658 A.D.

Shivaji was prudent enough not to invite any clash with Aurangzeb at that juncture and hence he sent his messenger[154] Raghunath-Pant to the Moghul court with a message of repentance[155] for his past activities. Aurangzeb was also too busy with his own problems and he granted pardon to Shivaji who accepted his authority over the forts and territories he had gained till then.

Although by this diplomatic move, Shivaji had gained some respite from Moghul danger but Bijapur had not digested the severe loss inflicted by Shivaji. Bijapur had lost twenty three major and seven minor forts by 1658 A.D. This was in addition to other losses. The depredation of Shivaji and his supporters had become a source of serious anxiety to the Bijapur king. Badi-Bagum viewed the activities of Shivaji with serious alarm. She asked her confident[156] general Afzalkhan to capture Shivaji by "pretending[157] friendship". With a staunch determination, Afzalkhan started on his mission[158] and marched towards Poona. He won over many Jagirdars and desecrated the temples (idols) on the way.

On hearing about this attack by Afzalkhan, Shivaji and Jijabai marched[159] from Poona towards Jaoli and took cover at Pratapgad which was well protected and safe. This move also indicates that Shivaji was aware of the futility of challenging Afzalkhan in an open encounter, instead, he wanted to await his chance to strike against Afzalkhan in an open encounter. Perceiving this move of Shivaji, Afzalkhan stopped his march towards Poona and proceeded towards Jaoli. He camped at "Wai" for nearly five months and sent[160] his envoy Krishnaji Bhaskar to Shivaji to invite him for an interview. He gave a promise[161] to influence the government of Bijapur to forgive Shivaji and to get him grant of the forts and land already won by him.

Both Shivaji and Jijabai doubted the words of Afzalkhan. Shivaji and Jijabai were aware that the march of Afzalkhan towards Jaoli was a part of his game plan to chastise Shivaji and to force him to submit before the authority of Bijapur. Hence, both mother and son decided to test the sincerity of the words of Afzalkhan. They sent Pantoji Gopinath to Afzalkhan with the request[162] that if a meeting between him and Shivaji was to take place, he should come to the foot of the plateau on which was the fort of Pratapgad. They posed as if Shivaji was afraid to go to war[163] in the plains of Jaoli to meet the Khan to discuss the proposal made by him.

The messenger visited Afzalkhan and communicated the desire of Shivaji. 10th Nov., 1659 A.D. was fixed for the epochal "meet" between Shivaji and Afzalkhan. Writers have differently stated the place where Jijabai stayed during the intended "meet" between Shivaji and Afzalkhan. Sabhasad and other Bakhars hold the view that she stayed at Rajgad[164] while the ballad by Shaheer Agyandas informs us that she was at Pratapgad. Sabhasad is a reliable source of information and Ballad has been proved to be a contemporary account. Apparently though the meeting between Afzalkhan and Shivaji had been fixed, yet, both had their own doubts and fear against each other. Meanwhile Jijabai had also her moments of anxiety and apprehensions for Shivaji's safety.

This was no fear without reasons, she had her own reason. It should be remembered that Afzalkhan was associated with the imprisonment[166] of her husband Shahji in 1647 A.D. and was responsible for the death[167] of her eldest son in 1657 A.D. at Kanakgiri. Therefore, it is obvious that she had no faith in Afzalkhan. She had witnessed political upheavals all through her life. She wavered as to whether Shivaji should at all proceed to meet Afzalkhan or avoid meeting at all. According to "Ballad"[168] Jijabai had become so anxious when she heard about the proposal for a meeting between Shivaji and Afzalkhan that she rushed to see Shivaji for being available by his side in the hour of need. Mother had her own apprehensions regarding the safety and well being of her son.

She was so worried that even on the eve of the departure of Shivaji on his mission to meet Afzalkhan, she pleaded[169] with him to avoid the meeting. However, Shivaji was reluctant to accept her advice and reminded her of the atrocities Afzalkhan had committed on the people and the temples which were desecrated by him and for which she had great reverence and respect. Having been reminded of the misdeeds of Afzalkhan, she not only blessed[170] Shivaji for his victory but also charged him to take revenge of the death of her son Sambhaji, Shivaji's eldest brother. She also advised[171] him to remain careful, and asked his companions to keep him safe. Dr. Sarkar also writes,[172] "As the party was about to descend from the fort, a saintly female figure appeared in their midst, it was Jijabai. Shivaji bowed to his mother. She blessed him saying, 'Victory be yours', and solemnly charged his companions to keep him safe."

Deep concern of Jijabai for the safety of Shivaji had given

rise to some hearsay and it seems that relying on such hearsay a letter sent by the Dutch[173] East India Co. to Batavia and another letter sent by Henry Revinton and Randolf Taylor[174] to Surat mention that Jijabai had visited Afzalkhan before his meeting with Shivaji, pleading for the safety of his son but there is no corroborative evidence to confirm this account and hence it is evident that the authenticity of this account is totally doubtful and the account is unreliable. A women like Jijabai who had known Afzalkhan for such a long time would have been quite aware of the futility of any such request. Moreover, if the details of the reasons given for the visit of Jijabai in the letters are scrutinised carefully it becomes evident that reason mentioned in the letters are widely different which make the letters unreliable.

During the meeting between Afzalkhan and Shivaji, Afzalkhan lost[175] his life and Shivaji was once more victorious against the Bijapur army. It was a matter of great rejoicing for the Marathas and to commemorate[176] this event Jijabai asked Shaheer Agyandas to compose verses for which he was handsomely rewarded.

Shivaji now reached Rajgad with a huge booty captured from the camp of Afzalkhan was bound to make Ali Adil Shah II of Bijapur wild with anger and spirit of revenge. Hence without giving a chance to the enemy to strike first Shivaji carried on his attacks and ravages on Bijapur territory and ravaged it incessantly. After reaching Panhalla[177] on 2nd Dec., 1660 A.D., he marched towards Kolhapur where he defeated the Bijapur General Rustam-I-Zaman and Fazlkhan. Maratha army continued to ravage different parts of Bijapur territory. Shivaji captured Dabhol[178] on 13th Feb., 1661 A.D. and raided the English Factory at Rajapur. Ali Adil Shah II felt seriously humiliated by the loss of his territories and he turned to the Moghul Emperor Aurangzeb for support to subdue Shivaji.

Having first hand knowledge of the politics and terrain of the Deccan acquired by him during his regime as the Moghul Subedar, Aurangzeb realised that the activities of Shivaji were not only a danger for the kingdom of Bijapur but in course of time might also emerge as a challenge and threat to the attempts for the Moghul supremacy over Deccan. Hence, despite Moghul hostility towards the kingdom of Bijapur, he took note of the request of Ali Adil Shah II for support against Shivaji and despatched[179] an army under Moghul general Shaistakhan to deal with Shivaji who had emerged as a danger both for Bijapur and the Moghuls.

While Shaistakhan marched towards Bheema to chastise Shivaji in February 1660 A.D. Ali Adil Shah II sent[180] for Siddi Jauhar and directed him to capture[181] Shivaji who was swiftly marching towards Miraj. In order to strike at an important power base of Shivaji, Siddi Jauhar launched an attack against Panhalla which forced Shivaji to turn towards Panhalla[182] on the 2nd March 1660 A.D. Shivaji sent Netaji Palkar and Siddi Hillal to ravage and plunder Bijapur territory in order to teach a lesson to Ali Adil Shah II. These tactics of Shivaji proved sound and he successfully resisted onslaughts of Siddi Jauhar. However, since Shivaji was busy at Panhalla, Shaistakhan was able to capture[183] Indapur and Chakan which made Shivaji to realise that Moghuls were enemy of Bijapur but both of them considered him a common foe and hence in future, he will have to deal not only with the Sultan of Bijapur but also to fight against the Moghuls. Besides this Jijabai and Shivaji were also witnessing that with the Moghul army were also marching Maratha Sardars like Rustamrao Jadhav, Kank, Trimbak Anant hailing from the house of Sindkhed distantly related with Jijabai. This scene was a sad commentary on the uphill task faced by the mother and son in their attempt to found a new Jerusalem.

During such adverse conditions the position of Shivaji at Panhalla was everyday growing more and more critical. He was surrounded by Siddi Jauhar, Rustam-I-Zaman and Fazl Khan, son of Afzalkhan, with the result that the siege at Panhalla assumed dangerous proportion for Shivaji. To add to his woe, Netaji Palkar and Siddi Hillal also returned to Rajgad without any success in the task assigned to them. Jijabai was now exasperated[184] to see the critical situation in which Shivaji had been placed at Panhalla. She burst in anger against Netaji Palkar and Siddi Hillal. She scolded them and declared that she would personally march to Panhalla and see that Siddi Jauhar was not only defeated but also killed.[185] She promised to bring the chopped off head with her. Here it may be remembered that she was not less than 60 years of age and yet she had not lost courage and determination to deal with such a tense situation when mother and son were fighting on two different fronts, son at Panhalla and mother at Rajgad.

Although she had scolded Netaji Palkar and Siddi Hillal for their failure but still she had faith in their loyalty towards her family and when she decided to leave for Panhalla, she asked them to remain at Rajgad to defend the fort. Her faith in them was well responded. Netaji Palkar and Siddi Hillal, who assured her that they would pay full attention to the task and demanded that they should be sent to break the siege of Panhalla laid by the enemy. Jijabai had to agree to their request and they left for Panhalla.

During this struggle Jijabai stationed herself at Rajgad. She was doing her best to defend[186] the fort. The mother and son were fighting on two fronts viz. Panhalla as well as round about Poona. This had adversely affected the general life of the people and their condition had deteriorated.[187] Business had been crippled and the people were seeking shelters in forests away from their homes. The Moghuls ravaged and plundered Saswad[188] and captured Poona as well as Shivpur. These attacks and the counter attacks between the Moghuls and the Marathas gave an adverse blow to the concerted efforts of Jijabai to rehabilitate and consolidate the Maratha State.

He was now surrounded by Siddi Jauhar, Rustam-I-Zaman and Fazl Khan with the result that their Panhalla seige assumed dangerous proportion for Shivaji. Meanwhile Shivaji was finding it most difficult to carry on the defence at Panhalla. To add to his harassment, Henry Revington[189], the chief of the English Factory, arrived with his assistant Mighaum Gifford to help Shivaji's opponents. Totally surrounded by such adverse circumstances, Shivaji had no alternative but to sue for peace. While negotiations were going on Shivaji left Panhalla in charge of Trimbak Bhaskar and escaped[190] from the fort on 13th July, 1660 A.D. He was hotly pursued by his opponents and skirmishes took place in more than one place. Baji Prabhu lost[191] his life. Shivaji reached Vishalgad safely. Panhalla was taken by Siddi Jauhar on 22nd September, 1660 A.D., after a fight of about four months and a half against Shivaji and his army.

At last Shivaji reached Rajgad.[192] It was quite a great consolation to Jijabai to meet him after nearly ten months. Instead of sitting back quietly Shivaji waited for a chance to strike Shaistakhan near Umarbhined. The attack of Shivaji was fierce that the Moghuls could save themselves with great difficulty and sought the mediation of Raibagin to find a way to come out of the net of Shivaji. The Moghuls had to pay heavy fine[193] to Shivaji. In March, 1661 A.D., Shivaji marched towards Rajapur and captured[194] six to eight English officers and thus avenged the help they had given to his opponents at Panhalla. He then marched towards Shringarpur in 1661 A.D. It belonged to Wagboji Shirkey and Suryarao Shirkey looked after its management. Shivaji won over Suryarao and took Shringarpur. He established[195] his sway over the Tal-Konkan by January, 1662 A.D. It was now apparent that he was quite strong to defy the Bijapur king openly.

At such a critical juncture there was a major change in Bijapur administration. Badi Begam of Bijapur left[196] for Mecca on pilgrimage by 1662 A.D., Ali Adil Shah II took over the management of the kingdom, with his known hatred of Shivaji and attempt to found an independent Maratha Power. This again posed a serious dilemma for Shahji who was still in the service of Bijapur. However, by now Shahji had made up his mind to display his affection for Shivaji and Jijabai openly. Shahji was still serving him but that he visited Shivaji and Jijabai with his second wife Tukabai. They reached Jejuri, Jijabai, Shivaji and his wife Soyarabai awaited Shahji's arrival at Jejuri. No sooner Shivaji saw his father, then he greeted him with great respect. The ladies spent some time together worshipping[197] and performing various social rituals. Thereafter, Shahji visited many places in Maharashtra. It is said that it was he who suggested to Shivaji to choose Rairi as a suitable place for Maratha capital and after some time the name of Rairi was changed to Raigad. Shahji stayed at Maharashtra for two months and then returned to his fief in 1662 A.D.

Despite the reverses faced by him, Shivaji had become emboldened again by the favourable condition in which he found himself. Hence, he made a surprise attack[198] on Shaistakhan on 5th April 1663 A.D. at Poona. In the melee, Shaistakhan's fingers were cut off[199] and he barely escaped with his life but his son was killed. Shivaji did not wait at Poona. He hurried[200] towards Sinhgad and asked Moropant Pingle to defend the fort and then quietly marched towards Surat, in order to plunder[201] and ravage it in 1664 A.D. It was a big loot and he returned with huge booty to Lohgad. Meanwhile as anticipated by Shivaji, Sinhgad was attacked by Jaswant Singh who laid a siege but the Marathas so ably defended the fort that he decided to lift the siege and marched away from the scene.

While this struggle was going on, Jijabai and Shivaji suffered a terrible personal blow when Shahji died[202] in 1664 A.D. in an hunting expedition. Ranade and Telong state[203], "Jijabai at first insisted on preparation for sacrificing herself as a sati". However, she was prevailed upon not to do so on the ground that "it might endanger the life of Shivaji and the empire established by him would at once cease to exist." Finally, she gave up the idea of committing "Sati". Ekoji succeeded[204] the personal fief and property of Shahji. However, the death of Shahji broke off all consideration which Shivaji had towards Bijapur king and he again emerged as a terror in the Deccan which could not be tolerated by the Moghul Emperor Aurangzeb.

Aurangzeb appointed[205] Mirza Raja Jaisingh as subedar of the Deccan to subdue[206] Shivaji. The Moghul General Dilerkhan, Daudkhan, Rajaram Singh Sisodia, Surjan Singh Bundela and Kirat Singh were deputed to assist Mirza Raja Jaisingh. They crossed the Narmada on 13th February 1665 A.D. and soon Mirza Raja Jaisingh won over the confidence of the Portuguese,[207] the English and the Naiks of Bednur who were the staunch enemies of Shivaji before he launched his direct attack against Shivaji and reached Aurangabad. On the 3rd March 1665 A.D., he arrived at Poona and with Dilerkhan besieged the fort of Purandar.

At this juncture Shivaji was at Rajgad and Jijabai was at Singhad with the result that Moghuls were forced to open two fronts against the Marathas but that had also created serious defence and logistic problems for the Marathas as well as they were now to defend two forts and to fight out on two fronts of Purandar fort. There was tough fight between the Moghuls and the Marathas. Morar Baji fell[208] fighting on the battlefield in May 1665 A.D. It was a tragic situation for Shivaji and Jijabai to protect the territories under their control and occupation against such powerful attack.

As mentioned Shivaji being confidant that he would rout Afzalkhan, had boldly faced him. Though Afzalkhan was a soldier of robust disposition, he suffered from over-confidence which led to his death, but Mirza Raja Jaisingh was of a different type. He was a shrewd[209] politician and seasoned general as well. He had attacked[210] Shivaji though pretending as if object of his campaign was to launch an attack against Bijapur and Golkunda. His shrewd strategy and his military onslaught had created highly critical situation for Shivaji. His mixture of political and military pressure created such a serious and adverse situation for Shivaji that he was obliged to send[211] his messenger Raghunath Pant to Jaisingh with an offer[212] of treaty which the Moghul Generals were reluctant[213] to accept in the first instant. However, this gave Shivaji an opportunity to meet him on 11th June, 1665 A.D.

Shivaji met Jaisingh and asked him to enter[214] into an understanding with him. It is said that Shivaji pleaded[215] with him for the revival of Hindu kingdom. However, Dilerkhan was not in favour of relaxing the military pressure on Shivaji but despite this, Shivaji and Mirza Raja Jaisingh concluded the treaty[216] of Purandar on 12th June, 1665 A.D. According to the terms of the treaty, Shivaji agreed to cede twenty three forts and kept only twleve fortresses with him. He also agreed to support Mirza Raja Jaisingh in his attempt to subdue other kings and to visit[217] the Moghul court alongwith his son Sambhaji. Thus, by keeping Shivaji with him Mirza Raja Jaisingh was sure that he would cease to be an obstacle in his Bijapur campaign. Shivaji also agreed to supply a contingent of 5000 cavalry to stand by the Moghul army but the Moghul General Dilerkhan was annoyed[218] with this move of Mirza Raja Jaisingh as he was already victorious at Purandar.

As promised, Shivaji prepared himself to march towards the north. He made arrangement for the administration of the estate in his absence. Dr. Sarkar writes[219], "His (Shivaji's) mother Jijabai was left as regent with Moro Pant, the Peshwa Niloji Sondev, the Majumdar under his orders." He cautioned everyone to remain vigilant against surprise attack or fraud. Jijabai took[220] over the responsibility from Shivaji who started for the north on 5th March, 1665 A.D., with his son Sambhaji. Dr. Sarkar commends his arrangement, stating it to be a "masterpiece of fore-thought and organisation." Shivaji met[221] Aurangzeb on 12th May, 1666 A.D., with his son Sambhaji. He was given a seat among the Panj-Hazari[222] which enraged him. With the result that Shivaji and his son were imprisoned[223] by the Moghul Emperor.

Meanwhile, Shivaji's principality was being well managed by Jijabai and the councillors, which drew the attention and praise of Mirza Raja Jaisingh who said,[224] "For although Shivaji had remained absent for nearly six months, Swarajya was not reduced by an inch in spite of the enemies like Siddi II of Bijapur." As if to continue Shivaji's tradition of not allowing any respite to the enemy, Raoji Somnath from Tal-Konkan was sent to take the fort of Rangna which was captured on 5th September 1666 A.D.

Though Shivaji was imprisoned, he managed to escape[225] with Sambhaji on the 17th August, 1666 A.D. Aurangzeb was extremely vexed[226] and Mirza Raja Jaisingh was soon called back. He left for Aurangabad instantly. This time he was not the general of a victorious army with a feather in his cap, yet a conscientious[227] Rajput soldier returning to the Emperor. While he was yet at Burhanpur, the general died, supposedly, of poison.[228]

Shivaji reached Rajgad on 20th November, 1666 A.D. Jijabai's happiness knew no bounds. Festivities were held for a few days to commemorate the happy occasion. Aurangzeb came to know about Shivaji's arrival at Rajgad, when he was busy suppressing[229] the Yusufzai rebellion at Peshawar. Hence, he could not pay personal attention to the Deccan affair. Prince Muzzam[230] was however sent to the Deccan as Subedar.

Shivaji had yet not broken off the Purandar treaty. He sent[231] Sambhaji to the Moghul camp at Aurangabad with Prataprao Gujar and Anandrao. Aurangzeb conferred on him the title of "Raja" and assured him to consider his other demands. But later events prove that Moghuls and the Marathas could not remain on friendly terms for long. It is held that Prataprao Gujar and Niroji Raoji came to know about Aurangzeb's general order to demolish[232] certain temples at Banaras and Mathura. This offended Shivaji who broke off the Purandar treaty. The Marathas prepared themselves to take back the forts they had ceded to the Moghuls.

Shivaji asked[233] his Peshwa Moro-Pant Pingle, Nilopant Majumdar and Annaji Surnis, "to capture the forts by diplomacy and exertion". He ordered[234] his Mavals, "Capture ye the forts".

Prince Muazzam, Subedar of the Deccan marched to attack Rajgad while the Marathas were also fighting against Moghuls on various fronts. Tanaji Malsure recaptured the much coveted fort of Sinhgad, though he lost[235] his life in this expedition. The Ballad of Shaheer Tulsidas narrates the part played by Jijabai to provoke[236] Shivaji for the campaign to capture Sinhgad which was of great strategic importance for the Marathas. After this notable success Shivaji again plundered[237] Surat and also captured Trimbak fort by November, 1670 A.D. It is stated[238] that Shivaji marched not as thief but as a conquerer. Further more Annaji Datto also recaptured Panhalla for Shivaji on 6th March 1673, A.D., Pandavgad on 13th October, 1673 A.D., Kelonja[239] on 24th April, 1674 A.D. He also captured various smaller forts with the result now Shivaji had practically become the master of the North Deccan and apparently he was no longer a vassal of the Moghuls. Moreover, the Marathas also had successfully almost subdued the power of Bijapur.

During these glorious days various accounts show that Shivaji was anxious to get himself crowned as a king according to the Hindu rites and after certain formalities[240] he was coronated[241] on 6th June, 1674 A.D. at Raigad amid splendour and grandeur, befitting a king. This has well been described by foreign visitors who attended the ceremony at Rajgad. It was indeed a "vision", a great achievement for Shivaji as much as for Jijabai. Various accounts show that they had kept the cause of an independent Maratha state above all other considerations and now that cause had been fulfilled. An independent Maratha State had been founded and the dream of Jijabai had been realised.

Facts and documents bear out that she was a 'friend', 'philosopher' and 'guide' to Shivaji. It was her keen understanding of situation that enabled her to take interest in revenue supervision and other affairs of the Estate. She was revered by all. Panhalla Siege is enough to show her courage, fortitude and boldness to meet any situation howsoever intricate, capably and tactfully.

Tomb of Jijabai (Pachad)

Having accomplished the highest objective of her life, Jijabai appeared to have no ambition left and resigned herself to an aloofness dedicated to religious offerings. She fell ill on 11th June and awaited the inevitable. She died[242] on the 17th June, 1674 A.D. at Raigad (Panchad) and left[243] to Shivaji "25 lakhs of Pagodas, some say more". Her active role and constant struggle from the year 1620 to 1674 A.D., till Shivaji's coronation bears ample testimony of her services to Shivaji and to the nascent Maratha state.

REFERENCES

1. Sharma, S.R., *Maratha History Re-Examined*, p. 58-59.
The Maratha sardars kept armies of Bargies and Shilledars. Bargies are soldiers, who are supplied with a horse by the state or the individuals to fight on for them, "while Shilledars provide horses at their own expense". A Shilledar is much more respectable than a Bargi. He is considered a sort of gentleman cavalry.

2. Sharma S.R. - *Maratha History Re-Examined*, pp. 58-59.
3. *Indian Historical Records Commission Proceedings*, Vol. XVIII, p. 28.
   "The Jadhavas family at Sindhkhed at present do not believe that they are the descendants of Deogiri Kings. They claim their descent from another Kshatriya King of Rajasthan". (Unpublished Paper - Keroli-Rajasthan).
4. Parasnis, D.B. - *Musalmani Amdaniteel*, Marathe Sardar, Bhag III, Nov.1909, pp. 39, 52.
5. B.I.S.M. - *Sammelan Vrutta*, VI, p. 88.
6. B.I.S.M. - *Swiya-Granthmala*, No.54, *Shiv-Charitra Sahitya*, p. 95.
7. Appendix 1.
8. Rajwade, V.K. - Khand IV, p. 23.
   Shiv-Bharat, Adhyay I, Shlokas 42, 43.
   दक्षिणस्यां दिशि श्रीमान् मालवर्मा नरूेश्वरः ।
   बभूव वशे सूर्यस्य स्वयं सूर्य इवौज सा ॥42॥
   महाराष्ट्रं जनपद महाराष्ट्रस्य भूमिपः ।
   प्रशशास प्रसन्नात्मा निजधर्मधुरन्धरः ॥43॥
9. Thus it is clear that Maloji had no reason to serve as guards at Lukhji Jadhavrao's place which has been mentioned in 'Bakhars' and other secondary accounts. 91 Kalami Bakhar, Kalam IV pp. 6-8 have not been supported by original or authentic sources.
10. Sardesai, G.S. - *Historical Genealogy*, p. 71.
11. *Shiv-Bharat*, Adhyay I, Shloka 49, Parasnis, D.B. - *Musalmani Amdani Teel*, Marathe Sardar, Bhag III, Nov. 1909, p. 32.
12. Sabhasad - *Life of Shivaji*, p. 5.
13. *Shiv-Bharat*, Adhyay 1, Shlokas 55, 56.
14. *Maathir-Ul-Umara*, Vol.II, p. 783.
15. *Modern Review*, Vol.XXII, Nos.1-6, 1917, p. 24.
16. *Ibid.*
17. *Madhya Yugeen Charitrakosh*, p. 756.
18. Sardesai, G.S. - *New History of The Marathas*, Vol.I, p. 51, mentions that Shahji was born in 1594 A.D. which appears to be doubtful. Reliable sources state that Maloji died in the battle of Indapur when Shahji was five years old (*Shiv Bharat*) Adhyay II Shlokas 2-5.
    As the battle was fought in 1605 A.D., it can be said that he was born not latter than 1600 A.D. besides Shahji had issued a Sanad

(*S.P.D.* Vol. XXXI L. No. 41) in 1606 A.D. which indicates that Maloji was dead by 1606 A.D.)

19. *Shiv Charitra Nibandhawali*, Anukram 2, p. 18.
20. Ferishta - *History of Dekkan*, Vol.II, p. 4.
21. *Shiv-Bharat*, Adhyaya 2, Shlokas 1 to 5.
22. *Shiv Charitra Nibandhawali*, p. 16.
23. *Modern Review*, Vol.XXII, 1917, Nos.1-6, p. 247.
24. *S.P.D.*, Vol.XXXI, L.No.4.
25. *Shiv-Bharat*, Adhyaya 2 Shlokas 42-44.
    Ibid., Adhyaya 2 Shlokas 38-40. "According to the above account Shahji appears to be not more than 15 years or less than 13 years of age at the time of his marriage with Jijabai. Thus, it can be said that his marriage must have taken place not later than 1614-15 A.D. Further the accounts of Bakhars and other texts mention that Lukhji Jadhavrao was forced to marry his daughter Jijabai to Shahji, son of Maloji Bhonsle, appears to be only an imagination.
26. Kincaid, C.A., & Parasnis, D.B. - *A History of the Maratha People*, Vol.I, p. 116.
27. Ferishta - *History of Dekkan*, Vol.I, p. 400.
28. *Jahangir's Memoirs*, Vol.I, p. 1; Beni Prasad - *History of Jahangir*, p. 131.
29. *Itihas Sangraha, Atihasik Charitre*, Vol.I, p. 10. B.I.S.M. - *Shiv Charitra Vrutta Sangraha*, Khand 3, p. 2, 5-7 (Futuhat-i-Adilshahi)
30. Sarkar, J. - *House of Shivaji*, pp. 17-18.
31. *Jahangir's Memoirs*, Vol.I, p. 344.
32. Sarkar, J. - *House of Shivaji*, p. 18.
33. Saksena, B.P. - *History of Shahjehan*, p. 30.
34. *Ibid.*, pp. 32 to 38.
35. *Shiv-Bharat*, Adhyay III, Shlokas 15-24; Ormes - *Historical Fragments*, p. 5.
36. Patwardhan, R.P. & Rawlinson, H.G. - *Source Book of Maratha History*, Vol.I, p. 21.
37. *Shiv-Bharat*, Adhyay III, Shlokas 38-39.
38. Patwardhan, R.P. & Rawlinson, H.G. - *Source Book of Maratha History*, Vol.I, p. 21 (The Tanajore Inscription)
39. Ormes : *Historical Fragments*, p. 5; English factory Record, p. 1 No.322. "One of the Lieutenants of Malik Ambar left him and went over to Moghuls".

40. *Shiv-Bharat*, Adhyay IV, Shlokas 1 to 4.
41. *Maharashtriyan Gyan Kosh*, Vol.4 (VI) p. 256.
42. The distance between Verul and Daulatabad is hardly more than four miles.
43. *Madhya Yugeen Charitra Kosh*, p. 801. (Whether the birth year of Sambhaji is authentic cannot be said, however, he must have been born before the battle of Bhatvadi, fought in 1624 A.D. between the Moghuls and Nizamshah. As mentioned, Lukhji Jadhavrao had gone over to the Moghuls after the "Elephant Episode." In that episode, one of Shahji's cousins, Sambhaji was killed. So the son born to Jijabai immediately after the death of Sambhaji was named Sambhaji according to the custom followed by Maharashtriyans. As such it can be said he was born not later than 1623 A.D. and certainly not before the "Elephant Episode" and the desertion of Lukhji Jadhavrao to the Moghuls.
44. Surat letter, 15 Nov. 1626 O.C. Nos.1, 2, 4, Surat to Company.
45. Beni Prasad, *History of Jahangir*, p. 356.
46. *Shiv-Bharat*, Adhyay-4, Shlokas 22 to 27.
47. Sarkar, J. - *House of Shivaji*, pp. 24-25.
48. *Shiv-Bharat*, Adhyay-III, Shlokas 5 to 7.
49. *Vividh Gyan Vistar*, Varsh 60, Ank II, 91 Kalami Bakhar, Kalam 14, p. 25 (Rajwade)
50. *Ibid.*
51. *Madhya Yugeen Charitra Kosh*, p. 646.
52. Rajwade, V.K. Khand 15, L.No. 398.
53. *Modern Review*, Vol.XXIII-1 to 6, Sept., p. 246. (Basatim-I-Salatim), pp. 276, 277-Translated copy at B.I.S.M. Poona.
54. *Vividh Gyan Vistar*, Varsh 60, Ank 2, 91 Kalami Bakhar, Kalam 15, pp. 28-30. It should be noted that Jijabai's eldest son was born in about 1623 A.D. The youngest was Shivaji born in 1630 A.D. As such, the child to be born on the above occassion could not be Shivaji. *Shiv-Bharat*, Adhyay-V, Shlok 23.
55. *Vividh Gyan Vistar*, Varsh 60, Ank 2, 91 Kalami Bakhar Kalam, 15, pp. 28-30.
56. Ferishta - *History of Dekkan*, Vol.II, p. 5.
57. *Ibid.*, Vol.1, p. 402.
58. *Itihas Sangraha*, Aitihasik Charcha, Part-II, p. 11.
59. *B.I.S.M. Quarterly* Varsh 6, Ank 1-4, p. 50, Shak 1847-48; Saksena, B.P. *History of Shahjahan*, p. 63.

60. *Shiv-Bharat,* Adhyay V, Shlok 19.
61. Sharma, R.S. - *Maratha History Re-Examined,* p. 66.
62. *Ramdass - Ramdassi,* Ank 65, L.No. 5.
63. *Shiv-Bharat,* Adhyay VIII, Shlokas 15-16.
64. Abul-i-Hamid Lahori - *Badshahnama,* H.I.H., Vol.VIII, p. 11.
65. *Indian Historical Records Commission Proceeding,* Vol.XVII, p. 233.
66. Sarkar, J. - *House of Shivaji,* p. 30. "Girjabai was wife of Bahadurji, son of Jagdeo, brother of Lukhji Jadhavarao. Recent account show chart Girjabai was other name of Mhalsabai (B.I.S.M.).
67. *Maathur-ul-Umara,* Vol.2, p. 784.
68. *Shiv-Bharat,* Adhyay IV, Shlok 1 to 4. One of the Lieutenants of Malik Ambar left him and went over to Moghuls.
69. *Ibid.*
70. Abul-i-Hamid, Lahori *Badshahnama,* H.I.H., Vol.VII, p. 15-17.
71. *Ibid.,* p. 17.
72. Sardesai, G.S. *New History of the Maratha,* p. 1.
73. *Ibid.,* p. 1 Tukabai was married to Shahji after Jijabai. Other papers in Tamil and Marathi and other sources mentioned that Tukabai was married to Shahji about 1631 A.D.
74. B.I.S.M. *Shiv-Charitra-Vrutta Sangraha,* Khand-I (Kannadi) p. 54.
75. Abdu-i-Hamid, Lahori, *Badshahnama,* H.I.H., Vol.VII, pp. 16, 19, 20, 22.
76. Rajwade V.K. Anand XV, L.No.415.
77. *Sanada - Patre,* L.No.5, p. 102, L.No. 6, p. 103.
78. Abdu-i-Hamid Lahori - *Badshahnama,* H.I.H., Vol.VII, p. 35.
79. Sarkar, J. - *House of Shivaji,* p. 36.
80. B.I.S.M. - *Shiv Charitra Pradeep,* p. 16. (Jedhe-Yanchi-Shakawali)
81. Sarkar, J. - *House of Shivaji,* p. 33.
82. Abul-i-Hamid Lahori - *Badshahnama,* H.I.H., Vol.VII, p. 41.
83. *Riyasat,* Vol.II, *Shak-Karta-Shivaji,* p. 18.
84. Kincaid, C.A. & Parasnis, D.B. - *A History of the Maratha People,* Vol.1, p. 1 to 4.
85. *Maharashtriya Gyan Kosh,* Vol.XIV, p. 246.
86. *Sardesai Commemoration Volume,* p. 45.
87. *Maharashtriya Gyan Kosh,* Vol.XIV, p. 256.
88. *Patre Yadi Vagere,* L.No.6.
89. Abdu-i-Hamid Lahori - *Badshahnama,* H.I.H., Vol.VII, p. 51. Saksena, B.P. - *History of Shahjehan,* p. 145.

90. *Maathir-Ul-Umara*, Vol.II, p. 385.
    Basatin-I-Salatin, p. 566 (copy at B.I.S.M. Poona)
91. *Shiv-Bharat*, Adhayay 9, Shlok 44.
92. Riyasat, Vol.II, Shak Karta Shivaji, p. 18.
93. *P.D.* - Vol.III, p. 151.
94. *P.D.* - Vol.III, p. 150 (The place for its construction was bought from Jhambre, Patil of Poona. It was 52½' east-west, 82½ feet north-east & 30.9' high. *S.P.D.* Vol.XXII, L.N.126.
95. *S.P.D.* Vol.XXXI, L.N.126.
96. B.I.S.M. *Poona Nagar Sanshodhak Vrutta* Khandi, p. 10.
97. *Sanada Patre*, p. 162.
98. *Sanada Patre*, p. 146.
99. *Shiv-Bharat*, Adhyay 10, Shlokas 34 to 40 - According to historians Dadaji Konddeva was responsible for his (Shivaji's) education.

    The view held by some writers that Shivaji did not know reading/writing does not seem to be correct. This is indicated by the letters which he wrote to the ministers and also to relatives. He had himself written a letter to Raugy Pandit (F.R. Surat, Vol.103 p. 268, Phillip Gifford at Rajapur to Surat-12th April, 1663 A.D. *ERS* (I) L.N.60; Introduction, p.11. Yesterday a letter arrived from the Raja written himself to Rougy. Kincaid, C.A. & Parasnis, D.B. - *A History of the Maratha People*, Vol.I, p. 124.
    "Jijabai bade him never forget that he was descended both from the Yadavas of Devgiri and the Ranas of Udaipur. She recited the Puranas with the marvellous feats of war and daring. But she wished to see him pious as well as brave".
100. Sabhasad-*Life of Shivaji*, p. 3.
    दादाजी कोणदेव शहाणा चौकस ठेविला होता तो बेंगुलरास महाराजाचे भेटीस गेला त्या बरोबर राजेश्री शिवाजी राजे व जिजाबाई आऊ ऐशी गैली।
101. It further mentions that when Jijabai left Poona Shivaji was twelve yeard old. "ते समयी" meaning "निद्यते समयी" clearly shows this. Parmanand has also mentioned this particular incident शिववर्मा यदा वर्ष द्वादश प्रत्यपद्यत। तदा नृपश्शाह वर्मा नियोगेन पिनाकनः।।. It proves that Jijabai and Shivaji were at Bangalore for some time before 1642 A.D. However , when they had gone to Bangalore cannot be said definitely, it may be 1639-40, Sarkar, J., *Shivaji*, pp. 21, 22.
102. Shejwalkar, T.S. *Vijaynagar Samrajya Gaurav Granth*, p. 9 mentions that Shivaji might have visited "Hampi-virupaksh" Temple (Shiva)

and Vijayanagar Empire, and seeing ruined parts of the throne and palaces of Hindu Raja of Vijaynagar, he might have been inspired to erect a new Hindu kingdom".

103. *Riyasat*, Vol.2 *Shak Karta Shivaji*, p. 22.
104. Kincaid, C.A. & Parasnis, D.B. - *History. of the Maratha People*, Vol.1, p. 124.
105. *Riyasat*, Vol.II, *Shak Karta Shivaji*, p. 22.
106. Sarkar, J., *Shivaji*, p. 20.
107. Patwardhan, R.P. & Rawlinson, H.G. - *The Source Book of Maratha History*, Vol.1, p. 158.
108. *Letter - Despatches - Others State Papers*, Vol.1, p. 7.
109. Ferishta - *History of Dekkan*, Vol.II, p. 5.
110. Kincaid, C.A. & Parasnis, D.B. - *A History of the Maratha People*, Vol.1, p. 127.
111. B.I.S.M. - *Shiv Charitra Sahitra - Lekhan*, p. 82, *Sangraha*, Vol.1, L.No. .513.
112. B.I.S.M. - *Quarterly*. I Ank 2/3. p. 37.
113. *Ibid.*
114. Rajwade, V.K. Khand XVII, L.No. 7; B.I.S.M. - *Sammelan Virutta* IV p. 67.
115. Rajwade, V.K. Khand XVII, L.No. 7; *Shivaji Souvenier*, p. 124.
116. Shivaji alongwith Dadaji Konddeva and four or five others of his men solemnly took an oath in the temple of Raireshwar at Bhor that each one of them would support the other". (Rajwade, V.K., Khand XV L.No. 269).
117. *Ibid.*
118. B.I.S.M. *Shiv Charitra Pradeep*, p. 292.
     प्रतिप्पच्यद्रलेखे/वर्धिष्णूर्तिश्ववदिता/शाहसूनोःशिवष्टोघा भिृग्रमद्राय राजते।।
119. Balkrishna - *Shivaji the Great*, Vol.2, p. 29.
120. Shivaji expressed his desire to extend his territory. Dadaji Konddeva replied "What you think is all right but it is extremely difficult of accomplishment - Patwardhan, R.P. & Rawlinsen, H.G. - *A Source Book of Maratha History*, Vol.1, p. 48.
     "Contrary to the remonstrances of Dadaji, he raised a banditti and plundered neighbouring districts which conduct in his charge so affected the old man that he poisoned himself to avoid the imputation of assisting in his decision". - Ferishta - *History of Dekkan*, Vol.2, p. 6.

121. *S.P.D.*, Vol.XXXI, L.No. 10, 18.
B.I.S.M. - *Shiv Charitra Sahitra*, Lekhank 120.
122. Sarkar, J. - *House of Shivaji*, p. 62.
123. *Shiv Charitra Pradeep*, p. 17.
124. *Vividh Gyan Vistar*, Varsh 60 Nov.1923 - Ank,II, 91, Kalami Bakhar, Kalam-24. British Museum, Persian Mss.6600, p. 29. *Sangraha*, Vol. 1, L.No.539.
125. Rajwade, V.K. Khand IV, p. 88.
126. B.I.S.M. - *Shiv Charitra Pradeep*, p. 50.
127. Sarkar J. - *History of Aurangzeb*, Vol.IV, p. 27.
128. *Shiv Bharat* - Adhyay, XV, Shlokas - 37 to 39.
129. *Shiv Bharat*, Adhyay XV, Shlokas 4, 38.
130. *Vividh Gyan Vistar*, Varsh 60, Nov.1929, Ank 11, 91 Kalami Bakhar, Kalam 29, p. 59.
131. Grant Duff - *The History of the Marathas*, Vol.1, p. 120 Marathi Mss)
132. Sabhasad - *Life of Shivaji*, p. 12; Sarkar, J. - *History of Aurangzeb*, Vol.IV, p. 27.
133. *Ibid.*
134. Rajwade, V.K. - Khand VIII, L.N.3; Prabhat - Lekh 1, *Sangraha*, Vol.1, L.No. 550; *Shiv Bharat* - Adhyay 15, Shlokas 51, 52.
135. *Vividh Gyan Vistar* Varsh 60, Nov.1929, Ank II, 91 Kalami Bakhar, Kalam 27.
"Nilogi brother of Chandra Rao, invited Shivaji and Jijabai considering the friendship that existed between him and Shahji when in Bijapur services. Shivaji accompanied by Jijabai with all Cavalry and 20,000 Mawalis misused the faith and imprisoned all the brothers and thus took the Purandar fort".
136. *Sanada Patre*, 112; *Sangraha*, Vol.1, L.No. 631.
137. *Bombay Gazetteer*, Vol.XIX, p. 3.
138. Patwardhan, R.P. & Rawlinson, H.G. - *A Source Book of Maratha History*, Vol.1, pp. 52-53.
139. Sabhasad - *Life of Shivaji*, p. 9.
140. B.I.S.M. - *Shiv Charitra Pradeep*, p. 202; Rajwade, V.K. Khand VIII, L.No.2.
141. Parasnis, D.B. - *Mahabaleshwar*, p. 18.
Chandrarao Morey had three beautiful daughters and it was the desire of Shivaji's mother to unite the two families by blood relation and cement the union for a heir purpose. But Chandrarao

Morey did not like the idea as he thought his dignity, rank and status far superior to those of Shivaji. Chandrarao vainly boasted of the titles and the honours conferred on his family by the king of Bijapur while he considered Shivaji's claim was never recognised by the Kings of Bijapur.

142. B.I.S.M. - *Shiv Charitra Vrutta, Sangraha*, Khand 2, p. 34.
143. B.I.S.M. - *Shiv Charitra Sahitya*, Khand VIII, L.No. 20.
144. Rajwade, V.K., Khand XX, L.N.279.
145. B.I.S.M. - *Shiv Charitra Sahitya*, Khand 1, L.No. 51, 53.
146. Rajwade, V.K., Khand VIII, L.No. 11.
147. Rajwade, V.K., Khand XVI, L.No. 16.
On the day Baba Jungarrao, Deshmukha of Kanadkhore, and his brother Maleji Patangrao, presented themselves before panchas and then the quarrel about their Vatan was settled and Mahjar was made.
148. *Shiv Charitra Sahitya*, Lekank-108; *Sangraha* Vol.II, L.N.1591.
149. *Prof. Potdar Commemoration Volume*, p. 29.
Shri S.V. Avalaskar (B.I.S.M.) in his article "Pratapgad Chi Bhawani" has given a vivid account of the fort and the other constructions which have now disappeared. The fort is in Satara district, four miles away from Jaoli and 3543 feet high. In the fort of Pratapgad, according to the writer, there was a Katchery "Jijabai Chllawada". Darukhana (artillery) and such other arrangement. The place had strategic defence qualities. It is said that Shivaji installed the famous Bhawani idol after his victory over Afzalkhan. The writer claims to have seen other original letters regarding the donation for the expenses of worship and establishment of "Anna-Chhatra". A marathi maxim also says. "राजगड़ राजा च प्रतापगढ़ जिजाबाई च"।
150. Sarkar, J. - *Anecdotes of Aurangzeb*, p. 6.
151. Sharma, S.R. - *Maratha History Re-Examined*, p. 134.
152. Sarkar, J. - *Anecdotes of Aurangzeb*, p. 7.
153. Khafi-Khan - Muntakhabu-l-Lubab, *H.I.H.*, Vol.VII, p. 229.
154. Rajwade, V.K., Khand VIII, L.No. 5.
155. Rajwade, V.K., Khand VIII, L.No. 6.
156. F.R. Rajapur, Henry Revington and Randolf Taylor to the company district Rajapur 10th Dec. 1659 A.D. *ERS* (I) L.No. 1.
157. *Ibid.*
158. *Indian Historical Records Commission - Proceedings*, Vol. XVI, p. 41-43.

That the campaign was taken up by Afzalkhan after full preparation is indicated by the article written by Dr. A.B. Powar, "Afzalkhan effetes Vishalgad fort". It refers to the six Farmans in Persian (original issued to the officers of Vishalgad Fort and others to meet the requirements, artillery-workshops at eight surrounding villages) and the sums received from Ali-Adilshah II of Bijapur from time to time. The article shows that though Vishalgad was 70 miles south of Pratapgad, Afzalkhan was prepared to meet any emergency requirements in his campaign, either to have a formidable northern defence against Shivaji or to corner him from all sides i.e. south-east.

159. B.I.S.M. *Shiv Charitra Pradeep*, p. 1.3
160. Sabhasad - *Life of Shivaji*, p. 13.
161. *Ibid.*
162. *Ibid.*, p. 16
163. Shyamaldas - *Vir - Vinod*, Vol.13.
    (Maratho-Ki-Tawarkh) *Ratnakar* - May 1927, p. 347.
164. Sabhasad - *Life of Shivaji*, p. 15.
165. Kelkar, Y.N. - *Aitihasik Powade*, pp. 2, 3.
166. *Patre Yadi Vagere*, L.N.6, p. 16.
167. *Shiv Charitra Nibandhawali*, Anukram 2, p. 159.
168. Kelkar, Y.N. - *Aitihasik Powade*, p. 17.

    खबर गेली जीजाउला, शिवबा जातो भेटायला।
    पालखीत बैसुनी माता आली भेटायला।।

    It should be noted that the distance from Rajgad to Pratapgad is not more than 40 miles which could easily be covered between 2 or 3 days in a palki used by people in those days. *Shiv Bharat* Adhyay Shlok 23. Jijabai had six sons, among whom only Shivaji had survived. As such it is quite natural that she would take any risk to reach him before he met Afzalkhan.
169. Kelkar, Y.N. - *Aitihasik Powade*, p. 17.,
170. Sabhasad - *Life of Shivaji*, p. 15.
171. *Ibid.*
172. Sarkar, J. - *Shivaji*, p. 76, (Pd. 1922)
173. Dagh Register - *Dutch Paper* - A, Folio 0636 (No. 1123, Year 1661, BATAVIA. (Appendix II) SANGRAHA - Vol.I, L.N. 812.
174. F.R. Surat, p. 89, Henry, Revington and Randoy Taylor dt. 10th Dec. 1659, ERS(I), L.N.1, p. 3.

175. *Basatin-i-Salatin*, p. 569 (Tr. Copy at B.I.S.M. Poona) Sarkar, J. - *History of Aurangzeb* - Vol.IV, p. 3.
176. Kelkar, Y.N. - *Aitihasik Powade*, p. 17, Verse 37.
177. *Basatin-i-Salatin*, p. 571, (Tr. Copy at Poona)
178. *Sangraha*, Vol.I, L.N.800.
179. *Indian Records Series - Indian Travels of Thevenot & Carwri*, p. 39.
180. *Basatin-i-Salatin*, p. 570, (Tr. Copy at B.I.S.M., Poona)
181. *Shiv-Bharat*, Adhyay 25, Shlok 12.
182. F.R. Rajapur, p. 140, M. Revington & Co. to Fort St. George, 5th July, 1660, ERS(1), L.No. 20.
 Basatin-i-Salatin, p. 351 (Tr. copy at B.I.S.M., Poona).
183. Sarkar, J. - *History of Aurangzeb*, Vol.IV, p. 46.
184. तंत्रं तं स्वमिनं हित्वात्रपां चाति महियसीम।
 अहो युवां परमिया परावृत्ता वुमावपि (13)
 तेथे त्या धन्यास सोडून सगली लाज गुंडालून ढेवूत तुम्हीं दोघेही शत्रुच्या भीतीने परतलांत हे आश्चर्य होय।
185. तमेंकात्मनों वत्सं विनोचयि तुमात्मना।
 प्रत्यतिष्ये हरिष्येय जोहरस्य शिरामुधि।(14)
 त्या माक्ष्या एकुलत्यास पुत्रास स्वतः सोडविण्याचा मी स्वतः करीन आणि जोहराचे मुंडके आज युद्धातून घेऊंन येईन..... I shall myself try to release my only son and would bring the chopped off head of Siddi Jauhar from the battlefield. (It should be remembered that Jijabai was 60 years old. She was born not later than 1600 A.D.) Jijabai must have been born two or three (or more) years after 1600 A.D.
186. *Shiv-Bharat*, Adhyay 26, Shlok 5.
 जननी शिवराजस्य सा राजगिरीवर्तिनी।
 निजानां गिरिदुर्गाणामवने वहितामवत्।।5।।
 राजगडावर राहणारी ती शिवाजीची माता आपल्या गडाच्यां रक्षणाच्या कामीं दक्ष झाली।
187. Khafi-Khan-Muntakhabu-i-Lubab, *H.I.H.* Vol.7, p. 262.
188. *Ibid.*
189. F.R. Rajapur, p. 145, Richard Napier & Co. to Surat, 15th June, 1660, *ERS* (1) L.N.21.

190. *Shiv-Bharat*, Adhyay 26, Shlok 66.
191. *Vir-Vinod*, Vol.13 (Marathon Ki Tawarikh No. 158).
192. *Shiv-Bharat*, Adhyay 27, Shlok 45 to 50.
193. B.I.S.M. - *Shiv Charitra Pradeep*, p. 21.
194. F.R. Surat, Vol.85, p. 257.
President and Council of Surat to the Co.-7th December 1661. *ERS* (I) L.N.30.
195. B.I.S.M. - *Shiv Charitra Sahitya*, Lekhank 344. *Sangraha* - Vol.1, L.N. 871.
196. Dagh Register : 11th July, 1661. *Sangraha* Vol.1, L.N. 812.
197. Patwardhan, R.P. & Rawlinson, H.G. - *Source Book of Maratha History*, Vol.1, p. 165 (Bhimsen Burhanpuri)
198. F.R. Surat, Vol. 103, p. 268, Phillip Gifford to Rajapur at Surat, 12th April, 1663 ERS(I) L.N. 60; B.I.S.M. - *Shiv Charitra Pradeep*, p. 22; *Maasir-i-Alamgiri*, p. 28.
199. *Maathir-ul-Umara*, Vol.2, p. 786.
200. B.I.S.M. - *Shiv Charitra Pradeep*, p. 22.
201. *Original Correspondence*, Vol. 28, No.3019. The President & Council of Surat to the Company, 28th January, 1663-64 *ERS*(I) L.No.78.
202. B.I.S.M. - *Varshik Ittivrutta*, Shak 1835, p. 378.
203. Ranade, M.G., & Telong, K.T. - *The Rise of the Maratha Power & Gleanings of Maratha Chronology*, p. 155.
"According to the Shastras women committed sati after the death of their husband but those women whose sons and daughters were alive were not permitted (by the Shastras) to commit sati; Umabai, mother of Shahji had not committed sati; This practice was also followed by Rajputs.
The widow of Jaswant Singh was not allowed to commit sati after her husband's death. She was forcibly prevented by Oada Kumpawat. (*Annals & Antiquities of Rajasthan*, Vol.II, p. 50).
204. Ranade, M.G. & Telong, K.T. - *The Rise of the Maratha Power & Gleanings of Maratha Chronology*, p. 155.
205. *A Preliminary Report of the Historical Records at Goa*, p. 8.
206. *Maathur-ul-Umara*, Vol.II, p. 786.
207. *A Preliminary Report of the Historical Records at Goa*, p.9.
208. Sabhsad - *Life of Shivaji*, p. 43.
209. *Indian Historical Record Commission Proceedings*, Vol.XII, p. 16.

210. Khafi-Khan-Muntakhabu-i-Lubab, *H.I.H.*, Vol.VII, p. 272.
211. Sabhasad - *Life of Shivaji*, p. 41..
212. B.I.S.M. - *Shiv Charitra Vrutta Sangraha*, Khand 2, p. 62; Sarkar, J. - *House of Shivaji*, p. 132.
213. *Sangraha*, Vol.I, L.No. 1065.
214. B.I.S.M. - *Shiv Charitra Vrutta Sangraha*, Khand 2, p. 69.
तुम्हीं मज़बरोबर दोस्ती कराल तर तुमचे असे काम करून देतो कीं तुम्हीं कध्री पाहिल् नसेल तुम्हीं मज़वर विश्वास ठेवा, भी तुम्हास सर्व दक्षिण घेऊन देतो।
Sarkar, J. - *House of Shivaji*, p. 132.
215. Deshpande, Rao Saheb - *The Deliverance or the Escape of Shivaji the Great*, From Agra, p. 27; *Sangraha*, Vol.I, L.N. 1042.
216. Saqi Mutad Khan - *Maasir-i-Alamgiri*, pp. 32-33.
217. *Public Record Office*, C.O.77, Vol. X, F61, letter from Surat by an unnamed writer sent to England by Return, Nov. 1660, *ERS*(I) L.N.133.
218. Sarkar, J.- *House of Shivaji*, p. 146.
"Hindus are one. They have taught to waste emperor's money and resources. But I do not worry, I shall defeat him myself". - *Shiv - Digvijaya*, p. 237.
219. Sarkar, J. - *Shivaji*, p. 136.
220. *Ibid.*
221. *Public Record Office*, C.O.77, Vol. X, F61, letter from Surat by England by *ERS*(I) L.N.133.
Saqi Mutad Khan - *Maasir-i-Alamgiri*, pp. 36.
222. Ferishta - *History of Dekkan*, Vol.II, p. 14.
223. *Public Record Office*, C.O.77, Vol. X, 61, letter from Surat by England by ERS(I) L.N.133.
Maathur-ul-Umara, Vol.II, p. 787.
224. Sarkar, J. - *Shivaji*, p. 136.
225. O' Correspondence, Vol.29, No.3183, Gifford and Chanterton to Surat, 5 Sept.1666, *ERS*(I) L.No. 128.
226. *Muasir-i-Alamgiri*, p. 37.
Indian Record Series - *Travels of Thevenot & Careri*, p. 42.
227. *Shiv-Charitra Nibandhawali*, Anukaram-II, p. 17.
228. Ormes - *Historical Fragments*, p. 24.
229. Sarkar, J. - *Anecdotes of Aurangzeb*, p. 9.
230. Ferishta - *History of Dekkan*, Vol.II, p. 16.
231. B.I.S.M. - *Shiv Charitra Pradeep*, p. 51.

232. B.I.S.M. - *Shiv Charitra Pradeep*, p. 24.
Sarkar, J. - *Anecdotes of Aurangzeb*, p. 10.
233. Sabhasad - *Life of Shivaji*, p. 55.
234. *Ibid.*
235. B.I.S.M. - *Ittivrutta*, Shak 1837, p. 19.
236. B.I.S.M. - Quarterly, Varsh 10, Ank. I, p. 13-16.
237. O, Correspondence, Vol.13, No.3515, Surat to Company 12th November, 1670, ERS(I) L.N. 237.
Mss. Dutch Records, Vol.29, DCC LXIII, FBS, pp. 384-385.
238. O, Correspondence, Vol.31, No.3415, Surat to Company, March, 1670-71, ERS(I) L.N. 185.
239. B.I.S.M. - *Shiv Charitra Pradeep*, p. 27.
240. *Shivaji Nibandhawali*, Anukaram 2, Part-I, pp. 15, 16.
241. B.I.S.M. - *Ittivrutta*, Shak 1835, p. 378.
242. B.I.S.M. - *Shiv Charitra Pradeep*, p. 27.
243. *Dutch Records*, Vol.XXXIV, (FBS.) p.387.

CHAPTER 2

SOYARABAI

Feudal Blood at Play (1674-1680 A.D.)

Jijabai was benign mother not only for the infant Maratha State but for the family of Shivaji as well. During her lifetime the entire household of Shivaji bore a homogeneous atmosphere despite the fact that most of the marriages were performed more due to political consideration. There is no account to show any type of mutual differences or friction among the queens[1] of Shivaji.

Saibai, the first wife of Shivaji and the mother of Sambhaji, who was born[2] on the 15th May 1657 A.D. at Purandar, was married to Shivaji in 1640 A.D. She was an asset in his (Shivaji's) struggle to lay the seeds of Maratha Power. She was cool tempered, generous and kind. She gave proof of her mettle and her cool temper during crises created by the threat given by Ali Adil Shah of Bijapur to arrest Shahji, holding him responsible for the activities of Shivaji in 1648 A.D. She died on the 5th September in 1659 A.D., after being in the service of Shivaji and the Maratha State for full nineteen years. In her death Shivaji not only lost a dependable companion but a sound adviser also[3]. After the death of Saibai and later on Jijabai in 1674 A.D., Soyarabai gained prominence in the house of Shivaji and thereby in the Maratha Court politics too. According to Shiv-Bharat she was from Mohite[4] family.

However, it is to be noted that after the death of Saibai, Sambhaji, the elder son of Shivaji and a boy of only two years at the time of the death of his mother was kept by Jijabai under the protective wing of her love and care but the death of Jijabai removed not only the affectionate hand of the grandmother from his head but he had now a chance to go wayward as there was now no one either to love him or to restrain him from his misdeed, with the result that the heir-apparent of the Maratha State and the natural heir of Shivaji figured as a rude, ill tempered and haughty youth.

During this period the coronation of Shivaji had been a drain on his treasury because of lavish expenditure incurred during the ceremony which made him to continue campaigns for the collection of money but this did not help much to improve his financial position in any substantial way. He was personally a soldier[5]–General and thoroughly understood the demands of the soldiers who were mostly mercenary. It was necessary to keep them financially satisfied. Moreover, the elderly generation of Sardars e.g., Nimbalkars, Mohites, Shirkeys, Ghorpades and few others were still either Jagirdars or vassals of the Mohammadan rulers, many a time resented[6] his acquisition of prominence and power within a short period. Thus, Shivaji found himself in a precarious financial and political condition among the clamouring sardars who were on the look out to gain power at his cost as soon as an opportunity arose. During this time Soyarabai naturally shared his worries and anxieties. This close association between Shivaji and Soyarabai during the crucial period appears to have brought on her the charge of influencing Shivaji in "Succession-Issue"[7], "Karnatak-Expedition" and "Poison-Episode"[8] by various writers, which are to be examined, keeping in view the events in their proper perspective vis-a-vis the conditions prevailing then.

This closeness of Soyarabai with Shivaji had been an important plank to involve her in what is known as succession issue cropped up between the two sons of Shivaji, Sambhaji and Rajaram but Sambhaji has been figured as a rude, ill tempered and haughty[9] youth and had totally disappointed[10] his parents by his wayward[11] attitude and behaviour while his step brother Rajaram was a calm and easy going person of sober[12] habits, with the result that the conduct of Rajaram appealed[13] more to them. At this juncture Sambhaji being an heir to the Maratha throne, it was necessary to be a man of responsible and balanced behaviour, more so during the troubled days, but commenting on the life and personality of Sambhaji Kincaid and Parasnis have observed,[14] "the young prince Sambhaji had all his father's bravery and share of his ability but he had been born in purple and had in idleness acquired vices from which his father's strenuous life had kept him free."[15] Further more Sambhaji could not gain confidence of and create good impression on Shivaji.

This type of life of Sambhaji might have been due to various facts. He had lost his mother at the age of two years and also probably with her the advantages of care and affection, he would have received if she were alive. Normally, such children do receive more attention from their grandmothers and other inmates of the household which sometimes results into an indulgent type of training and upbringing. Thus, Sambhaji probably could not be as staunch, as firm and as resolute as Shivaji was, in spite of his active life full of zeal and enthusiasm till his execution at the age of thirty-two on 11th March, 1689 A.D. It is regretted that he found none at home to whom he could look for affection. Moreover, the death[16] of Jijabai had created a void between father and the son which could not be filled by Soyarabai as is evident from the continued dissatisfaction of Shivaji towards Sambhaji.

Besides, during such a time of critical turn in the life and career of Sambhaji, a few ministers who appear to have nursed disgruntled[17] feelings towards him had looked ahead to find a person who would convey their anti-Sambhaji feelings to Shivaji. Soyarabai was naturally interested in the succession of Rajaram and such feelings of the members of the Maratha Court. It is difficult to say anything positively except that this gave her a chance[18] to groom Rajaram as the heir-apparent. It was not that Shivaji was not conscious of the happenings in his own house and the resultant[19] danger to the welfare of the State which rivetted round the succession problem and the part played in by different interested persons. He could not bear to see that the kingdom gained by hard toil should thus fall a prey to selfish designs of the individuals. However, at this juncture Shivaji planned to undertake, what is famous in Maratha history as "Karnatak-Expedition". This expedition has evoked mixed comments from the historians and those who had been critical about it have accused that the baneful influence which Soyarabai had over Shivaji was responsible for it. But before coming to such a conclusion historical forces operating in the Deccan during that time are to be analysed and assessed. Such an analysis illustrates that during this period the political[20] conditions existing in the south Deccan States like Bijapur, Golkunda and others offered a good respite[21] to Shivaji because none of these states were in a position to take any stern measures against him due to chaos and confusion prevailing. A good amount of their population specially of the rural areas were often on the verge of starvations and were suffering heavily by the exploitations and the devastation caused by the Sardars of these very states in order to meet their monetary needs. In fact these conditions were proving to be a boon to Shivaji to consolidate Maratha power in the Deccan. Being a far-sighted statesman Shivaji knew well that the decay set in the Muslim states of the Deccan offered much better fertile ground for realising his ambitions than what was available in northern India. Hence, he decided to concentrate his attention in the Deccan for the present. Moreover, because the rulers of these states were still wealthy, Shivaji decided to grab their wealth by his military exploits and campaigns. Shivaji was also aware of the fact that the Moghul Emperor had never lost sight on his early favourite scheme of annexing[22] the whole of the Deccan to the Empire. The declining States themselves suggested that any power could easily subjugate them. Luckily there were only two powers, the Moghuls and the Marathas. If the Marathas failed to utilise the opportunity to exploit the wealth and to annex the territories of these states, Moghuls were bound to do so.

Dr. S.N. Sen observes[23], "who planned the 'Karnatak-Expedition' and with what object?" Dr. Shrinivasanchari[24], "The plan was discussed as early as 1675 A.D." It has also been said[25], "Shivaji had claims against Ekoji with respect to Shahji's estate," and hence, this expedition was planned to settle these claims. S.R. Sharma says[26], "He (Shivaji) had no designs against his brother but only wanted a political lever in Karnatak". Holding such a view, notwithstanding these different views, it is generally agreed that there were high ambitions of Raghunath Pant, the minister of Shivaji's younger brother, Ekoji was much more responsible to provoke Shivaji to undertake this expedition, it is held that he wanted to be as prominent[27] as Balaji Avaji, the Chitnis, was to Shivaji, yet nothing definite can be ascertained in absence of more reliable accounts.

As mentioned, Shivaji had coronated himself on 6th June, 1674 A.D. and Ekoji also got himself coronated[28] on the 17th March, 1675 A.D. just after nine months. Besides, the recent experience with Mirza Raja Jaisingh at Purandar Siege had given him an opportunity to know the superior military and financial resources of the Moghuls, in spite of the skill of the Marathas in guerilla warfare. Sambhaji had not come up to the expectations[29] of Shivaji. Moreover, he had no peace of mind nor physical rest after the coronation as the succession issue had practically disturbed the whole of the household. That such a house stood all chances of being destroyed even by weak opponents, no less than strong one, bears historical testimony. It was all right so long as he lived, but did not augur well thereafter. Hence he was worried.

It was under such a condition of mental disturbance that Soyarabai asked him to declare her son Rajaram as future incumbent to the throne. In respect of this advice, different opinions have been expressed by writers. It is held[30] that Soyarabai prevailed upon Shivaji to get her son Rajaram succeed him (Shivaji) and whatever more was conquered was to be given to Sambhaji. Sardesai writes[31], "The next queen consort Soyarabai possessed a character far from amiable. She planned to supplant

Sketch Map Showing Places mentioned in the Account of Shivaji Campaign

Sambhaji with her son Rajaram". Kincaid and Parasnis observe,[32] "During her husband's life she and her kinsmen used their influence to remove from succession Sambhaji, as one unfitted by his evil habits and proved treachery to rule over the Marathas". Not satisfied with this, they have gone to the extent of holding her responsible for Shivaji's southern campaign and thus attributed to her very uncharitable and questionable motive of being selfish and ambitious.

Shivaji could have come in direct conflict with the Muslim States, already declining, but he waited till they collapsed. Even if he failed to win these States, it would not be a loss to him if the two halves of the Maratha kingdom were made so strong as would work like pincers to sandwich these States as and when required. This was not possible as long as Ekoji remained[33] powerful in the far south. Moreover, Ekoji's control on Karnatak highly raised his position. Therefore, the annexation of Southern States was necessary to carry on offensive as well as defensive operations in times of need. As such, there is no need to start with the hypothesis that Soyarabai instigated it even though she was interested in Rajaram's succession.

Once having made a decision, he only awaited the best opportunity which offered itself in 1676 A.D. The Rajputs had rebelled[34] against the increased fanaticism of Aurangzeb. Therefore, the Emperor's whole attention[35] was diverted to the handling of the Rajput menace with vigour and determination. The Moghul commanders were at ease to find that Shivaji's southern expedition would withdraw the pressure from them and relieve them from the southern provinces for the time being.

Before, Shivaji departed for south, he took measures so that no disturbance would crop up in his State during his absence. He sent Sambhaji to Shringarpur with his wife Yesubai and Umaji[36] Pandit in 1675-76 A.D. "to administer[37] the Pravalli district and learn the art of administration". Moropant Pingle had already marched[38] towards Dandarajpur with the determination not to return till he had taken it. Rajaram, Soyarabai, Annaji Datto and Raghoji Somnath stayed at Raigad. Shivaji also entered into an understanding with Bahlolkhan[39] of Bijapur and the English[40] at Rajapur. He wrote to Ekoji to give him share in his father's patrimony which he was enjoying for about 13 years since the death of their father Shahji in 1664 A.D. Further, he entreated him not to sow the seed of discord in the house by refusing his demands.

Thus, Shivaji prepared himself and started[41] on his campaign in January, 1677 A.D., with 500 troops and soon reached Hyderabad.[42] He marched through various smaller principalities[43] where he was accorded a warm welcome by the natives and the Sultans as well as the foreigners, viz., the Dutch, the Portuguese and the English, who expressed[44] that "Shivaji had grown great and famous". By the third week of July, 1677 A.D., Shivaji reached Koleroon, ten miles of Tanjore. He met[45] his brother Ekoji and tried to have a peaceful compromise with him regarding his share in the patrimonial estate. Ekoji disagreed. A battle was fought between them on November 16th, 1677 A.D. at Valigundapuram. Finding himself in an awkward position, Ekoji fled[46] away one night, leaving Shivaji with his minister Raghunath Pant. Shivaji only expressed surprise at this unexpected attitude of his brother. Ekoji opposed Shivaji for about a year, but did not succeed in his endeavour. Finding it useless to linger on, Shivaji managed to win over Raghunath Pant.

Ekoji's wife Dipabai seemed to realise the danger from the ambitious minister who agreed[47] to act in complete obedience to Shivaji. In that case, Ekoji would have lost all. Perceiving the intentions of the Pant and others, she entreated[48] Ekoji to come to terms with Shivaji. He reluctantly agreed. She was well compensated[49] by Shivaji for her efforts to bring about a peaceful understanding. Bakhars state that Shivaji made over the state of Karnatak to Dipabai and appointed Ekoji to supervise it on her behalf which shows that Shivaji not only limited Ekoji's Jagir but kept in his hands the right of appointment and wiped off any possibility of challenge to his authority. If Shivaji had given this right to Ekoji, it would have meant that Shivaji had yielded. It was, however, a piece of good luck that Dipabai became instrumental in maintaining the welfare of both the houses of Poona and Tanjore.

Shivaji started on his return journey from Karnatak in December, 1677 A.D. On the way, he was opposed[50] by Savtribai Desai of the village of Belwadi. She had her own grouse against Shivaji and plundered his army. Her fort was besieged. She heroically defended it for twenty-seven days, after which she was captured.[51]

Shivaji marched ahead. He asked the English people to meet[52] him at Panhalla where he reached in April, 1678 A.D. He reached[53] Raigad in May, 1678 A.D. The Karnatak campaign had its own advantage for Shivaji. His new[54] possessions were securely bound from sea to sea by a line of forty-four strongholds.

Sambhaji was at Shringarpur. Khafi Khan states[55] that his gross dereliction and disorderliness drew Shivaji's attention. He ordered him to move on to Sajjangad (Parali) in 1678 A.D. He was kept there as a royal captive. But more reliable accounts mention[56] that Shivaji was displeased with him as he had come to know that Sambhaji often excused the subjects from payment of the State's dues and that he also insulted the minister. Therefore, he was asked to leave Shringarpur. Dr. Sarkar also writes[57] that he was removed by Shivaji because he had antagonised the "Diwan". He also interfered in the administration. Besides, he set people against the minister and called him an oppressor. However, Sambhaji had made good impression in foreign camps. The English account states[58], "Sambhaji appeared to possess sufficient understanding".

Meanwhile, Sambhaji realised that the trends at Raigad would not favour his claims to the Maratha throne. He felt like revolting.[59] As known, the Moghuls had not discontinued their efforts to subdue the Marathas. At the same time, the Moghul General Dilerkhan assured[60] Sambhaji that "he would win his patrimony of Desh for him by the armed strength of the Moghul Govenment if he joined Dilerkhan". The promise induced[61] Sambhaji to join the Moghuls. He overlooked the fact that Shivaji had yet not given his assent to the possible succession of Rajaram.

Sambhaji escaped[62] from the fort Panhala on the 13th December, 1678 A.D. He reached Hyderabad and met Dilerkhan who had opposed any compromise with Shivaji when Mirza Raja Jaisingh was on the point of conquering[63] him. Dilerkhan received[64] Sambhaji with great honour and respect. He issued a 'farman' by which Sambhaji received the Subas of Khandesh and Varhad. Sambhaji was made "Sapt-Hazari"[65]. He received other presents also. Thus Dilerkhan was able to create a rift in the family of Shivaji. He was greatly pleased.[66]

Doubtless Sambhaji had acted unexpectedly. Shivaji greatly felt it.[67] But, unlike others, he had not yet lost hopes to bring Sambhaji back. Therefore, he kept an army within Sambhaji's approach, so that he might avail of the advantage in case of an emergency. Shivaji also helped[68] Adilshah against the combined attack of Dilerkhan and Sambhaji at Bijapur.

Meanwhile, Sambhaji being away and perhaps uncompromising, Rajaram's chances to succeed Shivaji grew stronger. Soyarabai was now more hopeful. As for Shivaji, the welfare of the Maratha State was more important than the question of the succession of any particular claimant. The recent act of Sambhaji had aroused his concern all the more. It was more likely now that he would be influenced by the supporters of Rajaram. The situation provided a much sought for opportunity to those who desired that Rajaram should succeed Shivaji. Later events also proved that Sambhaji could not be so popular during his life while Rajaram saved the Maratha State from 1689 to 1700 A.D. In this effort, he was helped by Ramchandrapant, Niraji Raoji and others. During this critical period, Rajaram's main assets were his non-aggressive and flexible temper, his capacity to take the strain of conflicting opinions in intricate problems, as compared with Sambhaji's haughty temper.

Shivaji still wavered on the succession issue. This indicates the intricacy of the problem, although the flight of Sambhaji to the Moghul camp had straightened Rajaram's succession to the Maratha throne. But he being of tender age, the success of the plan depended entirely on the co-operation he would get from the ministers and the Sardars. It was doubtful whether he would be able to overcome the opposition of Sambhaji and his supporters.

As known, the Moghuls were not slow to take full advantage of any weakness or mutual strife in the Maratha camp. Ordinarily, the Hindu law of succession vested the right to succeed his father on the elder son. But there were the nobles who viewed that if the younger one was completely ignored, there was every likelihood of a civil war. In that case, whether Rajaram would be able to deal squarely with the family as well as with the foreign powers was a delicate problem to be decided.

Meanwhile, Sambhaji and Dilerkhan proceeded[70] towards Bhupalgad. It was the main treasurehold of Shivaji. Many prominent Maratha families had resided there. There was fierce fighting between the inmates of the fort and the Moghul army, led[71] by Sambhaji. After tough fighting, Sambhaji won[72] the fort. Next, Sambhaji and Dilerkhan marched[73] on to Athani and Tikota. But the atrocities committed by Dilerkhan were not liked[74] by Sambhaji. Later on, Sambhaji also realised that Dilerkhan was not at all serious about his problem of succession. It is held that he came to know that "Dilerkhan planned[75] to send him off to Delhi to become a mansabdar or Moghul servant or more probably to be doomed to circumcision or death on refusal to apostasise." Besides, Mahadji Nimbalkar, son-in-law of Shivaji, informed[76] him about the intentions of Aurangzeb to get him (Sambhaji) imprisoned. No sooner had Sambhaji realised[77] the situation than he rode into Panhalla on 4th December, 1678 A.D. He had stayed at the Moghul camp for about a year where he had received only disappointment.

Shivaji visited Sambhaji. He talked to him and expressed[78] that he wanted to divide his kingdom between the two brothers. He desired that Sambhaji should take the kingdom of Karnatak (South Maharashtra) and let Rajaram have North Maharashtra. Dr. Sarkar writes,[79] "In 1678, Shivaji proposed a very understandable division of his Empire. The homeland of Maharashtra with its long settled peaceful territory and the families of hereditary and faithful ministers and generals was to go to Rajaram, a delicate boy of eight, because there was then no whisper of the Moghul Emperor, and the newly annexed country of the Karnatak (Jinji Vellore) could more reasonably be Sambhaji's share because the half subdued condition of the province demanded a vigorous grown up sovereign, to keep hold of it, for such a task Sambhaji was beyond question the fittest prince and Rajaram was unthinkable. Sambhaji cleverly put[80] off the talk about it. However, it was obvious that he was not in favour of division of the kingdom. Shivaji was worried. He stayed there for a few more days, and left for Raigad on 4th February, 1680 A.D. There he found that the executive body was not a homogenous one.

Shivaji reached Raigad and performed the thread ceremony of Rajaram on 7th March, 1680 A.D. He married[81] Rajaram to the daughter of Prataprao Gujar on 15th March, 1680 A.D. He had an attack of fever and died[82] in early April, 1680 A.D. The three successive happenings within a period of three weeks indicate that Shivaji was in no mood to leave the contending parties unbriefed. Apparently, he had made the position of Rajaram secure by winning[83] over to his support the allegiance of Ramchandrapant, Prahlad Niraji and Balaji Avaji.

Shivaji had yet not named his successor even under pressure, nor did he denounce Sambhaji. The death turmoil[84] described by the writers gives a vivid picture of the tense atmosphere at that time. Sane counsel had left Soyarabai and a few of the ministers at Raigad. Dr. Sarkar writes[85], "Immediately after his death, Soyarabai persuaded most of the ministers and generals present there that the accession of Sambhaji means disaster to the State and their own humiliation, while her son's character promised better times for his subjects." It is believed that a proposal[86] was made by Soyarabai to Sambhaji to divide the kingdom into two parts to be retained[87] by the two brothers. No accounts mention that Sambhaji ever accepted it. This brought in all the more trouble. Soon, on 21st April, 1680 A.D., arrangements were made to make Rajaram's position secure. The 'Manchakarohan' ceremony of Rajaram was performed by Annaji Datto and a few of Rajaram's supporters. It is also stated that Soyarabai expressed her concern over the accession of Rajaram, as she apprehended[88] troubles from Sambhaji and attack by the Moghul Emperor.

Sambhaji was at Panhalla.[89] He was being addressed as king by the foreign powers. Meanwhile the situation at Raigad changed soon. Chitnis states that differences cropped[90] up among the supporters of Rajaram and Soyarabai. It is said that Soyarabai wanted to send letters to Babaji Naik, Havaldar of Panhalla, Somaji Banki and Hiroji Farzand, instructing them to be more vigilant. But Balaji Avaji refused[91] to do that. However, he asked to get the work done through his son Avaji. How far the above statement is correct is difficult to say in the absence of reliable account. However, the vascillating attitude of the ministers had made it obvious that those who supported Rajaram had not taken his succession as final or were still doubtful whether Rajaram would be able to justify his claim.

Soon Annaji Datto, Moropant Pingle, Prahlad Niraji, started[92] for Panhalla. After some time, Prahlad Niraji did not proceed ahead and stayed[93] back. Meanwhile a messenger from Hambirrao Mohite met Annaji Datto and Moropant Pingle. Later both of them met Hambirrao Mohite, the commander of the army. He could know that Shivaji had not given his assent to divide[94] the kingdom and that opposition to Sambhaji's succession was started by a few ministers at Raigad. As a soldier of healthy disposition[95] and a wider outlook, he did not believe or indulge in a phase of shifting allegiance like others.

Hambirrao Mohite and others marched towards Panhalla and paid their respects to Sambhaji. Annaji Datto and Moropant Pingle were imprisoned[96] and kept at Panhalla under strict[97]vigilance. According to Bakhars Pilaji Shirke, Yesubai's father, supported Sambhaji and proceeded[98] ahead with 5000 of his men to arrange for his (Sambhaji's) arrival at Raigad. After some time, Sambhaji and Hambirrao Mohite marched[99] towards Raigad with an army. Sambhaji got possession of the fort on18th June, 1680 A.D. The quiet submission of the ministers and the Sardars was hardly expected by Soyarabai. However, there were factors which made the Sardars to take such a decision.

As known, the Sardars had committed allegiance to Rajaram. Probably they wanted to exercise[100] power in the regime of the minor, but had gained little from the new king and hoped to gain much more by going out to his rival and earning his favour. As mentioned, there existed differences among the supporters of Rajaram. Therefore, no sooner had Sambhaji arrived there than a few of them went over to him. There was confusion and demilitarisation. As such, they could not act in any other way than to march over to Sambhaji meekly. It is also apparent that the attitude of Hambirrao Mohite paralysed the opposing Maratha soldiers. Any resistance would have resulted into civil war which was not the aim of Shivaji.

Besides, Sambhaji being the elder son of Shivaji, no one opposed him. The tender age of Rajaram was also an important set-back. His success depended on the support of the Sardars. Under such circumstances, Soyarabai had no other option but to bear the consequences quietly.

No sooner had Sambhaji ascended[101] the throne then a reign of suppression was let loose. Those persons who had served

Shivaji and supported Rajaram were made the victims of his wrath as he apprehended trouble from them. Samarth Ramdass came to know of the activities of Sambhaji and wrote[102] to him "to be a king by deeds and not by tortures," but without any effect. Sambhaji, who could not get reverence, respect and co-operation, sought the same by spreading a reign of uncertainty and suppression. As such, he was feared more than respected.

Sambhaji imprisoned[103] Rajaram. He had yet not forgotten the influence wielded by Soyarabai and her supporters. Moropant Pingle was already dead, and his son Nilopant succeeded him. Next he put to death[104] Annaji Datto, Hiroji Farjand, Somaji Datto, Chitnis Balaji Avaji on the charge of intriguing against him and manouvering to bring in Akbar, the rebel son of Aurangzeb, on the Maratha throne. Kincaid and Parasnis write[105], "Annaji Datto and Soyarabai's kinsmen, of the great house of Shirkas saw, as they thought, in prince Akbar a fitting tool for their intended treason. They offered him the sovereignty of the Maratha Deccan, reserving only a small province as a provision for Rajaram." That Soyarabai and Rajaram's supporters would have gone to the extent of bringing in Akbar, needs to be tested.

It is well known that Akbar was himself seeking shelter[106] in the south[107] and was staying at Paligad. He aspired[108] to get the Moghul throne with the help of the Rajputs and the Marathas. In that case, he would not have antagonised Sambhaji. Therefore, if anybody could expect some advantage from Akbar, it was only Sambhaji and not the supporters of Rajaram or Soyarabai. Hence, it is difficult to think that they would have tried to bring Akbar on the Maratha throne. On the other hand, it can be said that Sambhaji and his supporters could not take advantage of the most opportune time when the father and the son were on fighting terms. As known, Akbar could not succeed. He left for Persia[109] in February, 1687 A.D.

Sambhaji had disposed of all his opponents except Soyarabai. She had wielded power. That she would continue to do so in the absence of those who supported Rajaram is difficult to imagine. Yet she was a participant in the 'Manchakarohan' ceremony. This could not have been forgotten by Sambhaji. Bakhars[110] states that he went straight to her apartment and accused her of having poisoned[111] Shivaji. Sarkar writes[112], "In Maharashtra there were some whispers of his wife Soyarabai, the mother of Rajaram, having administered poison to him (Shivaji) to prevent him giving the throne to Sambhaji." The accounts available further state that she was imprisoned in a room. This was nothing less than entombment. She died there within three days. Bendre states[113] that Soyarabai committed "suicide". Whether she died of entombment or suicide cannot be ascertained in the absence of more reliable accounts, yet the above statement indicates that her death was not natural. Hence, it would not be out of place to examine the circumstances that brought in the difficult situation for Sambhaji and Soyarabai to face.

Available accounts show that Sambhaji did not like Rajaram's succession to the Maratha throne. His dissensions with Shivaji, Soyarabai and Rajaram and a few of the councillors are not unknown. Besides, Shivaji neither confirmed nor criticised the anticipation of a few to get Rajaram declared as heir-apparent. His silence on such an important issue only added anxiety and concern[114] to Soyarabai for the welfare of Rajaram, he being younger and only about ten years. As the facts are, it cannot be denied that Shivaji had inclination towards making Sambhaji future king, though he was not well disposed towards him. Soyarabai and a few ministers could not rely on Sambhaji. As such, immediately after the death of Shivaji, they forestalled the succession of Sambhaji by the 'Manchakarohan' of Rajaram. This was probably either due to their (of the supporters of Rajaram) state of mind or fear that if the 'Manchakarohan' was not done, the consequences would be harmful to Rajaram because Sambhaji had never agreed to divide the kingdom even during the life time of Shivaji.

Under these circumstances, Sambhaji was feeling more insecure, although the had coronated himself. He had suppressed or executed those whom he suspected of evil designs against him except Soyarabai who had also participated in 'Manchakarohan' ceremony of Rajaram. Now it was necessary to get rid of her, although it is difficult to imagine that she would have been able to wield any influence on the councillors or other Sardars when her supporters were either imprisoned or executed. Sambhaji was also aware of the fact that any maltreatment of her without enough cause would certainly invite troubles for him. Therefore, charging her of having poisoned Shivaji was the best suited cause which would serve his purpose as well as invite public resentment and hatred towards her. But how far he adhered to punish her to the extent of getting her entombed is doubtful as no reliable account is coming forth to substantiate the same.

As known, intrigues and conspiracies are not unknown in royal houses. Yet the possibility that Soyarabai would stoop down to the abject level of poisoning Shivaji is simply unimaginable taking into account the benefit she would have derived by having Shivaji with her. She was bold and forthright. This is indicated by her request to Shivaji to declare Rajaram as his successor, fully knowing that the suggestion might bring in resentment and ill feelings towards her from Sambhaji and the ministers who supported him. The events show that the ministers and the Sardars were also not supporting either Rajaram or Sambhaji with one voice. It is obvious that they were deriving advantage of the shortcomings of Shivaji, Sambhaji and Soyarabai. Besides, the Sardars were always in the habit of sharing the spoils of the Maratha kingdom. The introduction of payment by cash system had debarred them from many advantages. They still preferred to be Jagirdars or independent Sardars to the immediate disadvantages of the nascent Maratha State. Doubtless, a combined approach by both of them (Sambhaji and Soyarabai) would have avoided the tragic situation which they had to face. It is apparent that they could not understand the trends of time that encircled the Maratha throne after Shivaji's coronation. Hence, it is all the more difficult to assign all blame to her.

The suggestion that her behaviour was haughty and that she wanted to rule with Rajaram is based on a very broad and slender presumption of her being from the Shirkey[115] class which she was not, as more reliable accounts say that she was from Mohite family.

Thus the available evidence does not justify the charges which have been brought by writers against Soyarabai either in the "Karnatak-Expedition" which was a political necessity, or the Succession-Issue which falls flat as Shivaji never declared his successor or the "Poison Episode". At the most, the poison episode was a figment of imagination and a means to exterminate Soyarabai. The charges seem[116] to be merely excuses that were brought forth by interested individuals.

REFERENCES

1. *Shivaji Nibandhawali*, Anukram II, Vol. 1 pp. 210, 211.
   Shivaji had eight wives :-

a. Saibai Malekar	Married in 1640-41 A.D. Died in 1659 A.D.
b. Sagunabai Shirke	Married in 1641 A.D.
c. Putlabai Shirke	Married in 1653 A.D. Became Sati.
d. Laxmibai Vichare	Married before 1653 A.D.
e. Sakwarbai Geakwad	Married in January, 1657 A.D.
f. Kashibai Jadhav	Married on 8th April, 1657 A.D.
g. Gunwantibai Ingle	Married on 15th April, 1657 A.D.
h. Soyarabai Mohite	Married before 1660 A.D. (Year not mentioned). Died in 1681 A.D.

   Bharatvarsha - Pant Pratinidhi Chi Bakhar, p. 25, mentions only four wives of Shivaji.
   Madhya Yugeen Charitra Kosh, p. 779, Apart from the names, the names of two more wives are found. They were : (1) Manohar and (2) Man Santosh.
2. B.I.S.M. - *Shiv Charitra Pradeep*, p. 118.

3. *Vividh Gyan Vistar* - Varsh 60, November, 1929, Ank 11, 91 Kalami Bakhar, Kalam 29, pp. 58, 59.
   Shivaji wanted to go to the rescue of his father in 1647 A.D. She replied, "To my humble mind, it appears best for you not to go to Bijapur for any reason at all, because your father is at court and you have committed irregularities".
4. *Gaekwad's Oriental Series*, No. CXX, p. 29, Verse 107.
   सर्वार्थ साधिनी वीरकन्या मोहितवंशजा।
   वीरमाता वीरबन्धुर्वीरव्रत परायणा।।
   Hence the belief that she was from Shirkey clan as mentioned in Bakhars and other sources is not correct.
5. Sen, S.M. - *Military System of the Marathas*, pp. 14, 15.
6. *Vividh Gyan Vistar*, Varsh 60, Ank 3, 1923, p. 123.
   "आम्ही घरन्दाज सरदार शिवाजी काल चपोर"
7. *Gaekwad's Oriental Series*, No. CXX, p. 59, Verse 47, 48.
8. Chitnis, M.R. - *Lives of Shivaji and Rajaram*, p. 5.
   Grant Duff - *History of the Marathas*, Vol. 1, p. 258.
9. Kincaid, C.A., & Parasnis, D.B. - *History of the Maratha People*, Vol. I, p. 265.
10. Khafi Khan - Muntakhabu-i-Lubab, *H.I.H.* Vol. III, p. 305.
    Riyasat, Vol. III, *Ugraprakriti Sambhaji*, p. 21.
11. *Ibid.*
12. Dennis Kincaid - *The Grand Rebel*, p. 162.
13. *Vividh Gyan Vistar* - Varsh 53, Ank 3, March 1923, p. 123, Rajwade, V.K., Vol. IV, p. 26.
14. Kincaid, C.A., & Parasnis, D.B. - *History of the Maratha People*, Vol. I, p. 265.
15. Sarkar, J. - *History of Aurangzeb*, Vol. IV, p. 222.
16. Riyasat, Vol. II, *Shak Karta Shivaji*, p. 202.
17. Rajwade, V.K., Khand XV, L.N.142.
18. *Gaekwad's Oriental Series*, No. CXX, p. 59, Shalokas 44-48.
19. Sarkar, J. - *History of Aurangzeb*, Vol. IV, p. 230.
20. Sharma S.R. - *Maratha History Re-Examined*, pp. 187-191.
21. *Ibid.*
    F.R. Fort St. George, Vol. XXVIII, pp. 34, 35.
    Surat to Fort St. George, 1st May, 1676 *ERS*(II) L.N.159.
22. Grant Duff - *The History of the Marathas*, Vol. 1, p. 230.
23. Sen. S.N. - *Studies in Indian History*, pp. 134, 135.

24. Shrinivasanchari, C.S.R.B. - *A History of Jinjee and its Rulers*, p. 227. Surat letter, 20th December, 1675 A.D. Archives Coloniales, 234 Inde.
25. *Itihas Sangraha* - Tanjawar-che-Rajgharane, p. 26.
26. Sharma S.R. - *Maratha History Re-Examined*, p. 185.
27. Patwardhan, R.P. & Rawlinson, H.G. - *Source Book of Maratha History*, Vol. I, p. 125.
28. *Itihas Sangraha* - Tanjawar-che-Rajgharane, p. 10.
29. Sarkar, J. - *History of Aurangzeb*, Vol. IV, p. 239.
30. *Gaekwad's Oriental Series*, No. CXX, p. 59,Verse 48.
31. Riyasat - *Shak-karta Shivaji*, Vol. II, p. 208.
    New History of the Marathas, Vol. I, p. 253.
32. Kincaid, C.A., & Parasnis, D.B. - *History of the Maratha People*, Vol. II, p. 1.
33. F.R. Fort St. George, Vol. 18, p. 13, Fort St. George to Bombay, Dt. 13th May, 1676, *ERS*(II), L.N. 162.
    Historical Miscellany, Series No.31. "... had Eoji attached the town, as he had done in Tanjore, he would have taken the possession of the whole kingdom of Madurey". (p. 9)
34. Sarkar, J. - *History of Aurangzeb*, p. 11.
35. Ormes - *Historical Fragments*, p. 85.
36. Riyasat, Vol. III, *Ugra Prakriti Sambhaji*, p. 21.
37. "At Shringarpur, Sambhaji exercised himself in gymnastics in the morning, studied the mystical histories and books on law and morals (Itihas, Puranas and the Mamandaki and other Niti Shastras)".
    - Sarkar, J. - *History of Shivaji*, p. 197.
    Gaekwad's Oriental Series, No. CXX, p. 66,Verse 87.
38. Orme Mss. Vol. 114, Sect. 5, p. 53, Bombay to Surat, 9th August, 1676, ERS (II), L.N. 177.
    Sangraha - Vol. I, L.N. 1866.
39. F.R. Surat, Vol. 88, p. 71, Carwar to Bombay, Dt. 9th June, 1675. ERS (II), L.N. 95, 96.
40. O, Correspondence Vol. 37, No.4253, (Mr. Child) Surat to Bombay, Dt. 10th Jan., 1676/77, ERS(II), L.N. 198 Letter Book, Vol. 5, p. 408. The Company to Surat, Dt. 7th March, 1676/77, *ERS*(II), L.N. 209.
41. Sarkar, J. - *Shivaji*, p. 286.
42. Sangraha - Vol. II, L.N. 1901.
    (Saraswati Mandir Itihas Mandal)

43. Sarkar, J. - *History of Aurangzeb*, Vol. IV, pp. 97, 217.
44. O, Correspondence Vol. 37, No.4266, Ft.St. George to the Company. Dt. 19th June, 1677, *ERS*(II), L.N. 232.
45. FBS., p. 303.
    Patwardhan, R.P. & Rawlinson, H.G. - *Source Book of Maratha History*, Vol. I, pp. 127, 128.
46. Sarkar, J. - *Shivaji*, p. 299 (Martin's Diary).
47. *Itihas Sangraha*, Tanjawar che Rajgharane, p. 38.
    "The latter (Raghunath Pant) replied that he was in the service of His Majesty Shivaji".
    - Grant Duff - *History of the Marathas*, Vol. 1, p. 241.
48. Riyasat, Vol. II, *Shak Karta Shivaji*, p. 193.
49. *Itihas Sangraha*, Tanjawar che Rajgharane, p. 40(15).
    "The Pargana of Bengrul yields today - with the neighbouring stations of Baskot and Silekot - a revenue of two lakhs Barai. If they are brought under our administration, they might yield five lakhs. These I had conferred on Chi. Saubhagyawati Dipa Bai for Cholibangdi. These should be continued in the female line. The mahals should be managed by you but their revenue should be enjoyed by her on whom it might be conferred by Sau. Dipa Bai".
    - Sharma S.R. - *Maratha History Re-Examined*, p. 198.
50. F.R. Surat, Vol. 107, p. 60, Rajapur to Surat, Dt. 28th February, 1677/78, *ERS* (II), L.N. 285.
    Vaidya, C.V. - *The Founder of the Maratha Swarajya*, p. 287.
51. Sarkar, J. - *Shivaji*, p. 309.
52. F.R. Surat, Vol. 107, Fol. 145, Rajapur to Surat, Dt. 12th September, 1678, *ERS* (II), L.N. 328.
53. Sabhasad - *Life of Shivaji*, p. 94.
54. Sarkar, J. - *History of Aurangzeb*, Vol. IV, pp. 231, 232.
55. Khafi Khan - Muntakhabu-i-Lubab, *H.I.H.*, Vol. VII, p. 342.
    It is alleged that Sambhaji's indecent behaviour with women was a common thing. The matter precipitated when he misbehaved with a Brahmin woman and people fled away from the village.
56. *Gaekwad's Oriental Series*, CXX, p. 81, Verses 24, 25.
    प्रजाभ्यो हाभयं दत्वा निरूणत्सि घनागमम्।
    अवजानासि चामात्थान्ममात्मान हवान्वहम्।।
    उत्तिष्ठ शृंगारपुरात्तिष्ठ सज्वनपर्वते।
    इंगितज्ञाय कवया किं सौजात्यवतेर्वते।।
    Bendre, V.S. - *Chhatrapati Sambhaji Maharaj*, pp. 73, 74.

57. Sarkar, J. - *Shivaji*, p. 76.
58. O, Correspondence Vol. 37, No.4353, Mr. Child at Surat to Bombay, Dt. 10th Jan., 1676/7, *ERS*(II), L.N. 198.
59. O, Correspondence Vol. 37, No.4353, Mr. Child at Surat to the Company, Dt. 17th Feb., 1678/79, *ERS*(II), L.N. 352.
    Sen. S. - *Sequel to the History of Shivaji*, FBS, p. 246.
60. Sarkar, J. - *House of Shivaji*, p. 199.
61. Martin, F. - *Karnatak Expedition*, *FBS*, p. 348.
62. B.I.S.M. - *Shiv Charitra Vrutta Sangraha*, Kha. ' 2, p. 100.
63. *Vividh Gyan Vistar*, Pustak 16, Ank 7, p. 156.
64. B.I.S.M. - *Shiv Charitra Pradeep*, pp. 29, 51 (Shivpur Daltarateel Yadi).
65. B.I.S.M. - *Shiv Charitra Pradeep*, p. 29.
66. Sarkar, J. - *History of Aurangzeb*, Vol. IV, p. 222.
67. *Gaekwad's Oriental Series*, CXX, p. 86, Verses 12, 13, 14, 16 & 17.
68. Sarkar, J. - *History of Aurangzeb*, Vol. IV, pp. 226.
69. *Ibid.*
70. B.I.S.M. - *Shiv Charitra Vrutta Sangraha*, Khand 2, p. 104.
71. *Gaekwad's Oriental Series*, CXX, p. 94, Verse 90.
72. *Ibid.*, p. 95. Verse 93 says that Sambhaji won the fort and gave it to Dilerkhan.
73. (S) F.R. Surat, Vol. 108, Fol. 37, Rajapur to Surat, Dt. 16th October, 1679, ERS (II), L.N. 393.
    F.R. Surat, Vol. 108 (unpaged), Bombay to Surat, Dt. 1st January, 1679/80, ERS (II), L.N. 469.
74. Sarkar, J. - *House of Shivaji*, p. 199.
75. *Ibid.*
76. Riyasat, Vol. II, *Shak Karta Shivaji*, p. 205.
    Sarkar, J. - *House of Shivaji*, p. 199.
77. Sabhasad - *Life of Shivaji*, p. 93.
78. *Ibid.*, p. 94.
79. Sarkar, J. - *House of Shivaji*, p. 199.
80. Sabhasad - *Life of Shivaji*, p. 94.
    आपणास साहबांचे पायांचीं, जोड जाहे, आपरण दूधभात
    खाऊन साहेबाचे पायाचे चिंतन करून राहीन।
81. *Shiva Nibandhawali*, Anukram II, Vol. I, p. 30.
    Riyasat, Vol. II, *Shiv Karta Shivaji*, p. 208.
82. B.I.S.M. - *Shiv Charitra Pradeep*, p. 30.

83. Sabhasad - *Life of Shivaji*, p. 103.
84. Patwardhan, R.P. & Rawlinson, H.G. - *Source Book of Maratha History*, Vol. I, p. 139.
85. Sarkar, J. - *History of Aurangzeb*, Vol. IV, pp. 239, 240.
86. Riyasat, Vol. II, *Shakkarta Shivaji*, p. 22.
87. *Gaekwad's Oriental Series*, CXX, p. 33, Verse 10, p. 29, Verses 108, 109.

    अभिविच्य पदे मुष्मिन्राजारामं कुमारकम्। आसमुद्रं वसुमतीमवितारः स्वयं वयम्।

    भव प्रशाधिसवलांकिंकरान्वशवर्तिनः। राजारामं पुरस्कृत्य महासाम्राज्यदीक्षितम्। सप्ताम्वुथिपरिम्राजन्मेखला वलयान्विताम्। वसुन्धरां शास्तु चिरं राजारामस्वत-वात्मजः॥

    Sarkar, J. - *History of Aurangzeb*, Vol. IV, p. 240.
88. *Gaekwad's Oriental Series*, CXX, p. 32, Verse 38-40.
89. Chitnis - *Gharanyachi Sanshipta Mahiti Wa Kagad - Patre*, Aitihasik, June Lekh 1, pp. 15, 16.
90. Chitnis, M.R. - *Live of Sambhaji and Rajaram*, p. 3.
91. *Ibid.*, p. 3.

    "आम्ही दरखदार राजाचे सावंद वडील संभाजी महाराज असतां अशा पत्रे आम्ही लिहिणार नाहीं, तेब्हां तुम्हारा हा आग्रह करण्याचे कारण नाहीं.. . मीहित नाहीं, मूल आवजीबाबा आहे, त्यास स्वाधीन करतो, पांहिजे तसे करवा।
92. *Gaekwad's Oriental Series*, CXX, p. 36, Verse 1 to 6.
93. *Ibid.*
94. Bendre, V.S. - *Chhatrapati Sambhaji Maharaj*, p. 155.
    Gaekwad's Oriental Series, CXX, p. 37, Verses 13, 14, 15.
95. Chitnis, M.R. - *Live of Sambhaji and Rajaram*, p. 3.
96. *Gaekwad's Oriental Series*, CXX, p. 38, Verses 29, 30; Gupte, K. - *Nagpurkar Bhonsele Yanchi Bakhar*, p. 15.
97. Ormes - *Historical Fragments*, p. 121.
98. Bendre, V.S. - *Chhatrapati Sambhaji Maharaj*, p. 138.
99. Sarkar, J. - *History of Aurangzeb*, Vol. IV, p. 242.
100. *Gaekwad's Oriental Series*, CXX, p. 24, Verse 34:

     श्रुग्विरामं प्रपयस्व राजारामं त्वदात्मजम्।

     राज्ये स्मिन्नभिषेक्ष्यामः स्रक्ष्यामः स्वमनोरधम्॥34॥
101. *Patre Yadi Vegere*, L.N. 489 (6)

102. Chitnis, M.R. - *Lives of Sambhaji and Rajaram*, p. 6/7.
103. B.I.S.M. - *Shiv Charitra Pradeep*, p. 30.
104. Sarkar, J. - *House of Shivaji*, p. 220, 221.
105. Kincaid, C.A., & Parasnis, D.B. - *History of the Maratha People*, Vol. II, p. 9.
106. Irvine, W.W. - *Later Moghuls*, Vol. II, p. 160.
107. Saqi Must-ad-Khan - *Maasir-i-Alamgiri*, p. 130.
108. *Annals and Antiquities of Rajasthan*, Vol. II, pp. 55-57.
109. Irvine, W.W. - *Later Moghuls*, Vol. II, p. 160.
110. Chitnis, M.R. - *Lives of Sambhaji and Rajaram*, p. 5.
111. Grant Duff - *History of the Marathas*, Vol. 1, p. 258.
112. Sarkar, J. - *Shivaji*, p. 331.
113. Bendre, V.S. - *Chhatrapati Sambhaji Maharaj*, p. 192.
     (मराठी साम्राज्यांची छोटी बखर)
114. *Gaekwad's Oriental Series*, CXX, p. 58, Verses 26, 27, 32 and 33:
     The word 'रक्ष मां' has special significance (protect us) in :-
     अदः सुदुः सहं शल्यमन्तःस्थं सोढुमक्षमाम्।
     रक्ष मां पक्षमात्मीयं क्षमाजाने जहि क्षमाम्।।33।।
115. Riyasat, Vol. II, *Shak Karta Shivaji*, p. 62.
116. The charges are mainly laid down by the poet Parmanand and supported by other writers later. He is believed to have been present at Shivaji's coronation in 1674 A.D. He was the partisan of Sambhaji and patronized his activities.
     The exaggerations in the narratives appear to have been written to please Sambhaji as well as a sort of palliative to his cruel activities.

CHAPTER 3

YESUBAI

Trial of Patience (1680-1720 A.D.)

Role of Soyarabai in Maratha politics was followed by the role of Yesubai, the wife of Sambhaji, both presenting the two banks of the river, never to meet; whereas, the presence of Soyarabai had often been marked with tension and power struggle, presence of Yesubai was a soothing balm, and healing touch on the deep scars that were being inflicted by her husband Sambhaji on the Maratha body politics by his hot temper and cruelty towards the suspects and his opponents. Against this Yesubai was a gentle breeze but at the same time, she displayed iron will and courage, firm determination in her behaviour. She had the courage to admonish Sambhaji for the misdeeds in killing with scathing words to Sambhaji like, "You have killed Balaji Prabhu which is not right, even Shivaji Maharaj had entrusted him with the sole responsibility of running the administration. Moreover, his descendents should be given the same place as was given by Shivaji. How could you act like a child? All kartoons are dead by your injustice. All have gone one by one. How will the kingdom be managed," Hereafter she kept the royal seal[1] under her possession which also indicated that Sambhaji had all faith in her ability and capacity.

Yesubai was the daughter of Pilaji Shirkey,[2] the prominent chief of Shringarpur in 1660-61 A.D. As known Shivaji took[3] Shringarpur by defeating Shirkey Sardars who were famous for their ambition and equitting chivalry. Shivaji also married Soyarabai, the daughter of Waghoji, and to further strengthen relations, he got his son Sambhaji[4] married to Yesubai, and thus Soyarabai and Yesubai being related she (Yesubai) became a countable member of Shivaji's family. Yesubai's inclusion at the tender and impressionable age in 1667 A.D., equipped her with such qualities as were displayed later on in the more distinguished manner. Details of her early life are not available when she is found with her husband at Shringarpur. She had a daughter born[5] to her on 4th September, 1678 A.D. Sambhaji had quietly escaped on 13th December, 1678 A.D. with Yesubai and proceeded[6] towards the Moghul camp. However, Bendre states[7] that Yesubai stayed back as it was not possible for her to accompany him in his flight. However, after the attack on Bhupalgad Sambhaji found that Dilerkhan would not help him in any way. As such he was greatly disappointed. With remorse and regret, the only course left to him was to return to Panhalla. He left[8] the Moghul camp on the 20th November, 1678 A.D. and reached[9] Panhalla on the 4th December, 1678 A.D.

Sambhaji got possession of the Raigad fort after a strenuous effort. For this he had to put under arrest a few of the most influential Sardars. His fear[10] complex compelled him to start his career with an ordeal of suppression[11], amounting to executions of a few[12] of the most influential Sardars, including Balaji Avaji, Hiroji Farjand, Annaji Datto and Annaji Pant. Yesubai viewed these actions with disfavour and repugnance and fearlessly showed her disagreement and concern over the executions of those experienced[13] persons. The emphatic observations made by Yesubai regarding the cruel acts show her boldness to criticize a wrong deed when everyone else was afraid of Sambhaji. Not satisfied with this, she brought[14] up affectionately the two sons of Balaji Avaji, Khandoballal and Nilloballal who served[15] her later in many ways.

Apprehending further trouble, she secured[16] the 'Sikka' (the royal seal) from Sambhaji through Khandoballal. She was careful enough to keep it under her possession. Her action brought no objection from Sambhaji. The fact that she was allowed to keep the seal shows that she enjoyed the confidence of her husband.

Sambhaji had established[17] himsef well at Raigad and was free from any impending troubles at home. He proceeded on to subdue his enemies, such as Siddis of Janjira, the Portuguese[18] and the Moghuls. Sambhaji also devastated[19] the areas including Khandesh, Berar and Bhroach by 1685 A.D.

In this effort to subdue his enemies, Sambhaji had to remain away from Raigad. During this time Yesubai carried on all "Mulki"[20] arrangements. She issued Kaulnama and could use her own seal which had the words "Shree Sakhi[21] Ragyi Jayati". The words indicate the respect, reverence and confidence which she enjoyed from Sambhaji and others.

Unfortunately, only a few letters which were written by Yesubai are found. This might be due to the reason that Maratha State had to struggle against its enemies continuously and specially after 1689 A.D. Therefore, those records which might have included such informations were either destroyed or displaced at the fall of Raigad fort in 1689 A.D. However, only one such letter written by Yesubai to Diwakar Gosavi, a sage of the sect of Ramdass, residing at 'Chaphal' (district Satara), could be found. She wrote[22], "You are going to celebrate the festival of Shree Raghunath but you are afraid that our people will trouble you in the celebration of the ceremony. We hereby declare that we are sending orders to our people (from village to village) that the fair and the festival should be observed undisturbed. The village of Singamwadi is given in Inam to the temple of Shri Raghunath perpetually". The letter shows her regard for the religious sentiments of the people. She could issue orders on her own which had the words "Agnya" and those of which Sambhaji was aware had the words "Rajagnya"[23], which created the position of Pratinidhi even during the life time of Yesubai. However, Sambhaji was not totally aloof from administration, as is obvious from State papers.

While the scuffle for power between the Marathas and the Moghuls was going on, when the most capable and staunch supporter of Sambhaji, Hambirrao Mohite, was killed[24] at Wai. The Sardars deserted Sambhaji one by one, except Kavikalash who had gained prominence and Sambhaji's confidence[25] by his sincere and loyal services to him after the execution of a few prominent Sardars in 1680 A.D. Since then he had looked after the state administration. Writers have expressed different views about his antecedents and whereabouts. A few among them are of opinion[26] that he was sent by the Moghul Emperor Aurangzeb to capture or imprison Sambhaji. No other reliable account confirms this view. The Marathas nicknamed him Kalush, an instigator of feuds. Nothing can be said regarding Yesubai's attitude towards him in absence of any account. There is nothing to suggest that she ever came in conflict with him.

Since Sambhaji had quite a few reverses in the battles, he craved for success all the more. Moreover Sambhaji had to carry on struggle against a few Maratha Sardars who were either in the Moghul service or independent. Meanwhile, there was a fight[27] between Kavikalash and Shirkeys, in which the former was defeated. He took shelter at Khelna (Vishalgad).

Yesubai and Sambhaji were at Raigad. No sooner had he heard about the defeat of Kavikalash than he marched[28] on to help him. On his way to Khelna, he defeated[29] Shirkeys. Later Sambhaji and Kavikalash decided to come back via Ghat areas. In between, they stayed at Sangameshwar, a hilly tract. Maratha families resided there, it being situated on the confluence[30] of the rivers Alaknanda and Varuna. A Mahadeo temple also provided special significance to the place. It is mentioned[31] that Sambhaji, after taking the fort of Khelna and having provisioned it well, went to Sangameshwar where Kavikalash had constructed a garden and a building, and spent his time in merry making.

As known, Aurangzeb had successfully alienated[32] the combination of Durgadas, Sambhaji and his rebel[33] son Akbar. His activities had continued to subdue[35] the Marathas and to capture[36] Sambhaji alive, if possible. He had his agents to keep a vigilant watch[37] on Sambhaji's movements. Sheikh Nizam, one of the Moghul officers of Golkunda, looked for an opportunity to capture him. Due to his long services in the Deccan, he was aware of the hilly region and tracts leading to the place where Sambhaji resided. It is also stated[38] that Sambhaji was warned of the impending attack of Sheikh Nizam, but he did not pay attention to it.

Sheikh Nizam attacked Sambhaji suddenly, and an encounter[39] took place in which Sambhaji suffered heavy losses. Perceiving the futility of further resistance, he tried to escape but was captured[40] with Kavikalash on 1st February, 1689 A.D. Shedgoakar Bakhar and other writers mention[41] that Yesubai was also with[42] him as he was performing an "Anushthan" (puruscharan) to get victory over his enemies. But more reliable texts have not mentioned that she was with Sambhaji or had reached Raigad hurriedly after the attack by Sheikh Nizam. Khafi-Khan as well as Chitnis write[43] that Sambhaji did not take any precautionary measures to save himself from being taken into captivity. He was careless and therefore could be captured easily.

The allegation[44] that one of the Shirkeys informed the Moghuls about Sambhaji's whereabouts on account of his ill-treatment of Soyarabai who was supposed to be from the Shirkey clan, does not seem correct, as Soyarabai belonged[45] to the Mohite family. Besides, Yesubai was from the Shirkey clan, and they also enjoyed her sympathy and help. As such, it is most unlikely that they would enhance the difficulties of Yesubai by helping the Moghuls in capturing her husband Sambhaji. At the most, it can be said that the Shirkeys had defeated Kavikalash and Sambhaji had defeated them. This might have alienated the sympathy and support of a few of the Shirkey Sardars towards Sambhaji and led them to support the Moghuls. As known, the frequent changing of sides was not unusual for the Sardars in those days.

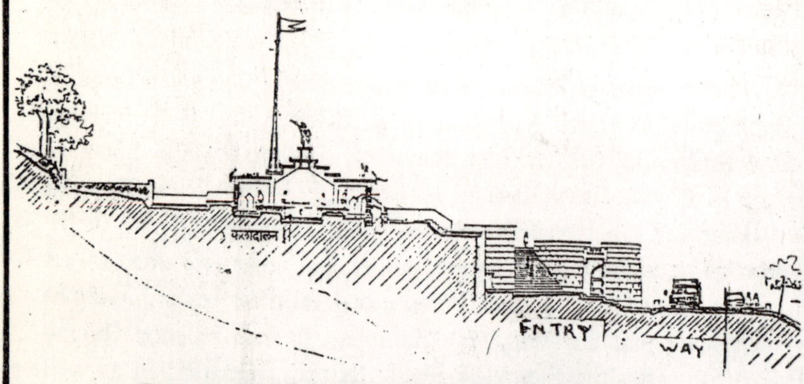

The memorial of Chhatrapati Sambhaji Maharaj at Sangmeshwar.

The Memorial of Sambhaji

The news of Sambhaji's capture was soon received[46] at Raigad through Santaji. The seriousness of the situation was realised by Yesubai and others at the capital. Shahu was only ten years old. As such, he was least expected to bear the responsibilities of a king as well as an efficient general to keep the Marathas united at the critical moment. No doubt, Yesubai had looked after the management of the estate affairs, specially when Sambhaji used to be on campaigns but whether she would be able to maintain internal solidarity as well as face the Moghul Emperor Aurangzeb till Shahu was old enough to undertake the responsibilities, was still to be considered.

Yesubai still paid attention to the management of various affairs in the State. This is indicated by her efforts at this critical moment. She gave the position[47] of Pratinidhi to Prahlad Niraji, son of Niraji Raoji. No one was yet declared Chhatrapati. Kincaid and Parasnis state[48] that a section of Sardars were interested in getting Shahu proclaimed king and Yesubai regent. But she had not given her assent to the proposal at once. She appeared to have thought over the problem from a different point of view, wherein she realised the difficulties she would have to face as a regent and avoided to accept the suggestion.

The other person nearest to the throne was Rajaram, whose 'Manchakarohan' ceremony was once performed[49] after the death of Shivaji in 1680 A.D. He was still a captive[50] but only in name. Further, no account shows that he had taken any initiative to usurp power from infant Shahu. It appears that he had confidence in Yesubai regarding succession or he realised that the ministers or Sardars might differ on his being made Chhatrapati. Moreover, there is nothing to show that Yesubai was either dissatisfied with or suspected any undesirable step by him in connection with the succession issue. Yet he was not to be ignored at the critical moment. Any ill-considered action on her part would have brought further troubles. She reposed[51] her faith in him and declared[52], "Let there be no coronation. Let Shahu be the king and Rajaram the regent." Accordingly, Shahu was declared[53] Chhatrapati unanimously.Thus, she could win the goodwill and the confidence of Rajaram and the Sardars. It was apparent that her cool calculation of the situation had warded off the likelihood of chaos and disturbance among the Marathas. The declaration indicated that the office of the Chhatrapati never remained vacant and that it continued in a conventional way which alienated any possibility of Rajaram being reduced by others against Shahu.

Though Aurangzeb had captured Sambhaji, his (Sambhaji's) fate was yet undecided. He counted on his willingness to be a vassal[54] of the Moghuls, and hoped that he would embrace[55] Islam, as is evident from the conditions he put to Sambhaji to obtain his release. He also promised[56] him freedom if he named such of his officers as were secretly working against him

(Aurangzeb). As known, Sambhaji refused to consider these suggestions. At last, Sambhaji and Kavikalash were executed[57] on the 11th March, 1689 A.D. at Koregaon (Tulapur Vadu) with cruelty and much torture. This enraged the Sardars to avenge[58] the death of their Chhatrapati.

Disappointed by Sambhaji's attitude, Aurangzeb would have been too glad to consolidate his position by bestowing favours on Rajaram and keeping him in his hand, so that he would not have become strong. Here he singularly failed in his expectations which were based on the Moghul practice rather than on the Maratha ways.

Rajaram, as known, had already taken over the task of the Marathas who had prepared themselves to resist the Moghuls vigorously and resolutely. Obviously, the execution of Sambhaji did not further the cause of the Moghul Emperor Aurangzeb. He commissioned[59] his general Itikadkhan to march on to Raigad. He attacked[60] the fort on 25th March, 1689 A.D. just after a fortnight of Sambhaji's execution.

Raigad was the seat of Maratha royalty[61] and was famous for treasure deposits and its impregnability. As mentioned, Yesubai and Rajaram had established themselves at Raigad. The Marathas had united and become a power to reckon with at this critical moment. Among them the prominent were Ramchandrapant Amatya, Sachiv Shankaraji Malhar, Yesaji Kank, Prahlad Niraji, Manaji More, Santaji Ghorpade, Dhanaji Jadhav and Babaji Bhonsle with others.

The Marathas continued to defend the fort, but the pressing siege by Itikadkhan disheartened them. They were losing hope in spite of their determined and continued struggle. Soon they realised the futility of resistance with the limited resources they had. They were also outnumbered by their Muslim counterparts who were duly armed with better equipment.

Yesubai, instead of giving way to despair and disappointment, advised[62] Rajaram to despatch a few eminent Sardars, supported by the pick of the Maratha forces to counteract the Moghul onslaughts. At the same time, she asked Rajaram to give a courageous[63] lead to the remnants of the Maratha army by escaping from the fort immediately. Rajaram reluctantly gave way to Yesubai's desire and hurriedly prepared himself to leave the fort with a few chosen ones. Before Rajaram left the fort, Yesubai got Shahu proclaimed Chhatrapati and, as a mark of allegiance, oath[64] was taken by all to remain faithful to him.

Rajaram delivered an inspiring message when he visited Yesubai for the last time. Yesubai blessed him and said,[65] "There is no cause for grief. Victory will be yours and you will reconquer your father's kingdom." Rajaram embraced Shahu. He escaped[66] from Raigad on the 5th April, 1689 A.D. He was accompanied by Ramchandrapant Amatya, Prahlad Niraji, Shankaraji Malhar Sachiv who were detailed by Yesubai to look after his safety and security. Further, she proved to be rather alert and active and adopted such a course of sustained policy as would maintain high order of morale in the army and common men against incoming adversities.

The impact of continued siege was felt by the besieged and the bisiegers alike. Since the Marathas were besieged, they could not secure any outside help. Thus the general tone and tenor of the soldiery was far[67] from satisfactory. No help from Rajaram could be secured as he was constantly[68] on the move from fort to fort being shadowed by the Muslims. At last, he reached[69] Jinji via Vishalgad, Panhalla and other smaller forts and by coastline, often in disguise.

It is apparent that after some time, Yesubai felt that if she did not deliver the fort herself, some one else who was suspected of treachery might do so. Among those on whom suspicion[70] had fallen was Narsoji Gaekwad of Birwadi. She assembled the Sardars and addressed[71] them. She explained that the best course under the circumstances was to hand over the fort to the Moghuls, failing which no assurance or security could be expected from them.

Ramchandrapant and Prahlad Niroji were at Khelna. How far they could have helped the inmates at Raigad is not beyond imagination. Meanwhile, Yesubai managed[72] to send away Tarabai, Ambikabai and Rajasbai, wives of Rajaram, to Vishalgad, taking it to be the next safest fort and so were the treasures removed to a safer place. It was decided that the fort should be handed over to the Moghuls. Finally, the fort was surrendered[73] to the Moghul General, Itikadkhan, on the 25th March, 1689 A.D. Yesubai, Shahu, Bhavanibai, Sakwarbai (Shivaji's queen), Madansingh and Madhosingh, sons of Champabai, were taken captive[74] along with Sardars[75] as Kesarkar, Moropant Sabnis and Uddhavji Yogdev. They were taken to Koregaon where Aurangzeb had encamped.

Yesubai, Shahu and others were received[76] cordially by the Emperor's establishments. They received all the facilities offered to royal captives, though they were guarded well. Aurangzeb honoured them by granting awards and other privileges according to their ranks. Accordingly, Shahu received[77] a mansab of 7000 and the title of 'Raja'. Aurangzeb also gave a Khilat[78] of Rs.4000/- to Shankaraji, son of Harje Raja Mahadik, who was married to Yesubai's daughter Bhavanibai. By and by, Yesubai got into the favour of Begam Zinnatunnissa, while Shahu claimed filial affection of Aurangzeb who fondly called him 'Sao'[79]. In spite of such favours, the Moghul Emperor did not relax his efforts to wipe off the Maratha power from the Deccan completely. He asked his General Itikadkhan, designated now as Zulphikar Khan, to press on his victory and to pursue Rajaram who was at Jinji.

Rajaram had established[80] himself well at Jinji. As asked by the Emperor, Zulphikar Khan attacked him on 13th November, 1689 A.D The Marathas were fighting against the Moghuls on two fronts; one in the north Maharashtra, organised[81], with Vishalgad as its seat, by Ramcandrapant Amatya and a few of the Sardars who remained there, and the other in the south Maharashtra, conducted[82] by Rajaram and Prahlad Niraji from Jinji. Besides, roving groups of Maratha Sardars roamed[83] about carrying on their ravages and plunders in the Moghul territory under Santaji Ghorpade and Dhanaji Jadhav. Both the fronts carried on pincer like attacks with full virulence more of an embarrassing nature as envisaged by Shivaji as early as 1677 A.D. The Marathas were able to ward off complete subjugation of the Moghuls.

Yesubai and Shahu remained[84] a part of the Moghul Emperor Aurangzeb's entourage and had to move from place to place and fort to fort along with him. During this time, Aurangzeb also tried to know the feelings Shahu had developed towards him or his uncle Rajaram. Once he (Aurangzeb) asked him if he would like to go to his uncle. Shahu replied[85], "My uncle is my enemy as he was to my father too. If I go to him, he will keep me in rigorous confinement. I will go back only when Your Majesty puts me firmly on my throne as a legitimate Sovereign of the Marathas." This reply shows that Shahu and Yesubai were extremely cautious and careful in their talk to the Emperor. In due course of time, she convinced him that Rajaram had left her at a most critical time.

Being always near to the Moghul Emperor, it was probably easy for Yesubai to get information of political importance. Whether she could derive any advantage from it and communicate the same to Rajaram in the far south is difficult to say. However, Chitnis States[86] that she utilized the services of Bhaktaji Huzre and Banki Gaekwad in passing intelligence to Rajaram at Jinji. Further, he writes that Yesubai was anxious to get rid of her captivity as early as possible. As she communicated to Rajaram, she was "though living most comfortably, yet in infinite peril." She also conveyed to him that her understanding with him was personal and secret and as such should be guarded well. It appears that Rajaram could realize the significance attached to the incident of being sent away in the company of trustworthy Sardars. According to Chitnis, she advised Rajaram to take[87] away his queens Tarabai, Rajasbai and Ambikabai from Vishalgad to Jinji.

Whether it was due to her suggestion or because of any other consideration, the queens were taken[88] to Jinji, undergoing a hazardous journey.

As mentioned,[89] Shahu moved with the Moghul camp. Yet he could be trained in riding, hunting and such other arts as were necessary for a man in those days. As far as knowledge of letters was concerned, Dr. Sardesai writes,[90] "He did not know Sanskrit, nor did he have any occasion to have his own education or traditional Hindu mythology. Placed as he was in an alien atmosphere, it was difficult for him to learn them, yet his mind was quite alert and more to human behaviour." However, there is a paper[91] which shows that Shahu could read and write well. According to a few writers, Jotyaji Kesarkar was responsible for all such training as he got in the Moghul camp.

At the same time, it is obvious that circumstances had made him more pliant and adjustable. This was quite noticeable even when he became Chhatrapati. Even then, he followed a policy of compromise, and tried to win his opponents thereby. Just as Jijabai had brought up Shivaji at Poona, so also was Yesubai bringing up the future Chhatrapati of the Marathas. However, the entirely different atmosphere and circumstances evidently left an indelible impression on the respective minds of Shivaji and Shahu.

The Moghul siege of Jinji continued without any decision till 1698 A.D., i.e., for nearly seven years. This made Aurangzeb all the more anxious to force a victory. He sent Prince Kambaksh to Jinji in 1696 A.D. This was perhaps resented by the Moghul Commander Zulphikar Khan who thought it to be a challenge to his efficiency. This is further strengthened by his (Zulphikar Khan's) highhanded action whereby he imprisoned[92] Prince Kambaksh for initiating a treasonable[93] negotiation with Rajaram. Meanwhile, Rajaram also realised the futility of carrying on the resistance and therefore desired to leave the fort at a favourable moment. It appears that this was a matter of convenience to Zulphikar Khan also.

Rajaram decided to leave the fort. Before he left Jinji, he managed[95] to send away Tarabai, Rajasbai and Ambikabai to Vishalgad. He escaped from the fort on the 7th February, 1698 A.D. The escape is said to be with the connivance of Zulphikar Khan through Rajaram's son Rajkarna. He (Rajaram) reached Vishalgad on 22nd February, 1698 A.D. The family reunited there. He did not stay there for long, and engaged himself in all round attack on the Moghul camp with his staunch supporters. In this effort, once he even reached[96] the very camp of Aurangzeb. He wanted to take away Shahu, but was unsuccessful in his attempt. Soon he had to return as he could no longer sustain the rigours of constantly changing life. He fell ill at Satara. At the same time, Dhanaji Jadhav again attacked[97] the Moghul camp at Brahmapuri without any success.

Aurangzeb laid siege to the Satara fort. Rajaram proceeded to Sinhgad, another invulnerable fort. His health deteriorated. He died on 2nd March, 1700 A.D. when he was about thirty years old. Ambikabai committed[98] 'Sati' at Vishalgad.

It is held that Shahu was distressed to learn of Rajaram's death. This was noticed[99] by Aurangzeb who inquired of him as to the reasons of ill health, to which he gave an evasive answer. It is not surprising that Yesubai's reaction on the sad event is neither known nor accounted for. For it should be remembered that, though the captives were treated with all human care, Aurangzeb's policy to seduce[100] the Marathas had never discountinued.

Finally, Aurangzeb asked[101] Shahu to embrace Islam. Shahu resented. Dr. Sarkar writes[102] that Shahu did not agree to conversion. Yesubai registered[103] her repugnance at the very thought of conversion. It is held that "she requested Begam Zinnatunnissa to relieve Shahu from the sad plight." Maratha historians assert that the 'order of conversion' of Shahu was because of the religious fanaticism of the Moghul Emperor Aurangzeb. However, the religious conversion was not forced upon Shahu. The reason for this is not beyond one's comprehension, even though it was the least expected of Aurangzeb that he would change his orders having once passed them.

As known, Aurangzeb had stayed in the Deccan for nearly twenty-five years. Yet his efforts to subdue the Marathas had not achieved success. Therefore, he thought of other ways to achieve his aim. The order of conversion was thus issued as a last ruse. However, the revision of the order proves that he wanted to settle the southern affairs amicably but with the dignity of a Moghul Emperor. He could perceive that obstinacy in getting the order obeyed would further diminish the chances of Maratha submission. In the circumstances, there were only two alternatives. The first was acceptance of Islam by Shahu and the other was to fall in line with the imperial policy and work for it. It can be said that if Shahu would have embraced Islam, no useful purpose would have been served, as there was least possibility that he could have stayed in the South.

The second alternative was, however, practised by Shahu even after the Emperor's death. Therefore, it can be said that the promulgation of the order of conversion and its revision were not only because of Aurangzeb's religious fervour or Begam Zinnatunnissa's effort to relieve Shahu from the sad plight, but also because of the aforesaid reasons. Since the orders issued must be obeyed, two Marathas, Khandoji and Jagjiwan, sons of Senapati Prataprao Gujar, were converted[104] to Islam and were named Abu-ur-Rahim and Adb-ur-Rahman. Thus, to the great relief of Yesubai and Shahu, an atmosphere of suspense and anxiety had ended without causing much bitterness.

Yesubai further had the satisfaction to see Shahu married[105] to two women of the most influential families of the South in 1703 A.D. They were Savitribai (Rajasbai) of Kanerkhed, a village 10 miles from Koregaon, and Ambikabai, the daughter of Manaji Rustamrao Jadhavrao of Sindkhed, the house of Jijabai. In between the marrige festivities, Aurangzeb carried[106] on his campaigns, but the tide turned and soon the Marathas started taking back the forts.

It was now twenty-three years since Aurangzeb had stayed in the South. His long stay in the Deccan affected him and his Empire in more[107] ways than one. He was 84 years of age, and the sad demise[108] of his sons and daughters in 1704 and 1705 A.D. had affected him adversely. He was suffering mentally and physically. The officers and the soldiers equally suffered[109] the hardships during the unsettled life and were keen to return to north.

However, Aurangzeb continued his march with Yesubai, Shahu and other Maratha Sardars. His camp suffered from epidemic, and the daily mortality was heavy. The armies and their followers had to march on flooded rivers, muddy roads and hilly tracts. Scarcity of grains was ever present in camps. His old and loyal officers were dead, one by one. Mutual jealousy existed[110] among the new officers, and they often corresponded with Maratha leaders. The Sardars had organised[111] themselves into a strong power, and were not afraid of giving up an open battle to the Emperor. Aurangzeb's march from Devpur to Ahmadnagar appeared like a 'mourning procession'.

The wretched[112] condition of the camp had affected Yesubai and others in the camp. This is indicated by the letter she wrote to Narayan Deo Moraya of Chinchawad on 19th April, 1705 A.D. "My son Daji has accompanied the Emperor and we were sent here along with the Zenana some five months ago. We are experiencing a dreadful predicament caused by the want of provision and cash. Our assigned allowances have not long been paid to us, all cash was either plundered by the Marathas or appropriated by the Moghul officers. For a long time, we have had to live on loans, but now no banker hazards loans to us. My debt already amounts to rupees seven thousand and we are heavily pressed for its repayment. It is indeed providential unkindness that such extreme misery should befall the great Shivaji's daughter-in-law. Every passing moment adds to our troubles. In this extremity, we approach as to your holiness as our last resort. If you kindly send me a loan of seven thousand rupees with the bearer Rayaji Jadhav, we can pay back our debts to our bankers here and obtain sums from them. The bearer will fully explain our situation. I will pay back this loan to your Holiness as soon as better days return. Your Holiness must not reject my prayer out of memory of what my father-in-law might have done for your Holiness's shrine. Trusting you will not disappoint me."

While Aurangzeb was suffering the tragic fate in the South, chaos and confusion prevailed[113] in northern India. The Bundelas fought for their own independence. Rajputs, Jats and Sikhs rose in rebellion agaist the Emperor. The Marathas started to benefit[114] themselves, taking advantage of the existing situation.

Aurangzeb appears to have realised that his end was approaching.[115] This is indicated by the letters he wrote to his son, Prince Mohd. Muazzam, in which he asked[116] him to take care of the people of Dohad as it was his birth place. He also prepared[117] a note and divided his empire among his three sons, Princes Shah Alam, Azamshah and Kambaksh. His eldest son, Prince Sultan, was in prison and Prince Akbar was already dead, in 1704 A.D. Aurangzeb died on 3rd March, 1707 A.D. He was buried at Khuldabad now called Roza in a low simple tomb without any marble platform.

With Aurangzeb's death, there occurred a sudden cessation of the campaigns against the Marathas. Prince Azamshah proclaimed[118] himself Emperor on the 5th March, 1707 A.D. and marched towards north.

Yesubai, Shahu and a retinue of about two hundred persons had to move on with Azamshah. He presented[119] to Shahu the robes of honour (khilat). Shahu remained in the army of Zulphikar Khan, but as the camp proceeded northwards, he grew impatient. Akhabarats indicate[120] that he wanted to return to Maharashtra.

Prince Azamshah was busy in his own affairs and concentrated his attention to the forthcoming contest against his brother Shah Alam. It is stated that Begam Zinnatunnissa asked[121] Shahu "not to wait for formal sanads and appointments from Azamshah and proceed on to south." How far the above statement is correct cannot be said in absence of more reliable accounts. However, Shahu left[122] the camp at Doraha about 20 miles north-west of Bhopal, and started for the south. Yesubai, Savitribai, Ambikabai, Sakwarbai, Madansingh and others of the family as well as Jotyaji Kesarkar moved[123] on to north with the Moghul camp.

Shahu's release from the Moghul camp has been differently viewed by writers. According to Akhabarats, Shahu was released because of Zulphikar Khan's connivance as he aspired to become the Viceroy of the Deccan in the near future and knew that Shahu in Maharashtra would be a great help to him. Dr. Sinha asserts[124], "Shahu's release would be a more potent weapon against the Marathas than Shahu in captivity." Dr. Mazumdar, Raichaudhary and Datta state[125], "Zulphikar Khan pointed out that Shahu's return to his kingdom would inevitably cause a disunion among the Marathas." However, it will not be an exaggeration to say that Shahu was an important piece on the chess-board of the Deccan politics in the hands of the Emperor, Aurangzeb. Failing other means, he would have used him as an instrument to have his hold in the Deccan. He had tactfully secured[126] his goodwill before his death. Curiously enough, Shahu always had respectful regards for Aurangzeb even after his death.

At the same time, Yesubai stayed back in the Moghul camp. This is another aspect of the circumstances in which she had been placed. That she would not like to accompany Shahu to south is unimaginable when she had already remained in the Moghul captivity for nearly eighteen years. Besides, the possibility that Shahu would have taken her with him, if it was possible, cannot be rejected.

As known, both the Moghuls and Shahu were unaware of

their respective future, as no agreement[127] was concluded between Shahu and the Moghuls when the former proceeded to south. Hence it will not be an exaggeration to say that if Shahu's release was a more potent weapon against the Marathas, Yesubai's stay back at the Moghul camp was a guarantee that Shahu would not jeopardise the Moghul interest in the Deccan.

While Shahu started for Maharashtra, Yesubai moved on with the Moghul Emperor and stayed at Gwalior with Begam Zinnatunnissa. Azamshah, who had earlier proclaimed[128] himself Moghul Emperor, was defeated[129] by Prince Muazzam on 20th June, 1707 A.D. He ascended the throne as Bahadurshah. He sent letters[130] to Vizier Asadkhan and his son Zulphikar Khan to bring Begam Zinnatunnissa and other members of Aurangzeb's and Azamshah's families to Agra from Gwalior where they were staying during the battle between Azamshah and Prince Muazzam. In July 1707 A.D., Asadkhan and Zulphikar Khan arrived[132] at Agra with Begam Zinnatunnissa and others. With Begam Zinnatunnissa, Yesubai had also to move to Agra.

Detailed account of Yesubai's life and activities now in the Moghul camp is not available. Yet it appears that she still received the same attention and facilities as were given to her by Aurangzeb. She had her seal, bearing the words, "Yesubai Walida Raja Shahu – Ihide"[132].

Bahadurshah died on 27th February, 1712 A.D. He was succeeded by Jahandarshah on 29th March, 1712 A.D. But he could not remain long on the Moghul throne. Farrukhsiyar succeeded[133] him as Moghul Emperor on 12th February, 1713 A.D. Thus, the quick changes in the Moghul Empire had affected the administration to the extent that the Emperor had become merely a puppet[134] in the hands of Sayyid brothers. Further, the court politics compelled[135] the Emperor to send Sayyid Hussain Ali as Nizam-ul-Mulk in the Deccan in 1715 A.D.

Sayyid Hussain Ali arrived in the Deccan on 5th April, 1715 A.D. His main purpose was to subdue the growing power of the

Marathas. But instead of fighting against the Marathas, he sought their goodwill.[136] However, he could not remain for long in the Deccan. The court politics in the north made him leave the Deccan. He proceeded to the north in 1718 A.D. with Balaji Vishwanath. Before Balaji Vishwanath left south, Shahu asked him to obtain a "Farman"[137] from the Emperor to release Yesubai, Durgabai, Madansingh, Jankibai and others who were still in the Moghul camp.

Sayyid Hussain Ali promised to help Balaji Vishwanath obtain the 'Farman' of Yesubai's release with others as demanded by Shahu on condition that the Marathas would extend him all help to obtain power in the Moghul court. Soon Balaji Vishwanath reached Delhi with Sayyid Hussain Ali who met the Emperor on 23rd February, 1718 A.D. On this occasion, Sayyid Hussin Ali demanded[138] many facilities from the Emperor to the extent that all officers round his Majesty's person must be made over permanently to the Sayyids and their nominees. At the same time, he informed the Emperor that the son of Prince Akbar was in custody[139] with him and would be produced if the Emperor accepted his demands. The Emperor, thinking that the presence of Akbar's son would be harmful to his interests, conceded the demands of Sayyid Hussain Ali on the promise that he (Sayyid Hussain Ali) would hand over the Prince to him (the Emperor).

Without going into the details about the happenings that took place in the capital, it is enough to say that Balaji Vishwanath succeeded in getting Yesubai and others released[140] according to the treaty that was concluded between Sayyid Hussain Ali and Balaji Vishwanath. He also obtained[141] the grant to realize Chouth and Sardeshmukhi and such other facilities which Shahu had earlier demanded.

Yesubai reached[142] Satara in 1719 A.D. and had the satisfaction to see Shahu firmly established on the Satara throne. She once again reverted to her indifferent attitude and passed the rest of her life at Satara.

Different accounts and events show that Yesubai had to face rather unexpected and intricate situations on more occasions than one. At home, she was esteemed well by the Maratha gentry and soldiery alike. Her timely interference had saved many of them from losing their lives when Sambhaji wanted to establish himself well at Raigad. Sambhaji relied on her and she carried on "Mulki arrangements" at Raigad. Thus, she was obeyed everywhere except on the battlefields where Sambhaji commanded his soldiers and had his own way.

She remained at the Raigad fort during 1689 A.D. Her declaration that Shahu was to be the king and Rajaram the regent avoided confusion and conflicts at a critical moment among the Marathas after the execution of Sambhaji. It enabled her to face the Moghul attacks and onslaughts. Her resources were extremely limited, friends few and handicaps many. Yet she played up her part well and enthused Rajaram to action.

She spent the period of her imprisonment in a normal and individualistic way, keeping with the honour and tradition of her family. She showed repugnance at the very suggestion of Shahu's conversion, knowing well that Sambhaji had lost his life by refusing the same condition put forth by Aurangzeb in 1689 A.D. But she was not afraid of the consequences. Thus, she brought up not only the Chhatrapati but also served the cause of the Marathas as well. She died in 1730 A.D., greatly mourned by all.

REFERENCES

1. Chitnis, M.R. - *Lives of Sambhaji and Rajaram*, p. 12.
2. *Itihas Sangraha*, Pracheen Marathe Sarda, p. 13.
3. D.I.S.M. - *Shiv Charitra Pradeep*, p. 22.
4. *Madhya - Yugeen Charita Kosh*, p. 670.
   Her maiden name was Jijabai or Rajasbai.
   Shivaji-Nibandhawali, Anukram 2, Vol. I, p. 224.
5. B.I.S.M. - *Shiv Charitra Pradeep*, pp. 29, 267.
6. F.R. Bombay, Vol. 8, p. 15, Bombay to Surat, 10th March, 1678/9, *FRS*(II), L.No. 355.

7. Bendre, V.S., *Chhatrapati Sambhaji Maharaj*, p. 75.
   Mentions that Yesubai did not follow Sambhaji in his flight because Bhavanibai was to be born. He states that she was born on 29th January, 1679 A.D. and refers Jedhe Shakawali as the source of information. But, according to *Sampurna Shivkaleen Shakawali* from Purandare Collections, the birth of Bhavanibai is "Shak 1600 Bhadrapad Viddya 14". It is obvious that the writer of Jedhe Shakawali forgot to mention 'month and miti'. He has mentioned only the day, i.e. Wednesday (See *Shiv Charitra Pradeep*—Introduction, p. 4 and p. 267), perhaps this has not been considered by Shri Bendre and therefore he has referred Jedhe Shakawali. Hence his conclusion that she would not have been able to follow Sambhaji due to her advanced pregnancy is difficult to accept. More authentic accounts would be required to establish his conclusion.
8. B.I.S.M. - *Shiv Charitra Pradeep*, p. 30.
   Basatin-i-Salatin, p. 716 (Copy at B.I.S.M. Poona)
9. F.R. Bombay, Vol. 108 (unpaged), Rajaput to Surat, Dt. 24th December, 1679, *ERS*(II), L.No. 467.
10. Sarkar, J. - *History of Aurangzeb*, Vol. IV, p. 222.
11. Ormes - *Historical Fragments*, p. 133.
12. Chitnis - *Gharanyachi Sanshipt Mahiti*, Aitihasik, June Lekh, Pustak 1, p. 4.
13. Chitnis, M.R. - *Lives of Sambhaji and Rajaram*, p. 11.
14. *Madhya Yugeen Charitra Kosh*, p. 670.
15. *Chitnis Gharanyachi Sanshipt Mahiti* - Aitihasik, June Lekh, Pustak 1, p. 5 :
    It is held that when Yesubai, on behalf of King Sambhaji, managed internal affairs of the country, Khandoballal helped her. She issued sealed documents to Watandars and Mokasdars.
16. Gupte, K. - *Nagpurkar Bhonsle Yanchi Bakhar*, p. 17.
17. F.R. Surat, Vol. 108, p. 105, Rajapur to Surat, Dt. 26th June, 1680, *ERS*(II), L.No. 510.
18. Ormes - *Historical Fragments*, pp. 143, 144.
19. Sharma, S.R. - *Moghul Empire in India*, p. 204.
20. Bendre, V.S. - *Chhatrapati Sambhaji Maharaj*, p. 651.
21. *Shree Sampradayachi Kagad Patre*, Vol. IX, Lekhank 67 (Ramdass Ramdassi), Appendix II.

22. *Ibid.*, Appendix IV.
23. Bendre, V.S. - *Chhatrapati Sambhaji Maharaj*, p. 651. While issuing orders, she wrote : अजरख्त खाने सौ। येसुबाई
24. Riyasat, Vol. III, *Ugra Prakrati Sambhaji*, p. 85.
25. Sarkar, J. - *History of Aurangzeb*, Vol. IV, pp. 253, 254.
26. Rajwade, V.K. - Khand IV, p. 26.
27. Riyasat, Vol. III, *Ugra Prakrati Sambhaji*, pp. 94, 95.
28. Khafi Khan - *Muntakhabu-l-Lubab, H.I.H.* Vol. VII, p. 38.
29. B.I.S.M. - *Shiv Charitra Pradeep*, p. 34.
30. Ormes - *Historical Fragments*, p. 170.
31. Sarkar, J. - HOUSE OF SHIVAJI, p. 229.
    Vir-Vinod - Marathon ki Tawarikh, No. 1592 (No page No.).
32. Riyasat, Vol. III, *Ugra Prakrati Sambhaji*, p. 75.
33. *Annals and Antiquities of Rajasthan*, Vol. I, pp. 56, 57.
34. Saqi Mustad Khan - *Maasir-i-Alamgiri*, p. 190.
35. Ormes - *Historical Fragments*, p. 170.
36. Khafi Khan - Muntakhabu-l-Lubab, *H.I.H.* Vol. VII, p. 337.
37. *Ibid.*, p. 190.
38. Chitnis, M.R. - *Lives of Sambhaji and Rajaram*, p. 23.
39. B.I.S.M. - *Shiv Charitra Pradeep*, p. 34.
40. B.I.S.M. - *Quarterly*, Varsh 11, p. 15.
    Sarkar, J. - House of Shivaji, p. 227.
41. B.I.S.M. - *Quarterly*, Varsh 11, p. 15.
42. *Vir Vinod*, Marathon Ki Tawarikh, No. 1592 (No page No.) mentions that the members of Sambhaji's family (wife and daughter) were with him. They were also captured. This, however, does not seem correct as shown by later events.
    Gaekwad's Oriental Series, CXX, p. 6 :
    "Tantrik Abhyas" was an important cult brought from Bengal into Maharashtra in Shivaji's time by a Chit-pavan Brahmin, named Shiv-yogi.
    It is said that Shivaji once snubbed Sambhaji and asked him not to practise "Tantric Abhyas", as early as 1677 A.D., when he was at Shringarpur. But no reliable evidence could be found for it. At the most, it suggests that he was under the influence as early as 1676 or 1677 A.D.
43. Khafi Khan - Muntakhabu-l-Lubab, *H.I.H.*, Vol. VII, p. 339.
    Chitnis, M.R. - *Lives of Sambhaji and Rajaram*, p. 23.

44. Sarkar, J. - *House of Shivaji*, p. 226.
45. Refer p. 72, Chapter II, F.N. No. 4.
46. Chitnis, M.R. - *Lives of Sambhaji and Rajaram*, p. 23.
It is also said that Khandoballal was with Sambhaji in the battle of Nawadi in 1689 A.D. and when he found that it was impossible to save king Sambhaji, he came hurriedly to Raigad with Ghorpade and thus joined Yesubai again at Raigad.
47. Ramdass-Ramdassi, Vol. 9, p. 118.
48. Kincaid, C.A. & Parasnis, D.B. - *A History of the Maratha People*, Vol. II, p. 62.
49. Refer p. 96, Chapter II, F.N. No. 1.
50. F.R. Surat, Vol. II, p. 1, Bombay to Surat, Dt. 12th June, 1680, *ERS* (II), L.No. 511.
51. *Vividh Gyan Vistar*, Varsh 56, March 1925, Ank 3, p. 131.
52. Kincaid, C.A. & Parasnis, D.B. - *A History of the Maratha People*, Vol. II, p. 62.
53. Khafi Khan - Muntakhabu-l-Lubar, *H.I.H.*, Vol. VII, p. 344.
54. Ormes - *Historical Fragments*, p. 208.
55. *Ibid.*, p. 108.
56. Riyasat, Vol. III, *Ugra Prakriti Sambhaji*, p. 98.
57. *Itihas Sangraha*, Aitihasik Charitre, Vol. 1, Pustak 1, p. 23.
Ormes - *Historical Fragments*, p. 208.
58. Gupte, K. - *Nagpurkar Bhonsle Yanchi Bakhar*, p. 19.
Itihas Sangraha, Aitihasik Charitre, Vol. 1, Pustak 1, p. 23.
59. B.I.S.M. - *Shiv Charitra Pradeep*, p. 35.
60. Sarkar, J. - *House of Shivaji*, p. 233.
61. Patre Yadi Vagere, L.N. 6, p. 26.
62. Riyasat, Vol. 4, *Sthirbudhi Rajaram*, p. 18.
63. Chitnis, M.R. - *Lives of Sambhaji and Rajaram*, p. 12.
64. Kincaid, C.A. & Parasnis, D.B. - *A History of the Maratha People*, Vol. II, p. 63.
65. Chitnis, M.R. - *Lives of Sambhaji and Rajaram*, p. 32.
66. *Indian Historical Records Commission Proceedings*, Vol. XVII, p. 222.
67. Khafi Khan - *Muntakhabu-l-Lubab*, *H.I.H.*, Vol. VII, p. 368.
68. Sarkar, J. - *History of Aurangzeb*, Vol. IX, p. 405.
Indian Historical Records Commission Proceedings, Vol. XVII, p. 222.

69. Saqi Mustad Khan - Maasir-i-Alamgiri, p. 197.
Rajaram Charitam - Diary R.Ft.St.G., p. 92 :
(Constitution book of 1689) - "Wee having certaine advice that Ramraja, king of the Maorattaes, is come privately from his kingdom of Punnaree to the Chinjie country leaving his uncle (?) nephew Sahu in charge of the kingdom and family to manage to war against the Moghuls".
70. B.I.S.M. - *Shiv Charitra Sahitya*, Khand 10, L.N.24, 3rd November, 1695 A.D., p. 24, states that Narsoji Gaekwad conspired to convey the secrets of the fort to Itikadkhan.
71. Chitnis, M.R. - *Lives of Sambhaji and Rajaram*, p. 27.
72. *Ibid.*, p. 32.
73. *Indian Historical Records Commission Proceedings*, Vol. VII, p. 35.
B.I.S.M. - *Shiv Charitra Pradeep*, Khand 6, p. 169.
74. Irvine , W.W. - *Later Moghuls*, Vol. II, p. 160.
75. *Itihas Sangraha*, Aitihasik Charitre, p. 7.
Riyasat, Vol. IV, *Sthir Budhi Rajaram*, p. 102.
76. *Patre Yadi Vagere*, L.No. 6, p. 26.
77. B.I.S.M. - *Shiv Charitra Pradeep*, p. 35.
78. *Itihas Sangraha*, Aitihasik Charitre, p. 8.
He was also given a seal which had the words "Shankaraji Raje Mahadik Banda-I-Badshah Alamgir". Similarly, Madan Singh, son of Champadi, had a seal, "Alamgir Gaz Khanhizad Badshah; Madansingh".
— Sanada Fadnisi Shahu Daftar, Rumal No.2, Pudhka No.1, Kramank 1.
B.I.S.M. - *Sammellan Vrutta*, Varsh III, p. 55.
79. Riyasat, Vol. IV, *Sthir Budhi Rajaram*, p. 103.
80. B.I.S.M. - *Shiv Charitra Pradeep*, Khand 6, p. 70.
Itihas Sangraha, Aitihasik Charitre, Vol. I, Pustak 1, p. 23.
81. *Itihas Sangraha*, Aitihasik Charitre, Vol. I, Pustak 1, p. 23.
82. *Indian Historical Records Commission*, Proceedings, Vol. XVII, p. 222.
83. Khafi Khan - Muntakhabu-l-Lubab, *H.I.H.*, Vol. VII, pp. 346, 347.
84. Saqi Mustad Khan - *Maasir-i-Alamgiri*, p. 200.
Their camp was erected near that of the Moghul Emperor. They lived there with all respect and privacy.

85. Riyasat, Vol. IV, *Sthir Budhi Rajaram*, pp. 104, 105.
86. Chitnis, M.R. - *Lives of Sambhaji and Rajaram*, p. 46.
87. *Ibid.*, p. 47.
88. *Itihas Sangraha*, Aitihasik Charcha, Part II, p. 21.
    Vir Vinod, Marathon Ki Tawarikh, No. 1593 (No page No.)
89. Refer p. 130, F.N. No. 1.
90. Riyasat, Vol. IV, *Sthir Budhi Rajaram*, p. 103.
91. This is an original document, a paper, 13" x 9" written by Shahu in bold letters (B.I.S.M., Poona)
92. Khafi Khan - Muntakhabu-l-Lubab, *H.I.H.*, Vol. VII, p. 349.
    Sarkar, J. - *Anecdotes of Aurangzeb*, p. 69.
93. Khafi Khan - Muntakhabu-l-Lubab, *H.I.H.*, Vol. VII, p. 349.
94. *Indian Historical Records Commission, Proceedings*, Vol. XIX, p. 160, mentions that in 1697, peace negotiations were held between Zulphikar Khan and Rajaram through Rajkarna.
95. Chitnis, M.R. - *Lives of Sambhaji and Rajaram*, pp. 47, 48.
96. *Patre Yadi Vagere*, L.N. 9, p. 31.
97. Khafi Khan - Muntakhabu-l-Lubab, *H.I.H.*, Vol. VII.
98. Chitnis, M.R. - *Lives of Sambhaji and Rajaram*, pp. 83, 84.
99. Riyasat, Vol. IV, *Sthir Budhi Rajaram*, p. 104.
100. There are examples when Aurangzeb had indulged in such conversions and matrimonial alliances between Hindus and Muslims, if he so desired. Daughters of Rajaram and Sambhaji, while they were captives with Yesubai, were married to Muslims. Similarly, Netaji Palkar was converted before he was sent on Afghanistan campaign.
101. Riyasat, Vol. IV, *Sthir Budhi Rajaram*, p. 133.
102. Sarkar, J. - *History of Aurangzeb*, Vol. V, p. 206.
103. Riyasat, Vol. IV, *Sthir Budhi Rajaram*, p. 133.
    Saqi Mustad Khan - *Maasir-i-Alamgiri*, p. 187.
104. Riyasat, Vol. IV, *Sthir Budhi Rajaram*, p. 114.
    It is held that Yesubai tried that these persons should embrace Islam to save Shahu from the sad plight.
105. Bharatvarsha - Pant Pratinidhi Chi Bakhar, p. 43.
    Riyasat, Vol. IV, *Sthir Budhi Rajaram*, p. 134.
    Indian Historical Records Commission, Proceedings, Vol. XVIII, p. 233, mentions about the marriages that were contracted between the descendants of Lukhji Jadhavrao and Shahji Bhonsle.

Ambikabai was perhaps the daughter of Bahadurji, grandson of Bhutji of the Sindkhed family.

106. Manucci, N. - *Storia Do Mogor*, Vol. IV, p. 115.
107. Sarkar, J. - *History of Aurangzeb*, Vol. V, p. 16, 17.
108. Irvine , W.W. - *Later Moghuls*, Vol. I, p. 2.
"Alamgir had five sons and five daughters. The eldest, Mohd. Sultan, born in 1639, died in 1676 without issues. The fourth son, Akbar, born in 1657, had rebelled against his father in 1681-82, and had gone over to Persia. He did not come back though Aurangzeb tried to bring him back".
— "*Khatut-i-Shivaji*, Royal Asiatic Society's Ms. Nos. 71, Fols.25 & 30.
109. Manucci, N. - *Storia Do Mogor*, Vol. IV, p. 116.
110. Manucci, N. - *Storia Do Mogor*, Vol. IV, p. 175.
Akbar's letter from Persia to Aurangzeb : "... in your Majesty's reign all are lords, governors, Generals, but none has any loyalty".
111. *Aitihasik Patra Wyawahar*, L.N. 5.
Bombay Gazetteer, Vol. XVIII, Part II, p.2
112. Saqi Mustad Khan - Maasir-i-Alamgiri, p. 277.
Varshik Itivrutta, 1837, p. 298.
113. Irvine , W.W. - *Later Moghuls*, Vol. I, pp. 86, 87, 88.
114. Manucci, N. - *Storia Do Mogor*, Vol. IV, p. 246.
115. Sarkar, J. - *Anecdotes of Aurangzeb*, p. 21.
116. *Indian Historical Records Commission, Proceedings*, Vol. III, pp. 46, 116.
117. Khafi Khan - Muntakhabu-l-Lubab, *H.I.H.*, Vol. VII, p. 386.
118. Irvine , W.W. - *Later Moghuls*, Vol. I, p. 8.
119. *Ibid.*
120. Riyasat, Vol. V, *Punyashloka Shahu* - Peshwa Balaji Vishwanath - p. 22.
121. *Ibid.*
122. *Sardesai Commemoration Volume*, p. 60.
123. Khafi Khan - Muntakhabu-l-Lubab, *H.I.H.*, Vol. VII, p. 395.
124. Sinha, H.N. - *Rise of the Peshwas*, p. xii.
125. Mazumdar, R.C., Raichaudhary, H.C. & Datta, K. - *An Advanced History of the Marathas*, Part II, p. 543.
126. *Modern Review*, Vol. XXIX, 1921 - (Prof. S.N. Sen). p. 444, Rajwade, V.K., Khand VIII, L.No. 79, 80.

The contents of the letters state that three or four days before the death of Aurangzeb, he told Shahu that he was free and his kingdom was given back to him. No Persian record or any other evidence supports the above account.

127. *Indian Historical Records Commission, Proceedings*, Vol. XVII, p. 204.
128. Khafi Khan - Muntakhabu-l-Lubab, *H.I.H.*, Vol. VII, p. 391.
129. Irvine , W.W. - *Later Moghuls*, Vol. I, p. 37.
Khafi Khan - Muntakhabu-l-Lubab, *H.I.H.*, Vol. VII, p. 400.
130. Irvine , W.W. - *Later Moghuls*, Vol. I, p. 37.
131. *Ibid.*
132. Joshi, S.N. - *Arwacheen Maharashtretihas Kalanteel Rajyakarbharacha Abhyas*, pp. 229-30.
But no letter bearing the above seal could be traced, Appendix II.
133. Irvine , W.W. - *Later Moghuls*, Vol. I, p. 225.
134. *Ibid.*, pp. 300, 301.
135. *Ibid.*, p. 329.
136. *Ibid.*
137. Rajwade, V.K., Khand XV, L.N.301.
Aitihasik Patra-Vyawahar, L.No. 6.
138. Irvine , W.W. - *Later Moghuls*, Vol. I, p. 377.
139. *Ibid.*
140. Rajwade, V.K., Khand XX, L.N. 50.
141. *Ibid.*
142. Riyasat, Vol. V, *Punyashloka Shahu - Balaji Vishwanath*, p. 148.

CHAPTER 4

TARABAI

Moghul Maratha Struggle : House of Shivaji – A House Divided (1700-1752 A.D.)

If the role of Yesubai in Maratha politics was that of a soothing balm, the role of Tarabai after the untimely death of Rajaram assumed the role of a shining sword for the cause of Maratha survival in the fierce Moghul-Maratha struggle. However, later on Tarabai Peshwa relations clouded her role in controversy and dissensions

Death of Rajaram in 1700 A.D., was a heavy blow to the cause of Maratha struggle against Moghul Emperor Aurangzeb who was vigorously attacking[1] the Maratha positions and during the confusion and chaos, caused by the death of Rajaram, he captured the fort of Satara[2] on 21st April 1700 A.D. The need of the hour for the Marathas was to have a balanced mind and strong hands to prevent them from falling asunder. Tarabai, the wife of Rajaram, rose to the occasion and did not lag behind to shoulder the responsibility of giving leadership to the Maratha cause.

Tarabai hailed[3] from the traditionally martial and well spoken family of Rangrao Chouhan Mohite. His name occurs first in the battle of Talikota fought in 1564 A.D. He was a descendent of the Chouhan Kings of Delhi. He had come to the south with Muslim kings who were ambitious and who, from time to time, invaded the Deccan to have their sway there. Tarabai's father, Hansaji[4] Mohite, served[5] Shivaji as his Senapati after the death of Prataprao Gujar.

Nothing definite is known about the date of birth of Tarabai. It seems probable that she must have been born after 1670 A.D., because her husband Rajaram was born in 1670 A.D. and, according to the prevalent customs, the brides were to be younger than their husbands. According to Sardesai,[6] she was twenty-five years old in 1700 A.D. and, therefore, it can be said that she was born in 1675 A.D. As regards the family background, it can be said that her parents brought her up in the best traditions of the family.

Later she was married to Rajaram. She followed[7] him to Jinji via Vishalgad along with Rajasbai and Ambikabai. It can be imagined that the journeys[8] in those days were not safe and they had to travel through land and sea often in disguise. She reached Jinji in 1694 A.D. Thus, continued movements from place to place provided an opportunity to Tarabai to be acquainted with the changing conditions of the Deccan and the warfares on different fronts.

She had a son born[9] to her at Jinji in 1696 A.D. He was named Shivaji. The differences[10] between Moghul General Zulphikar Khan and Prince Kambaksh provided an opportunity to Rajaram to escape to Vishalgad. But, before he left Jinji, Tarabai and others had already left for Vishalgad. Finally, Rajaram escaped[11] from the fort and reached Vishalgad on 22nd February, 1699 A.D. He engaged himself in an all round attack on Moghul camps with his stout supporters. He was also blessed[12] with a son to Rajasbai on 23rd May, 1698 A.D.

Rajaram carried[13] on his attacks on the Moghul camps with his stout supporters in northern Maharashtra. As such, for most of the time, he had to remain away from Vishalgad and Tarabai had to take[14] important decisions pertaining to administration and army movements in different spheres. As a result, she had to despatch Krishnaji Sawant with 15000 cavalry towards Malwa to check the military progress of the Moghuls in 1699 A.D. Krishnaji Savant returned with plenty of booty after ransacking Malwa. Soon after this, Tarabai had to face the problem of succession to the Maratha throne due to Rajaram's demise.

As known, there were three parties advocating the claims of three incumbents for accession to Maratha throne. They were Shivaji, son of Tarabai, Sambhaji, son of Rajasbai, and Shahu, son of Yesubai and Sambhaji. Shahu was still in Moghul captivity and whether he would be able to return to the South was not known. Shivaji and Sambhaji being very young needed regency.

Besides, the condition of the Deccan was far from satisfactory, worse than what Soyarabai or Yesubai had to face. Different accounts show that there remained no central power to wield any co-ordinating influence over the warring interests of the Maratha State for, although Shivaji had established an independent kingdom and an executive[15] body of Astha-Pradhan had begun to function, he did not aspire to be an original[16] legislator. He lived for a short time after his coronation, and could not bring in more reforms. Again, he proceeded[17] on the 'Karnatak Campaign' and was in south for about two years, i.e., from 1677 to 1679 A.D. Sambhaji's reign was a constant struggle against the designs of a few of his own people at home and the foreigners[18], viz., the Dutch, the Portuguese, the English and the Siddis of Janjira. Besides, he had to resist Moghul attacks and onslaughts from time to time till his execution in 1689 A.D. Rajaram lived[19] at Jinji for nearly ten years and devoted his time to counteract the Moghul offensive in north and south Maharashtra. In the circumstances, he awarded[20] Fiefs and Watans to different Sardars to carry on the fight against the Moghuls as well as to administer the area. In due course of time, these Sardars supported[21] themselves by pillage and plunder, giving a part thereof to the State treasury. Later on, the personal and clan rivalry was more in evidence. Dissentions[22] had prevailed among them. As such, they could do little against their common enemy, the Moghuls. Plunder, loot and arson was in vogue on the slightest pretext. Sardars were in the habit of taking best advantage of the king's indisposition, grant of awards and lands, titles and army commands during the fag end of Rajaram's regime.

Moreover, Shivaji's kingdom was a military[23] State and was in a state of "chronic warfare". Again the demand and the thought

Photo of Tarabai

prevailing then never admitted to the vacuum created by the demise of the king. Besides, Tarabai was also aware of the plight suffered[24] by Soyarabai who depended on the vascillating councillors. Further accounts also indicate that differences existed among the councillors regarding the succession of a particular candidate. Sardesai writes[25], "Tarabai was ambitious to get her son coronated and not to wait for Shahu as was advised by Ramchandrapant Amatya." But Senapati Dhanaji Jadhav and Pratinidhi Parashuram Trimbak supported Tarabai's aspirations to get her son enthroned as Chhatrapati. In this effort, she had to imprison[26] Rajasbai and her son Sambhaji.

Tarabai coronated[27] her son Shivaji at Panhalla. She continued[28] Parashuram Pant as Pratinidhi. It is held that Ramchandrapant aspired to be Pratinidhi, but Tarabai did not prefer him because he had not supported Shivaji's coronation. As Shivaji II was quite young, she began to act as Regent.[29]

She made Panhalla the seat of administration. She issued her orders through Girji[30] Yadav, the guardian of the fort. He acted as her personal and trusted agent and communicated her commands to the Sardars and others whom they concerned. Thus, once more she had an opportunity to resist Aurangzeb's attacks and shatter his high hopes to subdue the Marathas during the regime of the minor.

Aurangzeb did not allow any respite to the Marathas. With concerted efforts, he laid siege[31] to Panhalla fort. Zulphikar Khan and Tarbiyat Khan also reached[32] there with 50,000 soldiers and 30,000 cavalry. A severe battle took place between the Marathas and the Moghuls. Dhanaji Jadhav and Baherji Ghorpade plundered and harassed the Moghul territory. Dado Malhar and Krishnaji Malhar lost their lives. At last, the Moghuls took[33] Panhalla on the 28th May, 1701 A.D. after five months of continued fighting. Meanwhile, Tarabai escaped from the fort. It is held[34] that the Moghuls had to bribe the killedar Trimbak with 55,000 rupees for their victory.

Tarabai prepared herself to defend the fort of Vishalgad (Khelna). She got it repaired well to enable it to withstand a long siege.

Aurangzeb followed up the victory of Panhalla and reached Vishalgad with Sawai Raja Jaisingh. Concentrated and planned battles were fought from both sides. Tarabai guided her Sardars individually and harassed the Moghul army on more fronts than one. In this context, her letter[35] to Prataprao More shows her deftness and courage in meeting the most astute of the Moghul Emperors, Aurangzeb. In that letter, she commended his (Prataprao's) sincerity and loyalty to her, because he had checked the progress of the army of Aurangzeb at Malkapur where he had encamped for some time. Further, she advised him to concentrate his efforts to attack and harass Aurangzeb wherever it was possible to do so with an advantage. According to her, Aurangzeb had become despondent and disspirited due to his old age and other[36] anxieties. She warned him, "Aurangzeb is knave and it is difficult to imagine and guess his intentions." She ordered him "to do his utmost to dishearten him by all possible means at his command, so that he might feel inclined to give up the idea of perpetuating his hold on Vishalgad." She advised him that his attacks should be on his camps in far off places to distract his attention from Vishalgad, though not very far away from "Swami" (Chhatrapati Shivaji II).

Aurangzeb took the fort on 4th June, 1702 A.D., and marched[37] towards Pedgaon on 13th November via Bhalwani and Indapur, and reached Singhad. Balaji Vishwanath, the Sar-Subedar of Poona, tried to defend the fort. The siege continued for three months. Soon he apprehended the fall of the fort in the absence of provisions. He asked Kashinath[38] and Ambaji Purandare to help him with gun powder, otherwise the fort was bound to be lost. Shahu had also accompanied Aurangzeb in this siege. Ultimately, the Marathas lost the fort on 8th April, 1703 A.D. and it was named "Bakshuda-Baksha".

Aurangzeb also took the fort of Purandar and named[40] it "Azamgad". Along with Pedgaon, he had taken Rajgad. Other minor forts were taken by him by 16th February, 1704 A.D. Next, he reached Khed on 17th April, 1705 A.D. where he encamped and captured Lohgad and Wakinkhera.

By 1703-04, the Marathas had lost many forts. It appeared improbable that they would win them back in the near future. But Tarabai, as dauntless as ever, plunged herself whole-heartedly in the task of defending the Maratha State with Dhanaji Jadhava, Shankaraji Narayan, Parashuram Trimbak and others. It is mentioned[41] that Tarabai won the hearts of her Sardars who took vigorous measures for ravaging the imperialists' territories, plundering and destroying wherever they went on. The desperate stand against the Moghuls has well been described by Kavindra Govind.[42]

Under the circumstances, the best arrangement to carry on the administration and, at the same time, continue the fight against Aurangzeb was to assign each fief or Jagir to a Sardar for his subsistence in lieu of payment of revenue in the central treasury. This had already been practised by Rajaram when he was in the far south.

Accordingly, Tarabai gave[43] east Berar up to Nagpur to Parsoji Bhonsle, Khandesh to Kathsingh Kadamrao, Gujerat to Khanderao Dabhade, Konkan to Kanhoji Angre and Miraj to Udhauji Chouhan. The above arrangement provided an opportunity to each Sardar to display his ingenuity and control in his sphere and fight out the Moghuls wherever it was possible. But Tarabai was careful, and never relaxed her authority over either fiefs or forts.

It was now twenty-five years from 1682 A.D. that the Moghul Emperor had constantly tried to crush the Maratha power but without success. Neither Shahu's captivity nor Rajaram's death had disappointed the Marathas. No account mentions that they had yet entertained any idea of reconciliation with the Moghuls.

The long stay of Aurangzeb in south had affected[44] the Moghul Empire in many ways. As mentioned, the financial condition in Aurangzeb's camp was critical and the Marathas were not slow to take advantage of the deplorable condition existing therein. They carried on ravages and plundered the Moghul camps. Shankaraji Narayan took back the fort of Panhalla and Pawangad. Parashuram Trimbak took Basantgad. Santaji Silimkar took the fort of Rajgad, though he lost his life in the struggle. Similarly, Dhanaji Visar took the forts of Rajmachi[45] and Lohgad[46] in 1705 A.D. The fort of Prachandgad[47] was taken. Thus, it is evident that most of the forts were taken back by the Marathas by 1706 A.D.

Aurangzeb had also become physically weak. He remained[48] ill. After suffering the vigours of the journey he died[49] on 20th Februry, 1707 A.D. As a result, there occurred a sudden cessation of the campaign against the Marathas, and, with it, the struggle[50] for the Moghul throne started among the contenders. Shahu[51] came to south with Moropant Sabnis, Mahadji Krishna Joshi, Gadadhar Bhat Nasikar and other Sardars. His release changed the course of events in Maharashtra as well.

Shahu informed Tarabai of his arrival[52] from Lumbakni. The news created a problem to Tarabai as well as to the Sardars, as it gave rise to the succession issue and created further troubles. As mentioned, Shivaji's coronation in 1700 A.D. was not a unanimous one. As such, there was little doubt that a section of Sardars would support Shahu.

The main difficulty was to decide whether succession should be in the line of Sambhaji or Rajaram, the sons of Shivaji. Shahu stood in the direct line of succession, being the only son of Sambhaji, the son of Shivaji, the legal successor to his father. Tarabai asserted[53] that Shahu, Sambhaji's son, was taken a prisoner indefinitely after 1689 A.D. and Rajaram continued to rule for all practical purposes. She stated that Shivaji never declared his successor and had maintained silence over such an important issue. According to her, Shahu had lost the claim to succeed to the Maratha throne after Sambhaji's execution and at the fall of Raigad fort in 1689 A.D. As such, according to her, the direct line of succession closed then and there. The second line of succession, as she upheld,[54] started from Rajaram, the younger son of Shivaji. He had all along tried to maintain good relations with the Sardars who had struggled hard for Maratha independence for eleven years, viz., from 1689 to 1700 A.D.

However, the important fact that Rajaram was never coronated completely nullifies the contention of Tarabai that Shahu had lost his claims after the execution of Sambhaji and fall of Raigad in 1689 A.D. Further, according to Kincaid and Parasnis, Rajaram and a few other Sardars and councillors had, as early as 1689 A.D., taken an oath[55] to remain loyal to Shahu who was declared Chhatrapati and Rajaram was to act as regent.

Apart from other considerations regarding the succession issue, the cruel execution of Sambhaji was still fresh in the minds of the Sardars. Though Sambhaji was hated during his lifetime, he was all the more respected and regarded after his death as a martyr for religious and political cause. This factor dominated average thought in which Tarabai's ministers also took part. Further, Yesubai's selfless advice to Rajaram, her voluntary imprisonment at Raigad and her sufferings[56] at the Moghul camp appealed to them most.

Besides, the Sardars thought over the problem in an entirely different light. The continuous struggles and warfare for thirty years from 1680 A.D. had affected them in various ways, materially, socially, politically and economically. Accounts show that the State had neither progressed nor had they benefitted by it. No doubt, they were jealous and looked more to their own interests, but to judge every Sardar by that standard is not the right approach. Therefore, it can be safely accepted that they decided to live peacefully. This prospect was offered more by Shahu than by Tarabai. Hence, neither the convincing argument nor the sentimentality was the decisive factor in the approach to the succession problem.

Not satisfied with her own argument, Tarabai assembled the highest officials of the State, e.g., Parashuram Trimbak Pratinidhi, Ramchandrapant Amatya, Dhanaji Jadhava, the Senapati, and Chitnis Khandoballal, and declared Shahu to be an impostor.[57] She asked them to take an oath[58] of loyalty to her son, Shivaji II. This indicates that she herself doubted the weight and influence of her words as far as allegiance was concerned.

Meanwhile, Bahiroji Pingle and Rakhmaji Kinhale reached Lumbakni. They informed[59] the Watandars about Shahu's arrival. Shahu desired[60] them to pay their respects to him. Rustamrao[61] Jadhav, Sajjansinh Raval and Parsoji Bhonsle responded, and promised to support him with men and money. Besides, Parsoji Bhonsle and a few other Sardars observed[62] certain formalities and accepted Shahu as their king. In due course of time, Haibatrao Nimbalkar,[63] Nemaji Sinde, Mutalik Chimnaji Damodar and others offered their support to Shahu.[64]

Meanwhile, Shivaji II (Tarabai) entreated[65] the Watandars to remain loyal to him and to abstain from injuring their interests. He was also anxious[66] to know why the Watandars had not informed him about the communications they had from Shahu's camp.

Shahu decided his course of action. He marched towards Chorwad and arrived at Kusumbi. He met Nilkanth Naik Purandarkar who offered[67] him his support. He had already evoked the support of Parsoji Bhonsle, Nemaji Sinde, Haibatrao Nimbalkar, Rustamrao Jadhav, Chimnaji Damodar, Shankar Sarnaik, Kesho Trimal, Hanwante Nimbalkar, Krishnaji Narasprabhu, Anandrao Mahadev-prabhu, Mahadji Yamaji Bokil and Purandares who were his staunch supporters. He marched towards Khed.

On his way[68] to Khed, Shahu defeated Sayaji Lokhande Patil who lost his life. Shahu brought up his infant son affectionately and named[69] him Fatehsingh Bhonsle. He was heartily welcomed by the people who accepted him as their king.

As mentioned, a few Sardars who had supported Tarabai had gone over to Shahu. Next, the wavering attitude of Ramchandrapant Amatya made Tarabai suspicious of his intentions.[70] She got aware of his correspondence with Shahu. She took it rather seriously, and imprisoned him at Vasantgad. She summoned[71] Kanhoji Angre, Pratinidhi Parashuram Trimbak, Senapati Dhanaji Jadhava, Shankaraji Narayan, Khandoballal and Khem Sawant. She asked them to march towards Khed where Shahu had encamped.

Shahu was clever enough and doubted his victory over the Senapati (Dhanaji Jadhava) in an open battle. As such, he thought of another device to win[72] his opponents through Chitnis Khandoballal, Balaji Vishwanath Bhat, Sar-Subedar of Poona, and Naroram. The armies of Tarabai and Shahu met at Kadu[73] on 12th October, 1707 A.D. Shahu won[74] the battle. Pratinidhi Parashuram Trimbak left the field. Dhanaji Jadhav, Khandoballal, Naroram and Balaji Vishwanath went over to Shahu. He offered the robes[75] of Senapati to Dhanaji Jadhav. Onwards, Shahu was addressed as "Kulawatans Shri Raja Shahu Chhatrapati". Thus, a majority of the influential Sardars joined Shahu. It was now easy for him to organise campaigns against Tarabai in right earnest.

Soon Tarabai lost the fort of Rohieda and, with it, the Killedar, Shankaraji[76] Narayan. Yet she continued to struggle against Shahu. Shahu halted at Shirwel and hurriedly[77] visited Supa, Jejuri, Veewalhe and other places. He also issued "Hathrokha"[78] for the realization of revenues. Soon the forts of Rajgad, Prachandgad and Vichitragad were taken by Shahu. He mainly resided at the fort of Chandan-Wandan.

He sent message to the Satara Havaldar to hand over the fort to him. He agreed. Tarabai had no other alternative but to leave the fort. She asked the Pratinidhi to defend it, and escaped with her son to Panhalla.[79] Shahu asked the Pratinidhi to submit the fort, but he refused and resisted. However, Shahu won over the Commandant of the fort, Sheikh Mira. He opened the gates to Shahu and imprisoned the Pratinidhi. Shahu took Satara. Rakhmaji Kinhale served[80] him well and received 2000 Hons as inam from him.

Tarabai's strength was considerably reduced because of the loss of the support of a few influential Sardars and the forts. She retired[81] beyond river Krishna and stayed at Kolhapur. She carried out her plans and issued orders from here as she used to do from Panhalla.

Shahu had brought the major portion of Maharashtra under his control. He celerabrated[82] his coronation on the 12th January, 1708 A.D. This enabled him to demand loyalty and obedience of other Sardars also. He appointed[83] Bahiropant Pingle as his Peshwa, continued the position of Senapati to Dhanaji Jadhav. Parsoji Bhonsle was made Sarsahebsuba. Similarly, many other appointments[84] were made at the time.

Tarabai prepared herself to contest Shahu more vigorously. She released Ramchandrapant and appointed[85] him to his old post. She once more assembled[86] Kanhoji Angre, Sawant of Wadi, Sidhoji Hindurao and Giroji Yadav, and held consultations with them regarding the future course of action. Further, she put Rangna fort in perfect condition to withstand long siege.

Shahu looked with concern to these preparations which were detrimental to his interests. He marched towards Panhalla, took Vasantgad and Pawangad, and reached Rangna or Prasiddhgad. Tarabai decided to defend[87] the fort herself from within while Kanhoji Angre and Sawant of Wadi were to harass the enemy from outside.

Tarabai defended the fort courageously; but, to her dismay, found that Kanhoji Angre did not turn up at all and Sawant of Wadi went[88] over to Shahu. The changed attitude of her allies naturally weakened the defence measures. She also wrote letters to Dhanaji Jadhav, Parashuram Pant and Khandoballal to desert Shahu and join her.[89] Meanwhile, she escaped[90] from the fort with her son and reached Malwan. Ramchandrapant Amatya remained behind to prolong the defence. After a while, Ramchandrapant Amatya and Dhanaji Jadhav reached to a secret understanding[91] to raise the siege. Dhanaji Jadhav pleaded[92] with Shahu to withdraw the siege. But Parsoji Bhonsle was not in favour of raising the siege when the fort was nearly captured. Shahu did not listen to Parsoji Bhonsle, and ordered the siege operations to stop. He returned[93] to Panhalla on the 24th June, 1708 A.D. Parsoji Bhonsle was posted near Kolhapur to observe the future movements of Tarabai. However, the fort remained in the hands of Tarabai.

As soon as Shahu returned to Satara, Tarabai came back and took possession of Vasantgad[94]. She took the territory south of river Warna and fixed Kolhapur as her permanent seat of administration. Once more she had begun to rule in her territory, leaving Shahu in the north. After some time, Shahu called Parsoji Bhonsle back.[95] It seems that both the parties were now tired of campaigns and settled in their own spheres for the time being.

While Tarabai and Shahu were trying to establish their sway in Maharashtra, the Moghul Princes were fighting[96] among themselves to succeed Aurangzeb. As mentioned, Shah Alam succeeded Aurangzeb as Bahadurshah on 3rd August, 1707 A.D. But soon he had to leave for Rajputana on an urgent mission.[97] He again returned to south and asked Shahu to help him with an army to settle his differences[98] with Prince Kambaksh. Shahu sent Nemaji Sindhe who was able to do a bit to get Bahadurshah victorious against Prince Kambaksh. Khafi Khan writes about him, "In spite of that, the infidel rendered singular service to the Emperor in his contest against Kambaksh." Prince Kambaksh was defeated.[99] He died on the 13th January, 1709 A.D.

As known, Shahu had not received the grant[100] to collect Chouth and Sardeshmukhi of the six Moghul Subas of Deccan for which he was anxious. The Moghul Emperor had nearly granted[101] it when claims from Tarabai reached him. She asked "for a *farman* in the name of her son, granting the nine rupees of the Sardeshmukhi, without any reference to the Chouth, for which he would suppress other insurgents and restore order in the country." Shahu and Tarabai were being supported by Zulphikar Khan and Munim Khan respectively. In the circumstances, the Moghul Emperor thought it best to let Shahu and Shivaji II settle[102] their differences among themselves. Thus "the orders about the sardeshmukhi remained inoperative."

Shahu prepared himself to meet Tarabai once more. He was more fortunate to secure the unflinching support of Balaji Vishwanath, Senakarte. As Dhanaji Jadhav had died[103] on 9th July, 1708 A.D., Shahu gave the robes[104] of Senapati to his son, Chandrasen Jadhav. He also gave the robes of honour to Rambha and Rajji Thorat. Shahu further declared[105] that the Moghul Emperor had given him the authority to realize Chouth and Sardeshmukhi of the six Moghul Subas of Deccan. He asked[106] his Sardars to realize the same or else carry on plunders in the Moghul territory to make up the amount.

The Sardars were again divided into three groups instead of two, i.e., the supporters of Shahu, those of Tarabai and those who neither supported Shahu nor Tarabai, but ravaged the territories of both occasionally. They were supposed to be the supporters of Tarabai. Among them, Damaji Thorat created a reign of terror in Supa and the adjoining territories. Shahu sent Balaji Vishwanath to subdue him. Instead, Damaji Thorat imprisoned[107] Balaji Vihwanath. Shahu could get him released after paying a heavy ransom[108] for him. Next, he sent Chandrasen Jadhav to defeat Damaji Throat and asked Balaji Vishwanath to accompany him. Chandrasen Jadhav resented this. It is also said[109] that they had grievance against each other since the days of Dhanaji Jadhav which got flared up on slight provocation.[110] The Senapati pursued Balaji who took cover at Pandavgad and immediatley appealed to Shahu for help. Shahu sent an army and saved[111] him from further trouble. He also called Chandrasen Jadhav back.

The patronizing attitude of Shahu towards Balaji Vishwanath

was looked down with contempt by Chandrasen Jadhav. He found a welcoming master in Tarabai. He fled[112] to Panhala in 1711 A.D. and joined[113] Tarabai's services. In due course of time, he could win over the goodwill of Haibatrao Nimbalkar, Damaji Thorat, Krishnarao Khatavkar, Udhauji Chouhan, Appaji and Santaji, and evoked their support[114] to Tarabai. The combined action of Tarabai and Chandrasen Jadhav did not augur well for Shahu. He realised the serious situation, summoned[115] his Sardars and ordered[116] them to remain prepared to face any eventuality.

Meanwhile, Tarabai was being supported by a few Sardars of Shahu's camp. This is indicated by her reply[117] to Jaisingh Jadhav, son of Dhanaji Jadhav. Jaisingh Jadhav wanted to enlist himself in Tarabai's services, but she was reluctant to take him in her army. Besides, the letter shows that she was scrupulously careful to enlist the disgruntled elements from the army of Shahu. She regretted that Dhanaji Jadhav had gone over to Shahu in the battle of Kadu, though he had pledged to remain faithful to her. Further, she said that Shahu had sent two persons whom she had met but found that Shahu wanted the whole of Maharashtra for himself. As such, no agreement could be reached at. She desired that if he really wanted to serve her, he should do so when the Moghuls attacked her. She reminded him the sufferings Rajaram had undergone to resist the Moghul attacks for a long time, and alleged that the present division was only due to the return of Shahu. Therefore, he must concentrate to defeat Shahu and take back Satara from him. She also commended[118] the services of Sawant of Wadi.

Shahu sent his Pratinidhi, Parashuram Pant, and Khanderao Dabhade to pacify Chandrasen Jadhav. They could not succeed in their efforts. On Ist October, 1711 A.D., Shahu gave the robes[119] of Senapati to Santaji Jadhav, brother of Chandrasen Jadhav. At the same time, he suspected[120] his Pratindhi, Parashuram Pant, of carrying on negotiations with Ramchandrapant. This was detrimental to his interests. Shahu imprisoned him.

It was unfortunate that while the battles were on between Shahu and Tarabai, the masses were suffering. Confusion and chaos existed, while only few were benefitted by it. It was not difficult for Shahu and his Sardars to understand that he would not be able to establish his sway in Maharashtra as long as Tarabai contested the same. As such, it was all the more necessary to subdue or defeat her and also her allies,[121] particularly Krishnarao Khatavkar, Kanhoji Angre, Udhauji Chouhan and Chandrasen Jadhav.

Krishnaji[122] Khatavkar had received the pargana of Khatav in 1689 A.D. from the Moghul Emperor, Aurangzeb. He refused[123] to accede to Shahu's authority and had become overbearing. Shripatrao, son of Pratinidhi Parashuram Pant, marched towards Khatav and defeated[124] him in a hard contested battle. He submitted to Shahu's authority. Shahu appreciated[125] the services of Shripatrao and released his father, Parashuram Pant. Henceforth, he remained loyal to Shahu for the rest of his life.

Kanhoji Angre, the other adherent of Tarabai, had become quite powerful on the western coast. Tarabai had granted[126] him the whole of Konkan between Bombay and Sawantvadi (sea-coast) and expected help from him in case of an attack from the Moghuls or Shahu. At the same time, he had incurred[127] the displeasure of the Peshwa by attacking the forts of Lohgad and Rajmachi which belonged to the Peshwa. Bahiropant Pingle and Niloballal marched with an army to subdue him. Kanhoji Angre defeated them. Bahiropant Pingle was imprisoned[128] and kept in the fort of Lohgad. Next, Kanhoji Angre prepared to march[129] on to Satara, the Maratha capital.

Shahu got anxious to defend Satara. He offered the position of Peshwa, in the absence of Bahiropant Pingle, to Pratinidhi Parashurampant. But he recommended the name of Balaji Vishwanath, because he happened to be more popular in the ranks of his army. Shahu made[130] Balaji Vishwanath his Peshwa, and Parashurampant his Pratinidhi.[131] He also appointed[132] Mansinh More his Senapati.

Balaji Vishwanath collected an army and marched towards Lohgad where Bahiropant Pingle and Niloballal were imprisoned. Instead of giving an open battle, he wanted to win Kanhoji Angre by other means. The fact that the Peshwa and Kanhoji belonged to the same coastal area and knew each other since long, enabled him to solve the problem in an amicable way. With this hope, he met Kanhoji Angre and induced[133] him to abstain from struggle in the interest of the Maratha kingdom. Moreover, Kanhoji Angre was surrounded[134] by his enemies, the English, Siddis of Janjira and the Portuguese at the time. This was another factor to be considered. As a result, Kanhoji Angre entered[135] into a treaty with Balaji Vishwanath on 28th February, 1714 A.D.

Thus, by 1714 A.D., Tarabai was deprived of the support of Kanhoji Angre, her most powerful ally with a few other Sardars. Besides, she had no funds to carry on an incessant struggle of long duration. Moreover, Chandrasen Jadhav had joined[136] Daudkhan Panni, the Governor of the Moghuls in the Deccan. He could win[137] the Moghul support and also receive the Jagir of Bhalki. Similarly, the other Sardars, who had followed Chandrasen Jadhav, were received[138] well by the Moghuls. However, Tarabai was not yet subdued totally by Shahu and his Sardars in spite of the defection of a few prominent supporters and the loss of some forts.

As known, Chandrasen Jadhav had joined Daudkhan. He hoped to further the cause of Tarabai and Sambhaji II of Kolhapur. But Daudkhan was called back to Delhi. On his way to Delhi, he was killed.[139] Sayyid Hussain Ali came as Nizam-ul-Mulk in 1715 A.D. He was first opposed to any Maratha aspirations. But, in due course of time, Shahu and Balaji Vishwanath could secure his co-operation. Thus, Chandrasen Jadhav failed in his attempt to uphold the cause of Shivaji II or Sambhaji II of Kolhapur.

Further, the opponents of Tarabai won a powerful section of the garrison and succeeded in getting her imprisoned[140] along with her son, Shivaji II, in 1714 A.D. She realised the futility of any resistance on being betrayed by Ramchandrapant and others so callously. She was helpless. She sadly expressed[141], "In due course of time, we were compelled to have a sad experience. Rajasbai and her son, Sambhaji II, managed through some of their agents to put us in confinement and inflict hardships on us." Thus, Tarabai, who had defied Aurangzeb and the Moghuls for seven years, found herself in a precarious situation. Finding no other alternative, Chandrasen Jadhav, who had come over to Tarabai, fled to Nizam-ul-Mulk.

Sambhaji II succeeded[142] Shivaji II at Kolhapur in 1713 A.D. His recognition as the king of Kolhapur proves that Rajasbai and Sambhaji II made easy the task of Balaji Vishwanath and Ramchandrapant to crush the power of Tarabai, which was otherwise difficult. It is also evident that Rajasbai had realised that her son had no chance to the throne as long as Shivaji II was there, besides, she was naturally grateful to Ramchandrapant[143] who must have felt elated as he himself was not in good grace of Tarabai. Rajasbai and Sambhaji were easier to deal with than Shivaji II and Tarabai.

The enthronement of Sambhaji II showed that Shahu and his sardars had recognised the existence of Kolhapur branch, though Tarabai and Shivaji were in captivity.

Sayyid Hussain Ali concluded[144] a treaty with Balaji Vishwanath in 1718 A.D. But, by a political revolution[145] in 1720 A.D., the power of Sayyid brothers was destroyed. Turanis came in power. Sayyid Hussain Ali and Sayyid Abdullah were murdered on 8th and 11th October, 1720 A.D., respectively. Henceforth, the province of Deccan was practically ruled[146] by the new Nizam-ul-Mulk Asaf-Jah who came to south in 1720 A.D.

After Tarabai, Sambhaji of Kolhapur was still supported[147] by Chandrasen Jadhav and the opponents of Shahu. They still anticipated to resist Shahu's power which was also noticed by Balaji Vishwanath. On his return[148] journey from Delhi, Balaji Vishwanath defeated Sambhaji II of Kolhapur at Umbrah on 20th

March, 1720 A.D. Thus, Balaji Vishwanath crushed Shahu's opponents once more. Next, he marched towards Saswad via Satara and died on 2nd April, 1720 A.D. Shahu gave the robes[149] of Peshwa's office to his son, Bajirao on 17th April, 1720 A.D.

Sambhaji II aspired to hold the major part of Maharashtra under him. This is indicated by later moves of Sambhaji. He entrusted Chandrasen Jadhav to win over the Nizam-ul-Mulk. They marched[150] towards Poona on 24th September, 1726 A.D. Sambhaji II joined them in October, 1727 A.D. and left Rajasbai in charge of administration[151].

Bajirao had gone towards south.[152] Shahu informed him of the recent developments and asked other Sardars to remain prepared to meet any eventuality.

Sambhaji II marched[153] towards Poona and pursued Chimnajee Appa. Chimnajee Appa took position at Purandar fort with Shahu. Sambhaji II was declared Chhatrapati[154] at Poona and was married to a Rajput princess of Ramnagar.

Soon Bajirao hurried to north. On his way, he raided north Khandesh and threatened to attack Burhanpur. He continued to subdue Nizam-ul-Mulk. Distressed by this situation, Nizam-ul-Mulk concluded[155] a treaty with Bajirao at Mungie Sheogaon on 6th March, 1728 A.D. after the famous battle at Palkhed.[156] According to this treaty, Nizam-ul-Mulk recognised Shahu as the "sole king of Maharashtra". He agreed to pay Chouth and Sardeshmukhi of the Six Subas of Deccan. He also reinstated Maratha tax-collector in his dominion. However, he refused to surrender Sambhaji II of Kolhapur, but promised not to offer further protection to him. Bajirao also did not press[157] for Sambhaji's surrender any more. Thus, it was apparent that the rise of the Peshwa and the consolidation of his power made the task of Shahu's rival most difficult.

But the hostilities between Sambhaji II and Shahu did not end here. Sambhaji appointed[158] Udaji Chauhan as his Senapati. Udaji Chauhan was the Chief of Miraj and rose in power during

Ramchandrapant Amatya's days. He still carried out his ravages and plunders. It is said that Sambhaji instigated[159] him to plunder Shahu's territory. He plundered Shahu's territories round the river Warna and created trouble for him. It is held that once when Shahu proceeded on a hunting expedition, Udaji Chauhan followed him and intended to murder[160] him. How far the above statement is correct cannot be said in absence of more reliable account. Shahu came to know about it. He could no longer restrain himself. He sent his army to invade Sambhaji's territory under Trimbakrao Dabhade. At the same time, Shahu encamped[161] near the river Warna.

Sambhaji's camp was on the other side of the river Warna. Pratinidhi Shripatrao attacked[162] him and a battle was fought. Sambhaji was defeated. He escaped[163] to Panhalla, leaving his womenfolk and other belongings behind. They were brought before Shahu whose magnanimity allowed[164] the womenfolk, Jijabai, Sambhaji's wife, his mother Rajasbai, Tarabai and others to go back to Kolhapur. Shahu gave up an attempt to pursue Sambhaji II. The statement[165] that Shahu did not pursue Sambhaji II due to the approach of monsoons is rather doubtful in view of the fact that the battle of Warna was fought in March 1730 A.D. and there still remained three months or so for the monsoons to set in.

Tarabai, on her own consent,[166] stayed back. Shahu asked her to reside at Satara with the comforts of a royal captive, looked after by Yadavgopal Khatavkar. She returned to Satara with Shahu. Whether her stay with Shahu had helped to promote amicable relations between the two cousins cannot be definitely said, though a channel[167] for communication and exchange of views was opened up in which Sambhaji II and his queen Jijabai II, took an active part.

Shahu sent[168] a few of his influential Sardars to Panhalla to invite Sambhaji to Satara. They paid their visit and respects to him with various valuable presents (nazrana). Sambhaji II also received them cordially. Shahu marched up to Karhad and awaited the arrival of Sambhaji who was accorded a grand reception. It is held that the meeting was celebrated amidst royal splendour. They spent a few days in gaiety and festivities. Finally, the treaty[169] of Warna was concluded. According to it, the territory north and south of Tungabhadra river was assigned to Shahu and Sambhaji respectively. Sambhaji II was to remain independent internally, but subordinate to the Chhatrapati as far as the foreign policy was concerned. Both of them agreed not to give shelter to each other's deserters. Shahu also promised his protection to Sambhaji II in case of an attack by any other power.

Afterwards, Sambhaji, and sometimes his queen also, visited[170] Satara for one or the other cause and the relations[171] between the cousins were cordial. Henceforth, Shahu and his Peshwa busied themselves in consolidating and further expanding the Maratha kingdom. In due course of time, expeditions[172] were led against Malwa, Gujarat and Janjira. The Peshwa was often successful in his attempts.[173] Bajirao died in 1740 A.D. His son Balajirao received the robes[174] of Peshwaship on 13th April, 1740 A.D. Mahadoba[175] Purandare was appointed Peshwa's deputy or Mutalik to look after the duties of the Peshwa in his absence.

Satara witnessed a peaceful atmosphere till 1745 A.D. when there cropped up the problem of future successor to the Maratha throne. As known, Shahu had no issues and did not hope to get one. The only[176] son he had died in 1730 A.D. at the tender age of three years. Therefore, he declared that a lawful heir to succeed him should be found out. A search for finding out any descendant of Maloji was vigorously made.

While efforts were being made to find out a successor to the State Gaddi, a few influential Sardars supported[177] Mudhoji Bhonsle, son of Raghuji Bhonsle of Berar, who was distantly related to Shahu's younger wife, Sagunabai. It is held that Sakwarbai and others supported[178] Sambhaji of Kolhapur. While the first was not in the direct line of succession, the claim of the second is said to have been nearly rejected on the ground that he also did not have

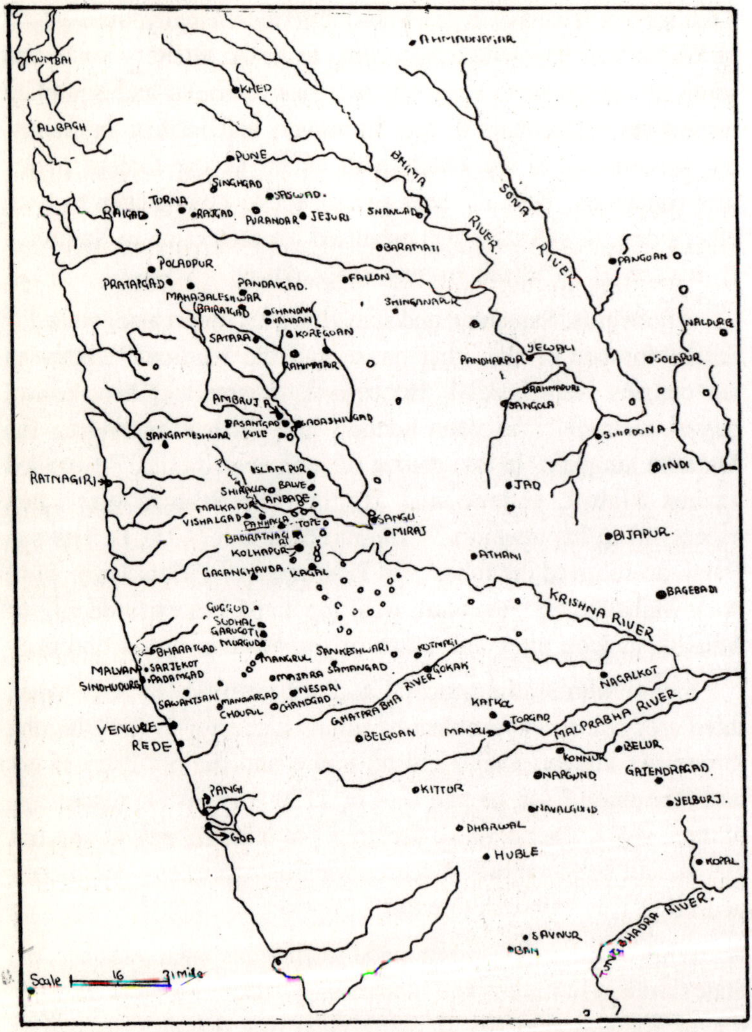

Map of Karbir State (Villages, Forts & Battlefields)

any issue and would be required to face the same problem after some time. The next candidate, as suggested by a few, was Nathaji,[179] son of Sawai Raja Jaisingh, a far fetched and exotic idea which could never materialise. There appeared to be a state of profound confusion and chaos. Various interests wanted to exploit the situation for their benefit.

In such a state of sustained anxiety, Tarabai seems to have looked at the problem from quite a different angle. It was with this mission that she sent a messenger to Shahu and declared that her grandson, Ramraja, son of Shivaji and Bhawnibai, was still alive.[180] She asked Shahu to consider him as his successor to the throne instead of Mudhoji Bhonsle or Sambhaji II or anyone else as suggested by others. Further, she earnestly pleaded[181] to Shahu, "Who else could be a better person to succeed you than one who belonged to the royal blood and was alive?"

She further declared[182] that Ramraja was a posthumous child and no sooner had he been born than he was sent out of the fort to be brought up in an atmosphere which guaranteed safety and security to his life. She said that she was afraid[183] of Rajasbai and Jijabai II and their tyranny to the child. In order to maintain secrecy, valuable services of a Rajput[184] woman, who belonged to Khasgi Chowki, were secured. She had a child born to her the same day, and, the child being dead, she wanted to go back to her home (*desh*).

Tarabai managed to send Ramraja with the woman to Bawda and let him grow there under the protection of Amatya. Next, the child was removed to a hiding place, i.e., Gagangad. For two years, Ramraja lived in obscurity, after which the woman died and the Rajput took the child to Krishnabai[185] (Daryabai Nimbalkar), elder sister of Shivaji II. As the child had been declared dead, it was not very difficult to bring him up safely.

Another account mentions[186] that Shivaji II died of small pox in 1726 A.D. and one of his queens committed 'Sati'. The other queen, Bhawanibai, gave birth to his son, Ramraja. It is held that

Shivrampant, younger son of Ramchandrapant, brought him up. For this, Shahu awarded[187] to his wife a "Vatan" later on.

Besides, Ramraja gave[188] an account of his own life. He said that he was born after Shivaji II was put into captivity at Panhalla by Rajasbai and Sambhaji II of Kolhapur. Next, he was put in charge of Shivrampant where he stayed for fifteen or sixteen years. He was then taken[189] to Pangaon and Tuljapur where he had to reside in obscurity, as others had come to know about him.

This version corroborates Bhagwantrao Amatya's declaration that he had taken Saheb to Bawda and brought him up for ten to twelve years with the help of Ghasiram and his wife. Once Jijabai II had visited[190] Bawda. She had inquired about Bhagwantrao Amatya and Ramraja, but the woman expressed her ignorance about Ramraja's existence while she managed[191] to send him away below the Ghats. Next he proceeded to Tuljapur through difficult routes and resided there for some time.

Shahu desired that the information should be verified before anything definite could be decided to declare Ramraja as the claimant to the Maratha throne. Pratinidhi Jagjiwan, Uppadhya and Chinto Mahadeorao came from Umbras and Shahu asked[192] them to find out if the said information about Ramraja was authentic. He desired that if the account was correct, Ramraja should be brought to Satara for his marriage, coronation and such other formalities. Santaji Mohite, Raghoji Mohite and Nagoji Ghatge[193] were to help on the occasion.

Finally, Shahu accepted[194] Ramraja to succeed him. He ordered the Peshwa to bring him and arrange for his succession to the Maratha throne. Thus, the hopes and ambitions of various other interested elements were done away with. It appears that Shahu continued to respect Tarabai and the presumption gained colour that she had influenced Shahu to accept her candidate as the future Chhatrapati.

Sakwarbai, elder queen of Shahu, did[195] not favour Ramraja's succession. The attitude[196] of Sakwarbai was noticed by Shahu and a few others at Satara. This is indicated by Shahu's letter[197] of February, 1745 A.D., to Bhagwantrao. In that letter, Shahu asked Bhagwantrao to send 'Chiranjeev' immediately to Daryabai Nimbalkar at Pangaon under great vigilance. Similarly, Tarabai had also asked[198] him to send him to Pangaon, as his existence had gained wide publicity which was not in his favour. Further, Bhagwantrao Amatya was to proceed[199] on to a pilgrimage (Mahayatra) for which the orders were being issued.

Shahu did not like to compel Sakwarbai to accept the succession of Ramraja, and desired that Ramraja should be brought after[200] his death and, as she would commit 'Sati' according to the prevalent custom, there would be no opposition to Ramraja's succession.

Thus, Shahu was now free from anxiety regarding the succession problem which had disturbed the peace of the palace and the State for some time. Shahu continued to remain ill. He prepared two notes,[201] with definite instructions to the Peshwa to carry on the administration of the kingdom. He ordered that the Peshwa should obey his descendants, and assured that they would not interfere with his office. From the notes, it is evident that he did not want Sambhaji of Kolhapur to succeed him.

Shahu died[202] on the 15th December, 1749 A.D. Sakwarbai committed 'Sati'. The Peshwa sent[203] Mahadoba Purandare, Chinto Vinayak, Lingoji Anant and Indroji Kadam to conduct Ramraja to Satara with due respect.

Daryabai Nimbalkar, who had looked after the welfare of Ramraja for all these years, satisfied herself as to the genuinness[204] of the message sent by the Peshwa. She escorted him personally to Satara with a section of her troops. Tarabai welcomed Ramraja, and honoured others with valuable presents, dresses, etc., offered on such occasions. Next, Ramraja was married to Tukabai Shirkey and Sagunabai, daughter of Burhanji Mohite.

Ramraja was coronated on 4th January, 1750 A.D. However, the two notes, found by the Peshwa after Shahu, had practically transferred the king's authority to the Peshwa. As Ramraja was new to the State policy and administration, many persons seemed to have played an important role at Satara. Among them, the Mutalik Purandare was of countable influence. Fortunately, Purandare's letters, including those which were written by Moreshwar, give a far clearer picture of the prevailing confusion and disturbance in the palace as well as in the administration.

Tarabai and the Peshwa could not remain amicable.[205] The scuffle[206] for power in the Maratha State had begun. Tarabai left[207] for Sinhgad to observe the commemoration of her husband on 20th March, 1750 A.D. The fort belonged to Chimnajee Narayan. He was not among those who supported the Peshwa. It is also believed that Tarabai had gone there to have a counter-plan to check the growing authority of the Peshwa or to start fresh intrigue against him. However, no account is available to prove the nature of the alleged intrigue or the actual plan that was chalked out by her. In between, it is also evident that the king tried to assert[208] his power.

Meanwhile, Daryabai Nimbalkar's Jagir[209] problem created further trouble at Satara. She asked the Peshwa to return her Saranjam which was given to her by the Moghul king and in absence of which she was completely ruined. She considered the Peshwa to be responsible for her sad plight and was much disturbed.

The king desired[210] that her Saranjam should be returned. He once said, "If the grant of Inamat to Daryabai is not sanctioned by the Peshwa, I will go back to Tuljapur along with Daryabai Nimbalkar." The understanding between the king and the Peshwa seems to have got strained.[211] Ramraja gave the robes of honour to Babuji Naik which was not liked by the Peshwa. It should be remembered that he was one of the contenders to the Peshwaship in 1740 A.D.

However, Ramraja, unmindful of the reaction, was firm. He met Raghuji Bhonsle who presented[212] him medals, gems and costly dresses with an elephant. The Peshwa resented it as he and Raghuji Bhonsle had remained opponents in the past, although now the relations between them had improved.

It is also held that Tarabai influenced Ramraja to the extent of domination. The Peshwa apprehended[213] obstacles in administration which he had been carrying on since the time of Shahu.

As mentioned, Daryabai Nimbalkar's problem was not yet solved. She was annoyed. She requested the king to decide about her Jagir problem as early as possible. Ramraja consoled[214] her and assured her that her interests would be well looked after by him. But the Peshwa was reluctant to return her Jagir, because he apprehended[215] that she would ask for more.

It is obvious that the interests of many persons in the administration at Satara palace and court caused deterioration in the state administration. The Mutalik Purandare was of opinion that the condition had deteriorated because of Tarabai's domination in the administration.

On 21st April, 1750 A.D., Balaji Vajirao had to leave[216] for his home (Poona) to celebrate the thread ceremony of his brother, Raghunathrao, and the marriage of Vishwasrao. He requested[217] Tarabai to visit Poona. She agreed, and reached there with Bhagwantrao Amatya and Sachiv Chimnaje Narayan on 9th March, 1750 A.D. On 14th August 1750 A.D., the king also arrived[218] at Poona to attend the functions. The rejoicings continued for a few days. Thereafter, Balaji Bajirao held a meeting to discuss the future policy of the State. A well fortified fort, Sangola,[219] was chosen for the purpose.

The assemblage consisted of a few dignitaries and the rising generation of the diplomats who later on played a more significant role in the politics of the day. They were Sadashivrao Bhau, Ramchandra Bawa, Mahadeo Purandare, Sarlashkar Somvanshi, Sindhia and Holkar. The Peshwa addressed[220] them and said that in the interest of the State, the executive authority must remain in his hands and that he would not tolerate any interference from the Pratinidhi or the Sachiv or anyone else. That Ramraja was not unaware of the purpose of the assembly can be infered from the letter[221] of Purandare. It is indicated that the king was keen to upset[222] the plan. However, he could not do so because of lack of either influence or resources.

It is evident that, by virtue of the 'Sangola Pact', the Peshwa became a de-facto ruler. It appears that Tarabai never expccted the sudden change and was overtaken by the decision of Sangola[223] Pact and the subsequent changes. Dr. H.N. Sinha writes[224], "The arrangement tied the hands and feet of Ramraja and tightened the hold of the Peshwa on him." It is also stated that the king was struggling to assert[225] his authority in administration. Purandare also advised the Peshwa to take strong measures[226] against Ramraja.

Next, the Peshwa demanded the fort of Sinhgad.[227] It was in charge of the Sachiv. The king was reluctant to give it to him. Tarabai did not like to part with it. However, he permitted the Peshwa to take it. The Sachiv resisted. The fort was taken by force[228] on 6th July, 1750 A.D. Similarly, the Peshwa also took the forts of Sangola[229] and Purandar. These were in charge of Pratinidhi Dadoba and Yamaji Shivdev, the supporters of Tarabai. Dr. H.N. Sinha writes[230], "Tarabai noticed all this, writhed as it were in bitter indignation." She had yet not come in direct conflict with the king or the Peshwa. The Peshwa also desired[231] that Govindrao Chitnis should not favour her and avoid differences of opinion being created between the king and the Peshwa. Tarabai appears to have been exasperated by the recent happenings. Later events show that she could not be cowed down by lack of resources or influence. She visited Shambhu Mahadeo Temple at Sinhgad on Ist October, 1750 A.D. It is believed that she met Umabai Dabhade and her other supporters there. They decided to subdue[232] the Peshwa.

Tarabai invited[233] the king to observe certain festivities at Satara fort. He obtained[234] the permission of Nanasaheb (Peshwa) to visit her. Sardesai writes[235], "Tarabai strongly remonstrated with him against his lending support to the Peshwa and advised him to be guided by herself alone". On 22nd November, 1750 A.D., she imprisoned[236] him after the festival (Champasasthi). This indicates that Tarabai and Ramraja had severe differences and therefore she took the above drastic action. She refused[237] to release him, which was greatly felt by his (Ramraja's) father-in-law, Burhanji Mohite. Further, she declared him an impostor[238] and informed[239] Sambhaji of Kolhapur about the recent events taking place at Satara. She also held consultations[240] with the killedar regarding the future course of action to be taken.

Ramraja could not return from the fort. The Peshwa and his adherents took this seriously. Meanwhile, Mahadji Ambaji inquired[241] from Nana Purandare whether the king was at Satara fort. He wanted to know if the killedar was also won over by him; whether Tarabai had opened[242] the treasury and had started distributing money to the inmates and gathered an army to support him.

At the same time, Ramraja was anxious to be released. He requested the Peshwa for the same. Mahadji Ambaji was worried as to the reaction of the people over recent developments. He wrote,[243] "If Tarabai had a complete hold on him (the king), we would lose in reputation and fame. So, it is our duty to see that the killedar and Tarabai are kept away from concocting any plans against him."

But the Peshwa's next move shows that he was thinking in a different way. He sent the king's belongings to the fort, and asked Tarabai to pardon[244] him if he had done anything wrong intentionally or otherwise. Meanwhile, Bhausaheb had informed Nana Purandare to take measures against Sambhaji's march towards Satara. The two villages on which Satara depended for its expenses were being looted by Trimbak Sadashivbhau and his Sardars. The Peshwa sent stern orders[245] to stop these ravages.

Sadashivbhau and Nana Purandare wanted to lay siege on

Satara fort. But the Peshwa, Balaji Bajirao, disagreed with the plan. He held[246] that any attack on the Satara fort would not further their cause. They would be considered unfaithful or traitors, and would be losing public support. Besides, he apprehended that the Moghul Emperor might take the advantage of the confusion that prevailed at Satara and in the State. Therefore, he advised them to be more cautious and polite.

Tarabai had already evoked[247] the support of Sheikh Mira of Wai, Trimbakrao Dhaigude, Shirkeys and Mohites. She also tried to take Yashwantrao and Govindrao to the fort. Thus, by now, she had become quite powerful.

The Peshwa was not able to bring down either Tarabai or the king from the fort. He laid[248] a counter-plan to create disturbance in Tarabai's camp. He declared that he was going to have Sambhaji of Kolhapur on Satara throne. Further, he won[249] over Puranik and Kasurde in his favour. He hoped that if the killedar of Satara fort also supported him, it would not be difficult for him to bring down Tarabai and Ramraja from the fort.

In between, the Peshwa had communicated[250] to the king to be patient as his release was a question of time. The names of the persons through whom the Peshwa sent the news to the king are not known. However, it suggests that, from among the supporters of Tarabai, there were a few who supported the Peshwa also. The Peshwa had hopes that, after some time, she would be fed up and the things would come down to their own natural course.

But the Peshwa was not unmindful of the recent situation, because he took special measures[251] to see that Tulaji Angre and Manaji Angre would not join Tarabai.

It was now more[252] than a month that Tarabai had not come down the fort. Nor had she allowed the king to leave the fort. Besides, she had recruited[253] new persons in the army and raised a new infantry. She had also established[254] new choukies. The old killedar of the Satara fort was ousted and a new person, named Partho, was appointed in his place. She honoured[255] Gode with a gift of palanquin and a few villages to maintain it. Arrangements were made to bring[256] Sambhaji II of Kolhapur to Satara. Bhausaheb sent information to Nana Saheb (Peshwa) that he should lead a siege against Satara fort, otherwise the king might be murdered.[257] If that happened, Tarabai would have overwhelming power. He further desired that the king should be with the Peshwa and if he would not lead the siege to Satara, he (the Peshwa) should proceed to Gujarat and then he would settle the Satara problem.

But the Peshwa was not in favour of storming Satara. Meanwhile, he had solved[258] Umabai Dabhade's affairs by 26th December, 1750 A.D. It was also decided that Bhausaheb would proceed on to meet the Moghuls. The Peshwa was to reside at Poona. Soon it became known that if the killedar of the fort could be appeased,[259] the king might be brought down from the fort. Besides, an impostor[260] of the king was also to be created. The Peshwa gave out that he should be sent to him, so that he could keep him in the fort; thereby he probably wanted to show that he was also able to keep impostors in the fort.

Tarabai had not come down from the fort; nor could the king leave the fort. It indicates that she could not be duped by the above measures. In between the time, Sadashiv Bhau wrote to Nana Purandare that he was going to see the Peshwa after five or six days and both of them would calm down the rebel[261] at Satara. They appear to be specially careful because Tarabai was being supported by Umabai Dabhade of Gujarat.

The much sought for opportunity for Tarabai came when the Peshwa had left[262] for Aurangabad (Karnatak). She sent her agent to Sambhaji II of Kolhapur and offered him the throne of Satara. The letter of Anandrao Girdhar indicates[263] that Sambhaji had not responded to her offer. He requested the Peshwa to return post-haste to Satara, as he apprehended that Sambhaji might side over with Tarabai. As known, she had requested

Sambhaji to reach Satara. Soon he sent[264] for Ramdasspant, the emissary at Nizam-ul-Mulk's court, to evoke his co-operation. In turn, she offered him Peshwaship which he also coveted.

Tarabai also got Satara fort well provisioned to withstand a long siege. She had with[265] her the Gujarat army under Senapati Damaji Gaekwad besides her own army and the support she anticipated from Nizam-ul-Mulk. Meanwhile, Damaji Gaekwad marched[266] towards Poona with lightening speed. Bapuji Reterekar had informed[267] the Peshwa of the march of Gaekwad towards Poona.

The inmates of the Peshwa's house took shelter[268] in the fort of Sinhgad, leaving behind Mahadev Purandare to command the Peshwa's forces. By marches, Damaji Gakewad reached Pargaon, a village 30 miles east of Poona on the 11th March, 1751 A.D. He encamped there. Instead of giving an open battle, Mahadoba Purandare called Damaji Gaekwad a traitor. Later, Trimbakrao Purandare, Balwantrao Mehendale and Bapuji Retrekar attacked him. Damaji Gakewad diverted[269] his course and marched towards Satara where Tarabai welcomed him warmly.

Trimbakrao Purandare attacked Damaji Gaekwad at Satara. On the banks[270] of the river Yenna, on 15th March, 1751 A.D., he defeated Damaji Gaekwad. Soon, the Peshwa hurried towards north. He was satisfied[271] to find that Purandare had handled the situation tactfully and had saved Poona from an open battle. The Peshwa stormed[272] Yavateshwar hill. He captured it along with other smaller forts. He pressed on his victory with Purandare. Damaji Gaekwad was compelled[273] to take a more difficult route through Salpa pass. During the fight, the Maratha forces of Tarabai left him. Damaji Gaekwad and his army were unable to either proceed on or to return, as they were not familiar with the place. Under the circumstances, Damaji Gaekwad had no other alternative but to sue for peace. The Peshwa allowed them to encamp near his own tent to discuss the terms of the treaty. The Peshwa demanded half of Gujarat. Damaji Gaekwad was not [274] prepared to accept the above condition. He pleaded that he was only a servant of Umabai. As such, she had all the rights to the final decision.

While the peace negotiations were on, the Peshwa attacked[275] the Gujarat army on 13th April, 1751 A.D. unawares. They were taken by surprise and could not resist. Damaji Gaekwad was captured[276] when he was taking his bath along with others who were present there.

In spite of the above incident, Tarabai had not yet lost all hopes to defeat the Peshwa. She sent her agent to Kolhapur and requested[277] Sambhaji of Kolhapur to come to Satara immediately. She also communicated to him that his lingering attitude was not tolerable to her. However, Sambhaji did not turn up. She was still giving a single handed battle to the Peshwa who concentrated to take Satara. Tarabai was enraged and increased the rigours of Ramraja. It was also rumoured[278] that once the king came down from the fort, he would run away or would only be a puppet in the hands of the Peshwa. She could not get any help either from the Sachiv or the Pratinidhi or Salabatjung, the Nizam-ul-Mulk, because the Peshwa had already entered into an understanding with him.

Thus, she was left without resources. At the same time, all was not well at Tarabai's camp. According to a few writers, she had differences[279] with Ramraja, while others state that a section of the garrison at Satara rebelled[280] under the leadership of Havaldar Anandrao Jadhav. She instantly beheaded[281] him for breach of faith, as she found him in direct correspondence with the Peshwa. But it was obvious that she had lost the battle. She sent Chinto Anand, Dewasthale and Moro Shivdev to the Peshwa at Poona to open up peace negotiations[282]. In return, the Peshwa sent Mahadji Nimbalkar, Dhodo Govind Vakil and Dinker Mahadeo to the Satara fort.

Finally, Tarabai came[283] down from the fort along with Ramraja. She stayed at Fatehsinh's Wada. Tarabai visited the

Peshwa at Poona where they reached to an understanding. Accordingly, the Peshwa could exercise full authority[284] in the administration of the State, while Tarabai could issue Sanads and perform other duties in internal affairs.

Henceforth, Tarabai remained in the background, but her call[285] for politics as a natural urge could never seem to leave her. This is indicated by her effort to send Dadoba Purandare to help Balaji when Nizam-ul-Mulk invaded[286] Peshwa's territory during the last month of 1751 A.D. But, Balaji, perhaps suspecting his sincerity of purpose, asked him to return.[287] Tarabai dismissed Dadoba, and gave the office of Pratinidhi to Babuji Naik. Being dissatisfied by her attitude, they became friendly to the Peshwa.

The final reconciliation[288] between Tarabai and the Peshwa took place on the 14th September, 1752 A.D., when the Peshwa returned after defeating Nizam-ul-Mulk. She solemnly[289] declared that Ramraja did not belong to the Bhonsle family and therefore Sambhaji of Kolhapur should be enthroned at Satara. The question whether Ramraja was an impostor was left aside.[290] No one was anxious to discuss it any more. The Peshwa enjoyed freedom of action in administration. But, in spite of this, she had not been able to compromise herself with the Peshwa and whenever any occasion arose, she gave vent to her feelings without let or fear.

The different accounts and events indicate that Tarabai's career was full of struggles, successes and failures. Fearlessly, she maintained her position and that of the Maratha spirit from 1699 A.D. She courageously fought against Aurangzeb in which she had to move from fort to fort like a soldier of fortune and saved the Maratha State from Moghul domination.

She founded the Kolhapur house which could continue even after her captivity in 1714 A.D. After the treaty of Warna in 1731 A.D. she stayed at Satara. This gave her one more opportunity to enthrone Ramraja as Chhatrapati of Maratha Kingdom.

Evidences are replete that Shahu respected her for intelligence, courage and experience. She was able, forthright and brilliantly tempestuous. At the most it can only be said that her approach was purely an individualistic thought and much ahead of her own times. Her failure could never disappoint her as long as she had the resources and the strength which she lacked in old age. She saw with dismay that while the Peshwa ruled and governed, the Chhatrapati remained a figurehead behind the bars. Greatly discouraged, she died on the 9th December, 1761 A.D. at Mahuli.

REFERENCES

1. Ferishta – *History of Dekkan*, Vol.II, p. 100.
2. *Bombay Gazetteer*, Vol.XVIII, Part II, p. 597.
   O.C.Vol. 56 IV, No.50C, 20th March, 1700-1, Factory records (Bendre Collection, Vol.12 p. 4360, B.I.S.M., Poona).
3. Parasnis, D.B. – *Musalmani Amdaneeteel*, Nov. 1900, Bhag 3,856.
4. Parasnis, D.B. – *Musalmani Amdaniteel*, Nov. 1900 – Bhag III, Marathe Sardars, p. 56.
5. *Madhya Yugeen Charitra Kosh*, p. 425.
6. Riyasat, Vol. IV, *Sthir Budhi Rajaram*, p. 106.
7. *S.P.D.*, Vol. 31, L.N. 60.
   Sen, S.N. – *The Military System of the Marathas*, p. 19. *Itihas Sangraha*, Vol. VII, Aitihasik Sphut Lekh (F.N. p. 10).
8. *Itihas Sangraha*, Vol. VII, Peshwa Daftar, p. 7.
9. *Madhya Yugeen Charitra Kosh*, p. 780. (According to this text, he was three and a half years old when he was coronated by Tarabai in 1700 A.D.).
   Riyasat, Vol. IV, *Sthir Budhi Rajaram*, p. 56.
10. Khafi Khan – Muntakhabu-l-Lubab, *H.I.H.*, Vol. VII, p. 348.
11. *Itihas Sangraha*, Aitihasik Charitre, p. 8
    Ferishta – *History of Dekkan*, Vol. II, p. 97.
12. Riyasat, Vol. IV, *Sthir Budhi Rajaram*, p. 56.
13. *Bombay Gazetteer*, Vol. XVIII, Part II, p. 239.
14. Rajwade, V.K., Khand VIII, L.N. 52.
    Raghuvirsingh – *Malwa in Transition*, p. 54, writes that the Marathas had crossed the Narmada for the first time, but Manucci, N. – *Storia Do Mogor*, Vol. IV, p. 246, says that the Marathas had gone to that side for the third time. Previous to this, they had

invaded Hindustan and gone as far as the province of Hrixas (Orissa).

15. Sen, S.N., – *Administrative System of the Marathas*, p. 62.
16. *Ibid.*, p. 117.
17. *Prof. M.M.D.V. Potdar Commemoration Volume*, p. 2.
18. Khafi Khan – Muntakhabu-L-Lubab, *H.I.H.*, Vol. VII, p. 341.
19. Saqi Mustad Khan – *Maasir-I-Alamgiri*, pp. 197, 238.
20. Riyasat, Vol. IV, *Sthir Budhi Rajaram*, p. 13.
21. Sen, S.N. – *Military System of the Marathas*, p. 55.
22. Sarkar, J. – *History of Aurangzeb*, Vol. V, pp. 69, 129.
23. Sen, S.N. – *Administrative System of the Marathas*, p. 117.
24. Refer p. 57, 58, F.N. Nos. 1, 4.
25. Riyasat, Vol. IV, *Sthir Budhi Rajaram*, p. 107.
26. *Ibid.*, pp. 107, 108.
    Chitnis, M.R. – *Lives of Sambhaji and Rajaram*, pp. 91, 92.
27. Sanada Patre, p. 204.
    Indian Historical Records Commission, Proceedings, Vol. XIX, p. 159.
28. Sarkar, J. – *History of Aurangzeb*, Vol. V, p. 201.
29. *Varshik Ittivrutta*, Shak 1835, p. 378.
    Patre Yadi Vagere, L.N. 9, p. 31.
    Khafi Khan – Muntakhabu-L-Lubab, *H.I.H.*, Vol. VII, p. 367.
30. Rajwade, V.K., Khand VIII, L.N. 68.
    Riyasat, Vol. IV, *Sthir Budhi Rajaram*, p. 125.
    Girjoji belonged to Karhad. He had managed the Jagir of Karhad well. He had a seal of his own.
    कन्हाडादि महालाना सरदेशमुखस्य हि,।
    गिर्जोजी यादवेरयेषा मुद्रा मूर्थोजिजन्मत।
31. Ferishta – *History of Dekkan*, Vol. II, p. 104.
32. Saqi Mustad Khan – *Maasir-I-Alamgiri*, p. 257, 258.
33. Miscellaneous Volumes –20, F.R. p. 120
    Bendre Collection Vol. 12 (B.I.S.M., Poona).
34. Khafi Khan - Muntakhabu-l-Lubab, *H.I.H.*, Vol.VII, p. 373.
    Riyasat, Vol. IV, Sthir Budhi Rajaram, p. 117.
35. *Aitihasik Patra-Wyawahar*, L.N. 2.
36. *Ibid.*, L.N. 2.
37. Riyasat, Vol. IV, *Sthir Budhi Rajaram*, p. 119.
38. *P.D.*, Vol.I, L.Ns. 21 to 24.

39. Khafi Khan - Muntakhabu-l-Lubab, *H.I.H.*, Vol.VII, p. 376.
40. Riyasat, Vol. IV, *Sthir Budhi Rajaram*, p. 120.
41. *Bombay Gazetteer*, Vol. XVIII, Part II, p. 5.
Khafi Khan - Muntakhabu-l-Lubab, *H.I.H.*, Vol.VII, p. 374.
42. Riyasat, Vol. IV, Sthir Budhi Rajaram, p. 122.
दिल्ली झाली दीनवाणी। दिल्लीशाचें गेले पाणी।।1।
ताराबाई रामाणी। मद्रकाली कोपली।।2।।
The account may appeal as an exaggerated narration, yet it conveys the qualities Tarabai possessed even as a good fighter, having knowledge of warfare.
43. Rajwade, V.K., Khand II, p. 5.
44. Saqi Mustad Khan – *Maasir-I-Alamgiri*, pp. 276, 277, 302.
Manucci, N. - *Storia Do Mogor*, Vol.IV, pp. 176, 241, 243, 244.
45. *S.P.D.* XXXI, L.N. 90.
46. *S.P.D.* XXXI, L.N. 88.
47. Rajwade, V.K., Khand XVII, L.Ns. 24, 29, 33.
48. Saqi Mustad Khan – *Maasir-I-Alamgiri*, pp. 301, 302.
49. O.C. m.o. 8535, Vol. 62, F.R. Mr. Wigmorie from Madras 8 Jan 1707/8 (Bendre Collection, Vol.14, P5183, B.I.S.M.)
50. Sardesai Commemoration Volume p. 60, Jaipur Akhabarats Ali Ibrahim Khan - Tarikh-i-Ibrahim Khan, *H.I.H.*, Vol. VIII, p. 259.
Indian Historical Records Commission, Proceedings, Vol. IV, p. 15.
51. *Varshik Ittivrutta*, Shak 1835, p. 378.
Gupte, K. - *Nagpurkar Bhonsle Yanchi Bakhar*, p. 25.
Patre Yadi Vagere, p. 503.
52. *Itihas Sangraha*, Junya Aitihasik Goshti, Pustak 2, October 1909, p. 17.
53. *Vividh Gyan Vistar*, February 1924 (Letter)
54. Riyasat, Vol. V, Punya Shloka Shahu, Peshwa Balaji Vishwanath, p. 35.
55. Chitnis, M.R. - Lives of Sambhaji and Rajaram, p. 31.
56. Refer, p. 3, F.No. 3.
57. Itihas Sangraha, Aitihasik, Sphut Lekh, Pustak 2, October 1909, Ank 3, p. 7.
58. Vividh Gyan Vistar, Pustak 18, Ank 1, p. 234.
59. Rajwade, V.K., Khand XV, p. 360.
60. Rajwade, V.K., Khand XX, L.N. 60.

61. Rajwade, V.K., Khand XX, L.N. 60. The letter is written at a later date when the king awarded him Rs. 5,000/- for his services.
62. Rajwade, V.K., Khand IV, p. 33.
63. *Itihas Sangraha*, Junya Aitihasik Goshti, II, p. 18.
64. *Shiv Charitra Sahitya*, Khand I, p. 102.
65. *Vividh Gyan Vistar*, Pustak 18, Ank 1, p. 234.
66. *Vividh Gyan Vistar*, February, 1924, Letter.
67. *Itihas Sangraha*, Peshwa Daftar, p. 10.
68. *Patre Yadi Vagere*, L.N. 495, p. 490.
69. *Itihas Sangraha*, Junya Aitihasik Goshti, p. 5.
Kincaid, C.A. & Parasnis, D.B. - *A History of the Maratha People*, Vol. II, p. 125.
70. Khare, W.W. - *Ichchalkaranji Sansthan Chitihas*, p. 22.
B.I.S.M. - *Aitihasik Sankeern Nibandhawali*, Khand II, pp. 74, 75.
71. Dhabu, D.G. - *Kulabkar Angre Sarkhel*, p. 9.
72. *Patre Yadi Vagere*, L.N. 495, p. 490.
73. Riyasat, Vol. V, *Punya Shloka Shahu, Peshwa Balaji Vishwanath*, p. 40.
74. *Ibid.*
Patre Yadi Vagere, L.N. 495, p. 490.
75. Rajwade, V.K., Khand XXI, L.N. 328
76. *Ibid.*, V.K., Khand XV, L.N.. 360.
77. *Ibid.*, V.K., Khand III, L.N. 64.
Patre Yadi Vagere, L.N. 495, L.N.. 491.
78. Riyasat, Vol. V, *Punya Shloka Shahu, Peshwa Balaji Vishwanath*, p. 43.
79. *Itihas Sangraha*, Peshwa Daftar, p. 33.
Bharatvarsha, Pant Pratinidhi Chibakhar, p. 41.
80. Rajwade, V.K., Khand III, L.N. 64. The inam was given at a later date.
81. *Bharatvarsha, Pant Pratinidhi Chibakhar*, p. 41.
Bombay Gazetteer, Vol. XVIII, Part II, p. 247.
82. *Patre Yadi Vagere*, L.N. 489 (17).
83. *Itihas Sangraha*, Peshwa Daftar, p. 321.
84. Rajwade, V.K., Khand XX, L.N. 44 (Sachiv)
Rajwade, V.K., Khand IV, p. 32 (Amatya)
Rajwade, V.K., Khand III, L.N. 135 (Sumant)
Watan Patre Niwab Patre, L.N. 17 (Mantri)

S.P.D., Vol. XXX, p. 226 (Nyayadhish)
Rajwade, V.K., Khand XV, L.N. 179 (Panditrao)
S.P.D., Vol. XLIV, L.N.41 (Pratinidhi)
Shahu Roznishi, No. 119.

85. Khare, W.W. - *Ichchalkaranjui Sansthan Ch Itihas*, p. 22.
86. Rajwade, V.K., Khand VIII, L.N. 68.
87. Rajwade, V.K., Khand VIII, L.N. 67, P. 88.
88. Sinha, H.N. - *Rise of the Peshwas*, p. xxiii.
89. Rajwade, V.K., Khand VIII, L.Ns. 64, 65, 66.
90. Riyasat, Vol. V, *Punya Shloka Shahu, Peshwa Balaji Vishwanath*, p. 55.
    Grant Duff - *History of the Marattas*, Vol.I, p. 359.
91. Sinha, H.N. - *Rise of the Peshwas*, p. xxiii.
92. *Ibid.*
93. *Itihas Sangraha*, Peshwa Daftar, p. 12.
    Riyasat, Vol. V, *Punya Shloka Shahu, Peshwa Balaji Vishwanath*, p. 55.
94. Khare, W.W. - *Ichchalkaranji Sansthan Ch Itihas*, p. 23.
95. Sinha, H.N. - *Rise of the Peshwas*, p. xxiv.
96. Khafi Khan - Muntakhabu-l-Lubab, *H.I.H.*, Vol.VII, pp. 396-400.
    Ferishta - *History of Dekkan*, Vol. II, pp. 54-56.
97. Irvine, W.W. - *Later Moghuls*, Vol. I, p. 46.
98. *Ibid.*, p. 57.
99. *Ibid.*, p. 61.
100. Jaipur Akhabarats - Riyasat, Vol. V, *Punya Shloka Shahu, Peshwa Balaji Vishwanath*, p. 30, mentions about the Sanad which Jotyaji Kesarkar brought for Shahu in 1707 A.D. This Sanad granted him the authority to collect Chouth and Sardeshmukhi from six Moghul Subas of south. He was also to rule the 'Swarajya' of his grandfather as a Vassal of the Moghul Emperor. In lieu, Shahu was to serve the Emperor with troops and other amenities, if required by him. Sardesai writes that the Sanad is not available. No other reliable account or Persian paper mentions about this Sanad.
     Rajwade, V.K., Khand VIII, L.Ns. 79, 80.
     The letters indicate that three or four days before Aurangzeb died, he had summoned Shahu and had told him that he was free and his kingdom was given back to him.
     Indian Historical Records Commission, Proceedings, Vol. XVII, p. 204.

101. Khafi Khan - Muntakhabu-l-Lubab, *H.I.H.*, Vol.VII, p. 409.
102. *Ibid.*
103. *Jadhava Kaifiyat*, p. 71.
104. *Shahu Roznishi*, No. 10(A)
105. Riyasat, Vol. V, *Punya Shloka Shahu, Peshwa Balaji Vishwanath*, p. 63.
106. *S.P.D.* Vol. VII, L.Ns. 4, 16 :
    Dues were to be collected from Hyderabad district and Satara also. *Indian Historical Records Commission, Proceedings*, Vol. XVII, p. 20.
    Zulphikar Khan, Viceroy of Deccan (1708-13), maintained a right understanding with the Sivajees.
    Letter Bombay to Surat, Jan 12, 1703 A.D. F.R. Bombay, Vol. I. A friendly agreement existed between Shahu and Daudkhan. Shahu might have declared his authority to realize Chouth.
    Bombay Gazetteer, Vol. XVIII, part II, p. 241.
107. *Varshik Ittivrutta*, Shak 1835, p. 382.
108. *Ibid.*
109. *Ibid.*
110. *S.P.D.* Vol. VII, L.N. 13 :
    Piraji Raut was a trooper in the service of Balaji Vishwanath. While Chandrasen Jadhav and Balaji Vishwanath had gone over to subdue Damaji Thorat, Piraji Raut pursued a black buck which entered the tent of Vyasrao, a Brahmin in the service of Chandrasen Jadhav. Piraji Raut asked Vyasrao to return the black buck. He refused. Piraji Raut wounded him and, frightened of his own action, escaped to Balaji Vishwanath and sought his protection. He offered him shelter. Vyasrao complained to Chandrasen Jadhav who demanded Piraji Raut from Balaji Vishwanath. He refused to hand over Piraji Raut to the Senapati who ordered his troops to attack Balaji Vishwanath's camp. Balaji Vishwanath escaped to the fort of Pandavgad, quickly followed by the Senapati, and appealed to Shahu for protection.
111. Kincaid, C.A. & Parasnis, D.B. - *History of the Maratha People*, Vol. II, p. 150.
112. *S.P.D.* Vol. VII, L.Ns. 14, 15.
    S.P.D. Vol. XXXI, L.N. 110.
113. *Sardesai Commemoration Volume*, p. 104.
114. *Ibid.*

115. *Shahu Roznishi*, No. 207.
116. Riyasat, Vol. V, *Punya Shloka Shahu, Peshwa Balaji Vishwanath*, p. 63.
117. *Aitihasik Patra Vyawahar*, L.N.5.
118. *Bawda Daftar*, Vol. I, L.N. 70.
119. *Shahu Roznishi*, No. 155.
S.P.D. Vol. XXXI, L.N. 110.
120. B.I.S.M. - *Aitihasik Sankern Sahitya Nibandhawali*, Khand II, pp. 74, 75.
121. *Varshik Ittivrutta*, Shak 1835, p. 382.
122. *Sardesai Commermoration Volume*, p. 104.
123. *Itihas Sangraha*, Peshwa Daftar, L.N. 18.
124. *Ibid.*
125. *Angrekaleen Shakawali*, p. 7.
126. *Ibid.*
127. *Ibid.*, p. 8.
128. *Bombay Gazetteer*, Vol. XVIII, Part II, p. 242.
129. *Ibid.*
130. *Itihas Sangraha*, Peshwe Daftar, p. 322.
Shahu Roznishi, No. 119.
131. *Patre Yadi Vagere*, p. 457.
132. *Shahu Roznishi*, No. 155 : S.P.D. Vol. XXXI, L.N. 113.
133. *Sardesai Commemoration Volume*, p. 104.
134. *Ibid.*, p. 109.
135. *S.P.D.* Vol. VII, L.N. 21 : Kanhoji Angre and Shahu met for the first time.
Unpublished paper - (Peshwa Daftar, Poona) : Sambhaji of Kolhapur donated a cocoanut grove to Vaijnath Jyotishi of Nagaon. The Sanad indicates that Kanhoji Angre had not come over to Shahu before 1714-15 A.D. After that, he left supporting Tarabai and Sambhaji of Kolhapur and joined Shahu.
— (Through the courtesy of Shri S.V. Avalskar)
136. Irvine, W.W. - *Later Moghuls*, Vol. II, p. 163.
137. Riyasat, Vol. V, *Punya Shloka Shahu, Peshwa Balaji Vishwanath*, p. 121.
138. *Ibid.*, p. 64.
139. *Maathur-Ul-Umara*, Vol. II, pp. 409 to 411.
Khafi Khan - Muntakhabu-l-Lubab, *H.I.H.*, Vol. VII, p. 446.
140. Khare, W.W. - *Ichchalkaranji Sansthan Ch Itihas*, p. 25.

141. Rajwade, V.K., Khand VIII, L.N. 169.
142. *Patre yadi Vagere*, p. 9 mentions : "Shri Raja Shambhu Chhatrapati 24-12-1714," i.e. he must have been coronated before the said date.
143. Ajnapatra : "The famous Ajnapatra, completed on 19th November, 1715, expounding Shivaji's policy, is addressed by Ramchandrapant to Sambhaji II, then 17 years old, as to a beloved pupil, conveying lessons in the art of governance and pouring forth all the accumulated wisdom of Shivaji's policy in which the Amatya was the principal instrument of execution. The language and diction are in harmony with the exalted subject, so that this treatise is considered to be of singular value in disclosing the high ideals of the founder. Ramchandra Nilkanth either died or retired after the issue of this Ajnapatra".
144. *Tah-wa-Kararmadar*, pp. 1-9.
Aitihasik Patra-Vyawahar, L.Ns. 77, 78, 80.
Indian Historical Records Commission, Proceedings, Vol. XVI, p. 2, 3, 4 : "The revenue of the provinces of Aurangabad, Berar, Bedar, Bijapur, Hyderabad and Khandesh was Rs. 18, 05, 17, 294."
145. Irvine, W.W. - *Later Moghuls*, Vol. I, p. 56, 57, 60.
146. *Indian Historical Records Commission, Proceedings*, Vol. XIV, p. 109.
Maathur-Ul-Umara, p. 411.
147. *Shahu Roznishi*, 9 (1723-24), 120 (p 89).
S.P.D. XXX, L.N. 51.
148. *Varshik Ittivrutta* (1835), p. 382 (10).
S.P.D. VII, L.N. 37 : Two days before his death, he was busy in collecting Maratha dues.
149. *Shahu Roznishi*, 100 (8)
Patre Yadi Vagere, L.N. 496, p. 495.
150. *Patre Yadi Vagere*, L.N. 489.
151. Rajwade, V.K., Khand VIII, L.Ns. 94, 96.
Available accounts show that Rajasbai took part in the activities of estate management. She had granted the village of Pedur in inam to Devdatta, son of Kavindra Parmanand. (*S.P.D.* XXXI, L.N. 118).
152. *Shahu Roznishi*, Nos. 22, 25, 212.
Balaji Bajirao Roznishi, Nos. 226-228.
153. *S.P.D.* Vol. X, L.N. 50.

154. Riyasat, Vol. V, *Punya Shloka Shahu, Peshwa Balaji Vishwanath*, p. 98.
S.P.D. Vol. X, L.N. 50.
155. Rajwade, V.K., Khand II, pp. 55, 56.
156. *S.P.D.* Vol. XXX, L.N. 362.
157. Rajwade, V.K., Khand II, p. 56.
158. *S.P.D.* Vol. XI, L.N. 2 : He was also addressed as Himmat Bahadur. (Rajwade, V.K., Khand VIII, L.N. 96).
159. Khare, W.W. - *Ichchalkaranji Sansthan Ch Itihas*, p. 36.
160. Kincaid, C.A. & Parasnis, D.B. - *History of the Maratha People*, Vol. II, p. 195.
161. *Ibid.*
162. Khare, W.W. - *Ichchalkaranji Sansthan Ch Itihas*, p. 39.
163. *Patre Yadi Vagere*, p. 9.
164. Khare, W.W. - *Ichchalkaranji Sansthan Ch Itihas*, p. 39. (The Pratinidhi took Rajasbai back to Panhalla).
165. Sardesai, G.S. - *New History of the Marathas*, Vol.II, p. 118.
166. Khare, W.W. - *Ichchalkaranji Sansthan Ch Itihas*, p. 39.
167. Sambhaji of Kolhapur visited Satara four times, on different occasions, during the life time of Shahu. — (*S.P.D.* Vol. XI, L.N. 19, 20, 21, 29, 31).
168. *S.P.D.* Vol. XI, L.N. 10.
169. *Patre Yadi Vagere*, L.Ns. 19, 20.
Shahu Roznishi, No. 175.
170. *S.P.D.* Vol. XI, L.Ns. 19, 20, 21, 29, 31: Sambhaji's visit to Satara on these occasions was to solve one or the other intricate problem.
171. *Itihas Sangraha*, Part 2 - Aitihasik Tippane, p. 34.
172. *S.P.D.* Vol. III, L.Ns. 182, 183.
Ibid., Vol. XIV, L.N. 1.
Ibid., Vol. XII, L.N. 46.
Irvine, W.W. - *Later Moghuls*, Vol. II, pp. 79, 278.
173. *S.P.D.* Vol. XV, L.N. 86, deals with various papers which show how the Peshwas Bajirao and Balaji Bajirao furthered the Maratha interests in expanding the Maratha kingdom.
174. *Nana Roznishi*, No.133.
175. *Shahu Roznishi*, No. 134.
176. Kincaid, C.A. & Parasnis, D.B. - *A History of the Maratha People*, Vol. II, p. 294.

177. Vaidya, C.V. - *Vaidya Daftar*, L.N.24, pp. 20, 21 (1748) Gupte, K. - Nangpurkar Bhonsle Yanchi Bakhar, pp. 30, 40 *Grant Gazetteer*, p. 304.
178. Grant Duff - *History of the Marathas*, Vol. I, p. 512.
Shyamaldas - *Vir-Vinod*, Marathon-Ki-Tawarikh (1594), no page No.
179. Sardesai, G.S. - *Historical Genealogies*, p. 119.
Ibid., - *New History of the Marathas*, Vol. II, p. 270.
180. B.I.S.M. - *Quarterly* (74), Varsh 19, Ank 2.
Shyamaldas - *Vir-Vinod*, Marathon-ki-Tawarkh (1595), no page No.
181. Riyasat - *Peshwa Balajirao*, p. 12, (Edn. 1953).
182. Rajwade, V.K., Khand VIII, L.N. 169 (p. 128) : "Why do you want to adopt a son when a boy belonging to Bhonsle family is alive?"
183. Khare, W.W. - *Ichchalkaranji Sansthan Ch Itihas*, p. 61.
184. B.I.S.M. - *Quarterly* (74), Varsh 19, Ank 2.
Riyasat - *Peshwa Balajirao*, p. 12.
185. Rajwade, V.K., Khand VIII, L.Ns. 170, 183.
186. *Patre Yadi Vagere*, p. 457 (27)
187. Rajwade, V.K., Khand VIII, L.N. 171.
188. *Itihas Sangraha* - Peshwa Daftar, L.N. 44.
189. Rajwade, V.K., Khand VIII, L.N. 184.
190. Khare, W.W. - *Ichchalkaranji Sansthan Ch Itihas*, p. 56.
191. Rajwade, V.K., Khand VIII, L.N. 184.
192. *Ibid.*, L.Ns. 169, 171.
193. *Itihas Sangraha* - Sphut Lekh, No. 5, p. 17.
194. Kincaid, C.A. & Parasnis, D.B. - *A History of the Maratha People*, Vol. II, p. 296.
195. *Ibid.*, p. 299.
196. *S.P.D.*, Vol.XL, L.N. 29.
197. Bawada Daftar, Vol. II, L.N. 186.
198. Bawada Daftar, Vol. II, L.N. 187.
199. Rajwade, V.K., Khand VIII, L.N. 170.
200. Riyasat, V, *Punya Shlok Shahu*, Peshwa Balajirao, p. 174.
201. Kincaid, C.A. & Parasnis, D.B. - *A History of the Maratha People*, Vol. II, p. 319 (Appendix III)
Rajwade, V.K., Khand VI, L.N. 198.
Ali Ibrahim Khan - Tarikh-i-Ibrahimkham, *H.I.H.*, Vol. VIII, p. 264.
202. Rajwade, V.K., Khand II, p. 111.
203. *P.D.*, Vol. I, L.N. 171.

204. Kincaid, C.A. & Parasnis, D.B. - *A History of the Maratha People*, Vol. II, p. 306.
205. *S.P.D.*, Vol.VI, L.N. 10.
206. *S.P.D.*, Vol.VI, L.N. 147.
207. Rajwade, V.K., Khand II, p. 113.
208. *S.P.D.*, Vol.VI, L.N. 20.
209. *S.P.D.*, Vol.VI, L.N. 73.
210. *Ibid.*
211. *Ibid.*
212. *S.P.D.*, Vol.VI, L.N. 76.
213. *Bombay Gazetteer*, Vol. I, Part II, p. 601.
214. *S.P.D.*, Vol.VI, L.N. 93.
215. *P.D.*, Vol.I, L.N. 234.
216. Rajwade, V.K., Khand II, p. 111.
217. Riyasat - *Peshwa Balajirao*, p. 27 (1953)
218. Rajwade, V.K., Khand II, p. 55.
219. Riyasat - *Peshwa Balajirao*, p. 30 (1953)
220. Sardesai, G.S. - *New History of the Marathas*, Vol.II, p. 291.
221. *S.P.D.*, Vol.VI, L.N. 79.
222. *Ibid.*
223. Rajwade, V.K., Khand II, pp. 115, 116 : Sangola was given in charge of Ranoji Mohite and Mangalvede was kept by the Peshwa himself. Gujarat, which had been given to Dabhade, was now divided between Gaekwad and the Peshwa. The Peshwa got the territory of Karnatak for himself on the promise of payments of subsidy to the royal treasury.
224. Sinha, H.N. - *Rise of the Peshwas*, p. 242.
225. *S.P.D.*, Vol.VI, L.N. 87.
226. *Ibid.*, L.N. 91.
227. *Ibid.* L.Ns. 57, 64.
228. *Balaji Bajirao Roznishi*, Vol.I, No. 43.
229. Khare, W.W. - *Ichchalkaranji Sansthan Ch Itihas*, p. 69.
230. Sinha, H.N. - *Rise of the Peshwas*, p. 242.
231. *Aitihasik Patra-Vyawahar*, L.N. 87.
232. Riyasat-*Peshwa Balajirao*, p. 30 (1953)
233. Kincaid, C.A. & Parasnis, D.B. - *A History of the Maratha People*, Vol. II, p. 315.
234. *P.D.*, Vol.I, L.N. 244.
235. Sardesai, G.S. - *Historical Genealogies*, Vol.II, p. 294.

236. *P.D.*, Vol.I, L.N. 242.
237. *S.P.D.*, Vol.VI, L.N. 152 : Burhanji Mohite also pleaded with her that she should do away with all of them as they had greatly suffered in prestige. But Tarabai was as firm as could be and thus lost their co-operation.
238. Kincaid, C.A. & Parasnis, D.B. - A History of the Maratha People, Vol. III, p. 7.
239. *S.P.D.*, Vol.VI, L.N. 13.
240. *P.D.*, Vol.I, L.N. 245.
241. *Ibid.*, L.N. 243 (A).
242. *Ibid.*, L.N. 243.
243. *Ibid.*, L.N. 244.
244. *Ibid.*, L.N. 251.
245. *Ibid.*, L.N. 274.
246. *Ibid.*, L.N. 253.
247. *Ibid.*, L.N. 259.
248. *Ibid.*, L.N. 260.
249. *Ibid.*, L.N. 266.
250. *Ibid.*, L.N. 253.
251. *Ibid.*, L.N. 264.
252. *Ibid.*, L.N. 260 : It was written on 23rd December, 1750 A.D. Ramraja was imprisoned on 22nd November, 1750 A.D. Hence, it can be said that he was not yet released by Tarabai.
253. *Ibid.*, L.N. 256; and 268.
    S.P.D., Vol.VI, L.N. 131.
254. *P.D*, Vol. I, L.N. 268.
255. *Ibid.*, L.N. 255.
256. *S.P.D.*, Vol.VI, L.N. 138; *P.D.*, Vol.I, L.N. 245.
257. *P.D.*, Vol. I, L.N. 255.
258. *Ibid.*, L.N. 270.
259. *Ibid.*, L.N. 271.
260. *Ibid.*, L.N. 296.
261. *Patre Yadi Vagere*, L.N. 71.
262. Sinha, H.N. - *Rise of the Peshwas*, p. 248.
263. *S.P.D.*, Vol.VI, L.N. 153 : This is a very important letter which gives an idea of the steps taken by the Peshwa to let Sambhaji remain aloof from Satara. Anandrao, the agent of the Peshwa, was quite aware of the talks that went on between Sambhaji and the agent sent by Tarabai which he communicated to the Peshwa. The letter

provides an interesting piece of information that Sambhaji wanted Ramraja to be killed first and then only he would proceed to Satara. But Tarabai said, "(You) come to Satara; I give you the throne". She insisted that Sambhaji should reach Satara first, to which the latter disagreed. Anandrao further informed the Peshwa, "Tarabai is trying to deceive Sambhaji by promises". He further adds, "There are still eight days when he would go" and that Sambhaji was also thinking that if the Peshwa was on his side, he had nothing to do with others (including Tarabai). The agent also said "Sambhaji is wavering between the two ideas". In the end, he warns the Peshwa, "The diplomatic steps you have taken to keep Sambhaji with us will be totally unsuccessful if he goes over to Tarabai," and suggests that if four or five thousand of army were kept round about Kolhapur, they (the Peshwa and his followers) would leave the politics of Satara". The agent concludes by saying, "I have no messenger to send you secret".

The above letter indicates that Tarabai had made all efforts for Sambhaji to come to Satara.

264. Kincaid, C.A. & Parasnis, D.B. - *A History of the Maratha People*, Vol. III, p. 3.
265. *Baroda State Records*, Vol.1, L.N. 40.
Rajwade, V.K., Khand VI, p. 55.
266. *S.P.D.*, Vol.VI, L.N. 173.
267. *Ibid.*, L.N. 154.
268. *Ibid.*, L.N. 163.
269. *Ibid.*, L.N. 166.
270. *Ibid.*
271. Rajwade, V.K., Khand VI, pp. 220, 221
272. *Baroda State Records*, Vol.1, L.N. 40.
Rajwade, V.K., Khand VI, p. 55.
273. *Bombay Gazetteer*, Vol. I, Part II, p. 601.
Kincaid, C.A. & Parasnis, D.B. - *A History of the Maratha People*, Vol. III, p. 3.
274. *Baroda State Records*, Vol.1, L.N. 40.
Rajwade, V.K., Khand VI, p. 55.
275. *Ibid.*
276. *Ibid.*
Kincaid, C.A. & Parasnis, D.B. - *A History of the Maratha People*, Vol. III, p. 6.
277. *S.P.D.*, Vol.VI, L.N. 200, pp. 70 71, 73 : The letter, written on 6.5.1751

A.D., is the answer to Tarabai after her defeat on 30th April, 1751 A.D. The purport was again communicated to the Peshwa by Anand Girdhar. The discussion in the letter and its conclusions give an idea of the desperate stand taken by Tarabai : if not Ramraja, then Sambhaji, "the own blood", but no one else. It is difficult to say whether she would have gone to the extent of killing Ramraja, as desired and proposed by Sambhaji; but the fact remains that she did not act as per Sambhaji's proposal for full three months (the first talk about it is found in L.N. 153, S.P.D. Vol. VI). Perhaps she apprehended that Sambhaji might not come, while Sambhaji was afraid of both Tarabai and the Peshwa. He was also worried to know that the Peshwa had brought a boy to be enthroned as king. Who that boy was and from where he had come is not yet known; but Sambhaji, on verification, found the information reliable and came to know that the boy was residing at Avaji Kavdey's house and was twenty-two years old. Sambhaji was sure that since that boy was called, the Peshwa never invited him to Satara. This made Sambhaji indifferent to Satara politics. He even remarked, "The Peshwa really wishes to keep these two kingdoms separate with the idea that they should not unite".

278. *Patre Yadi Vagere*, L.N. 81 (1751 May)
279. *S.P.D.*, Vol.VI, L.N. 202.
280. Kincaid, C.A. & Parasnis, D.B. - *A History of the Maratha People*, Vol. III, p. 9.
281. *Ibid.*
282. Riyasat, *Peshwa Balaji Rao*, p. 49.
283. *Ibid.*, p. 51.
     Rajwade, V.K., Khand VI, p. 500.
284. *Itihas Sangraha* - Part VII, Article 8, p. 7 : The article includes questions raised by Tarabai and answered by the Peshwa.
285. *Patre Yadi Vagere*, L.Ns. 114, 101.
286. Rajwade, V.K., Khand VI, LN. 234.
287. *Ibid.*, L.N. 237.
288. *Ibid.*, L.N. 276.
289. Rajwade, V.K., Khand VI, LN. 257.
290. *Itihas Sangraha* - Part VII, Article 8, p. 7.
     Rajwade, V.K., Khand VI, LN. 276, Nos. 1, 2, 4 to 10.

CHAPTER 5

SAKWARBAI

Clash of Ambitions (1740-1749)

Despite the house of Jijabai now being divided[1] into two – Satara and Kolhapur — the women of both the houses carried forward the initiative taken by Jijabai to play an active role in the affairs of the States. Whereas, Shahu had established himself at Satara, Sambhaji-II had also done the same at Kolhapur. Sometimes they worked in unison but for most of the time they maintained there separate identities which often harmed the general interest of the Marathas.

Tarabai, the commendable shining sword of Maratha struggle for survival against Aurangzeb, her determined opposition against the return of Shahu from the Moghul Camp to the Deccan as the successor of Shivaji had brought forth severe cleavage in Maratha politics. During these critical days for Shahu three women namely, Sakwarbai, Sagunabai and Virubai[2] played a memorable role in Maratha politics as protector of the personal and family interest of Shahu and for this purpose were even indulging in the affairs of the State.

Shahu on arrival in the Deccan had entered into matrimonial alliances[3] with two women - Sakwarbai and Sagunabai from prominent families of Maratha Sardars. Sakwarbai was the daughter of Ramoji Shirkey. Sagunabai hailed from Mohite family. Though Tarabai declared Shahu imposter yet these marriages tell of a different story as Shahu could win over the support of other Sardars, so essential at the time.

In spite of these marriages, Shahu had the unflinching devotion of "Dassi" Virubai[4] who had followed Shahu from the north towards

Deccan and had participated in the trials and tribulations Shahu had to face to be accepted Chhatrapati of the Marathas and the Maratha State. Besides, she had been able to gain full confidence of Sakwarbai and Sagunabai to such an extent that Virubai continued to have pull over Shahu and the Queens in the most respectful approaches.

Accounts show that her behaviour in the palace as well as in the Maratha Darbar brought her regard and respect from those who came in her contact. Virubai accompanied Shahu on important missions and also took part in various activities of the State. This is apparent from the letter of British Agent, Captain Gordon of Bombay. He stated[5], "As we could not see Virubai, a woman of consequence, we sent her letters and presents. She gave a civil profession in return." Though the purpose of the letter and the date of the incident could not be traced out, in the absence of any definite information on this point, yet it shows that she enjoyed respect and regard in foreign camp also.

On another occasion, Virubai came to the rescue[6] of Balaji Vishwanath from the most adverse circumstances. As known Balaji Vishwanath had taken shelter[7] in Pandavgarh to save himself from the wrath of the Senapati Chandrasen Jadhav. He sent[8] Ambaji Purandare to Shahu's Court to inform the king about the event. Ambaji Purandare related the incident to Chitnis Govindrao. Chitnis was quite sympathetic towards Balaji Vishwanath, but he showed his inability to help him. However, he advised Ambaji Purandare to convey the news of the event to Virubai. It should be remembered that Balaji Vishwanath had still to prove his capacity and superiority as compared to Chandrasen Jadhav. Kincaid and Parasnis state[9] that Virubai heard the details and brought them to the notice of the king. She also sought the support of Sagunabai. Shahu sent a section of his army to relieve[10] Balaji Vishwanath from the pressure of Senapati's army. He also asked the Senapati to present himself in the court. Thus, Virubai served the cause of Balaji Vishwanath and won over a willing and strong supporter to Shahu as well.

Besides, she was also interested in the activities concerned with the palace and Shahu's welfare. Her letters[11] to Brahmendraswami indicate amply her field of work. Meanwhile, different accounts show that Shahu's queens, Sakwarbai and Sagunabai, were interested in their own spheres of work. They had their income derived from Watans, certain privileges and trade carried on in a few ports of Kolaba districts (Khadi of Kundalika), as the queens had received the Sanad[12] from the king to carry on the trade in a few ports of westen coast, specially Ashtami and Roha. The trade was to be carried free of taxes. From these ports, commodities like fish, salt, rice, spices and coconuts were transported to other places. Sometimes, disturbances[13] occurred in these places due to a few interested persons and the queens were requested to check the activities of such persons.

Sakwarbai and Sagunabai had their own palaces to reside in, known as Darunimahal and Dhaktamahal. Sakwarbai resided in "Darunimahal" and Sagunabai in "Dhaktamahal". Both the queens had their separate establishments and their Chitnises to manage their affairs in their respective spheres. Besides, different accounts show that the queens kept themselves well acquainted with the events taking place in the kingdom, specially on the west coast. This is apparent from their correspondence and communications to Brahmendraswami[14] till 1746 A.D., i.e., till he lived and after him Narayanbaba.[15] They were also in communication with other Sardars from time to time. But Brahmendraswami happened to have enjoyed an enviable position among the Maratha Sardars. He had influence in the foreign camps also, such as the English, the Portuguese and Siddis of Janjira, for nearly half a century.

Originally, Brahmendraswami lived[16] at Chiploon, near the temple of Parashuram. Siddis of Janjira committed cruelties on the people on western coast. Siddi Sat desecrated the temple as early as 1727 A.D. As such, he (Brahmendraswami) moved away from there. Shahu offered him a suitable place at Dhawadshi near Satara. Here he lived for the rest of his life. Being near to

Satara, Shahu's queens, Sakwarbai, Sagunabai and Virubai, appeared to have come in his contact. They regarded him for his spiritual powers. Besides, Balaji Vishwanath, Bajirao and Balaji Bajirao, Radhabai, Kashibai, Umabai Dabhade, wife of Senapati Khanderao Dabhade of Gujarat, and others had great respect for him. They sought his advice on personal as well as political affairs. This is indicated by their communication to Brahmendraswami from time to time.

During 1733 A.D., Siddis of Janjira carried on hostile activities[17] against the Maratha king. Shahu was ill disposed towards them. He wanted to take back the old capital, Raigad[18], as well as the ports of Anjanvel and Govalkot along with other forts which belonged to Shivaji (Swarajya). He also wanted to punish the Siddis as they had destroyed[19] the temples. It is needless to say that the queens were also interested in western ports.

Bajirao marched[20] towards Janjira in 1733 A.D. He took many places, destroyed the Siddis navy in the creek of Rajapur. But he could not take the ports of Anjanvel and Govalkot. He wrote[21] to Shahu about the shortage of funds and asked him for monetary help. He also informed him that the Siddis were getting help from Surat[22] and Bombay. He was also awaiting the arrival of the Pratinidhi. At the same time, Shahu was annoyed, as he had received conflicting news about the campaigns.

Meanwhile, Sakwarbai asked[23] Brahmendraswami to see that the English did not help the Siddis. Further, the purport of her letter suggests that she hoped much more from him. She desired that the English and the Marathas should have friendly terms. She also warned him not to proceed to Bombay personally but to get the work done through any other agency.

As known, Shahu had no issues. The problem of an heir apparent to Satara throne worried him and the queens also. Sakwarbai and Sagunabai believed[24] that they would have issues through the blessings of the "Swami". Both of them wrote to him for the same.

At the same time, Brahmendraswami demanded money, other commodities and even villages from the queens. On the occasion, Sakwarbai wrote[25] to him, "Received your letters. You required us to donate one village to meet the expenses of the palanquin. You wanted the village of Pongare, but the village cannot be donated to you because of some political reasons." However, she promised that he would be given some other village.

Similarly, Virubai also communicated[26] to him that, as Bajirao was away on the pre-arranged visit to Nizam-ul-Mulk, nothing could be considered regarding the donation of the villages. She assured him that something worthwhile might be done when Bajirao returned. It is not known whether the villages asked for were the same as the Swami had asked for from Sakwarbai previously.

As mentioned, the queens were interested in taking the ports of Anjanvel and Govalkot. Brahmendraswami assured them that they would be able to have them. He again demanded certain villages and other facilities from them. He "gave high hopes that the king would be able to take the same at an opportune time[27]". But, he added, "I order you to donate the village of Dhamni and Songoan to us; if you do that, the king would be able to capture the sea ports Anjanvel.... .Give us one more village near Ambad where I shall keep my cattle." The letter is not dated; yet it suggests the influence that Brahmendraswami commanded over the queens.

It is also indicated by different accounts that the king had not been able to take Anjanvel and Govalkot. Meanwhile, the "Swami" had not received the demanded villages or other consideration and he wrote to Sakwarbai to return the four thousand rupees to him which he had given earlier to the queens. He again pressed[28] his demands and asked her to get the "Sanads" issued to him by the king for Dhamani, Songaon and Dhalevali. He gave out that if the above demands were not accepted, she should break off all relations with him. At the same time, he had complained that the king had not given any attention to his requests.

Meanwhile, Sekhoji Angre, the admiral of the Maratha navy, died[29] in 1734 A.D. This gave rise to dispute among his three sons, Manaji, Sambhaji and Tulaji, for the admirality of the Maratha navy (Sarkhelship). As known, Shahu and his queens were interested to have Anjanvel and Govalkot. The king laid the condition that whosoever would take the above ports would be honoured with the position of the Sarkhel. Among them, Manaji Angre was more pliant to the Peshwa and could evoke his support. Hence a dispute arose between[30] Manaji and Sambhaji Angre. Sambhaji Angre attacked the forts of Kolaba and Hirakot and other places. But he suffered serious reverses. He had to retreat. Meanwhile, Siddis of Janjira attacked Manaji Angre at Bankot and Govalkot. Manaji Angre faced the Siddis, but could not hold for long against them. Shahu sent Chimnajee Appa against the Siddis of Janjira. A bloody action took place between them at Chiraikamarley[31]. Siddi-Sat fell dead on the battlefield on 19th April, 1736 A.D., with his brave officers, 1300 soldiers and Siddi Yakut who was defending the fort. Shahu and other Sardars rejoiced[32] the victory of Chimnajee Appa over Siddi Sat.

The queens, Sakwarbai and Sagunabai, must have felt elated over the recent victory of the Peshwa. They were also interested in the events taking place on the western coast, because it also concerned the trade they carried on there. But the happiness in the palace could not last long. Virubai, who looked after the affairs[33] of the palace and who was greatly devoted[34] to Shahu, fell ill and died[35] on 24th December, 1740 A.D.

Her death was terribly felt by Shahu and the other inmates of the palace. Sardesai writes[36], "Shahu's household was long satisfactorily controlled by his illegitimate wife, Virubai, a capable woman who most carefully and lovingly looked after the personal comforts of the king and who exercised a healthy control over the queens. She died on 24th December, 1740 A.D. That her death, though a personal loss to Shahu, had affected the palace and thereby the State was evident in due course of time." After her death, Shahu found it very difficult to bring about "the balance[37] in the uncompromising attitude of the interested individuals". Yet another problem was that of Tarabai and the moves of a few interested parties such as Raghuji Bhonsle, Angre brothers and Ghorpades.

The occupation of Anjanvel and Govalkot was postponed for certain time. But the attention of the Peshwa was drawn towards their capture in 1745 A.D. By this time, Sambhaji Angre was also dead. Appaji Angre and Tulaji Angre aspired for the position of Sarkhelship of the Maratha navy.

Brahmendraswami appears to have written to Sakwarbai that the position should be given to Appaji Angre. In reply[38], Sakwarbai asked him not to worry on that account because the position had already been given to Tulaji. As for the donation of the villages, she said that the same would be given to him according to the promise of the king. She wrote to him that the four thousand rupees which he demanded would be returned.[39] She advised him to take the help of the English, the Portuguese and the Sawant of Wadi. It should be borne in mind that Brahmendraswami had written that they were ready to help him. She further added,[40] "Get their help if you can and let us have Govalkot and Anjanvel in our possession. Let them send their ambassador to us. The king will see them." She added, "These are political matters and the ladies should not trouble themselves by thinking over such affairs. Why not directly write to Shahu and discuss the matter?" But she entreated that the English should not help the Siddis of Janjira because Tulaji Angre had proceeded to take Anjanvel and Govalkot in 1745 A.D.

Tulaji Angre captured[41] the above forts after a hard and keenly contested struggle on 25th January, 1745 A.D. Siddis lost 200 of their soldiers. Sakwarbai sent the good news[42] to Brahmendraswami. He again demanded the villages of Ghargoan and Ropala. Sakwarbai refused[43] to donate the villages to him, particularly Ropala as it was already given to Jamrao Nimbalkar by the Nizam-ul-Mulk.

Thus, the above accounts and incidents show that the queens were interested in capturing the ports on the western coast; but were careful to see that the donations of villages, etc., would not bring in political disturbance or give rise to other difficulties. This is indicated by the fact that the queens had the courage to refuse even the demands of Brahmendraswami even though they had great regard and reverence for him. They tried to pacify him by donations of such villages as would not create any sort of problem or difficult situation to handle.

Besides, it is shown in different accounts that the financial position of the State was not satisfactory. The letter of the Peshwa to Ramchandrababa reveals[44] the deplorable financial condition of the State. The king also demanded any amount of money. This was difficult to procure. Shahu felt dejected if he did not receive the demanded amount from the Peshwa. The shortage of money was all the more felt in the palace. The Peshwa felt that the king's demand of money should be fulfilled, so that he remained satisfied[45].

Shahu was ill. His queens often disagreed between themselves, at least once a day, for one or another cause. Shahu felt disgusted. He neglected his health. The creditors pressed for money. He realised that if it was not paid, it would certainly harm his reputation and prestige in case they demanded to settle their accounts in a day or two. Further, he apprehended[46] "Dharna". He said that he had become a bankrupt. The queens were held responsible for the situation. It became more embarrassing when the bankers and creditors stopped advancing loans to the king. The impact of the then existing financial condition was felt in the palace severely. Accounts show that the queens were annoyed which often ended in quarrels which aggravated the situation all the more. Sagunabai tried to pacify[47] the king with the help of Govindrao Chitnis and Yashwantrao in whom she had confidence, but Sakwarbai was disgruntled.

It appears that because of the stringency of money, the queens had begun to draw money from wherever they could, more for their maintenance and probably for other purposes as no woman would tolerate seeing people sitting in 'dharna' before the house. Perhaps to meet the demands of the queen, Shahu gave[48] the Saranjam of Khandesh and Baglan to Sagunabai with an inam of ten to fifteen thousand of rupees. He also granted her the right to collect the Sardeshmukhi of that region.

Further, it is apparent that the queens also took advice of such persons as they thought fit to save the situation from further deterioration. This could easily lead to an assumption that the queens were acting as their confidants advised them. As is likely to happen in such situations, the Sardars and the confidants tried to exploit the opportunity to benefit themselves from the queens whom they advised. This also led to frequent quarrels and disagreements among the Sardars and between the queens. Shahu was disgruntled. He remarked that the queens would starve[49] him to death, which suggests a very abnormal and incredible phenomenon. However, it is obvious that the king was utterly disgusted with the then existing condition. As his prestige had suffered to an extent, the queens could not be allowed to continue the practice.

Shahu asked the Peshwa to arbitrate in their disputes and let them come to an understanding[50]. Accordingly, the Peshwa tried to secure their mutual understanding. He chalked out a document[51] according to which he asked the queens to abstain themselves from interferring in the State affairs.

The queens agreed to abide by the terms of the agreement. This indicates that they were ready to give up the adopted practice and thus cease to appropriate all that they had confiscated. Thus, it can be said that the queens did not indulge in such practice for pleasure, nor were they fascinated to hoard or to waste.

Further, the agreement reveals the economic tension and chaos that prevailed in the palace and the State at the time. Though the charges in the agreement have not been substantiated by facts or figures to enable one to deduce how far the queens were responsible for the financial stringency existing in the State, yet it is difficult to absolve them from all responsibility for the then existing state of financial affairs.

Beside the activities of the queens, there were other factors which were responsible for the financial muddle resulting into failure of exchequer and the subsequent results at Satara during Shahu's reign.

It is known that Shahu came to south without money. Prior to this, the Maratha State had undergone a long term[52] of war since 1680 A.D. Balaji Vishwanath and Bajirao had to proceed on to different campaigns. These campaigns resulted[53] into heavy military expenditure and other expenses. Therefore, the stringency[54] of money was all the more felt during Bajirao's last days. This is apparent from the fact that he was greatly in debt and had to remain on battlefields for most of the time.

The next Peshwa, Balaji Bajirao, had to face a worse situation from 1740 A.D. As known, his appointment as the Peshwa was a preference given to him by the king. Senior Sardars[55] aspired for the position because of their long and sincere services. They were disgruntled and were indifferent. This is indicated by different accounts. In due course of time, differences and lack of co-operation was visible among the responsible Sardars and the ministers. One of the aspirants to the position was Babuji[56] Naik. He had extended large sums of money to Bajirao. He asked Balaji to return the money. It was a difficult problem for Balaji. However, he managed to pay back the sum with the help of Mahadji Purandare. Later on he manoeuvred to oust him from Poona. Shahu arranged[57] for his stay at Baramati. He also gave him a Sanad[58] and the province of Karnatak.

The Maratha kingdom extended far and wide. Still Balaji followed[59] the policy, "War paid for by war," as was being done[60] by Shivaji. This policy was useful during the times of Shivaji but seemed hardly so now. Moreover, the annexation of any new territory or fort only increased the maintenance expenditure. The Peshwa had to depend on the Sardars and other officials to collect the revenue. How far they were scrupulous in the discharge of their duty is not difficult to imagine. Not to quote others, only the letters of Vaidya brothers, the bankers and agents of Raghuji Bhonsle of Nagpur at Satara, indicate[61] that even the Sardars and the State officials were not returning the money they had borrowed from them (Vaidya brothers). Most of the time, they had to write directly[62] to the Mokaddams and the Patils for the respective payments. Sakwarbai was quite intimate[63] with Vaidya brothers. Often money transactions were completed through her.

Different accounts show that the majority of the Sardars usually utilised the revenue themselves or only sent a part of it to the king as was being done by the Dabhades of Gujarat. As such, the State suffered heavily.

There is no account to show that the Sardars ever denied their respective debts, which shows that they themselves were in a desperate situation and that they could not realize the same from their respective spheres. Besides, there is nothing to show that they had been able to pursue a planned revenue policy. The Marathas continued to believe in raids and a sort of conquests. Further, the expansionists[64] policy of Bajirao was continued by Balaji Bajirao. Among the many expeditions, only the northern campaigns numbered four. These were also potent factors responsible for the approaching bankruptcy in the Maratha State.

Moreover, the Sardars were interested in their own affairs. This is obvious by their attempt to get the support of the queens and thus meet their ends with their help. One such instance occurred when the Peshwa had taken the fort of Bahirogad which belonged[65] to Manaji Angre. Manaji Angre wanted to take the fort back and therefore had come to see the king. Shahu and Sagunabai wanted to give the fort to Manaji Angre; but the Peshwa wrote[66] to Ramchandrapant, "If I accede to it, the elder queen asks to give Payagad to Bande." Under the circumstances,

Manaji Angre could not receive Bahirogad as the king did not want to give Payagad to Bande.

The above difficulties were yet not solved when there cropped[67] up another complex problem of accession to the Satara throne by 1745 A.D. As mentioned[68], Sakwarbai had not agreed to the succession of Mudhoji Bhonsle, son of Raghuji Bhonsle. No account is available to show that Shahu approved the succession of Mudhoji Bhonsle. However, Sagunabai's letter[69] to Raghuji Bhonsle appeared to have constituted a good cause to the Sardars to assume Shahu's approval of Mudhoji Bhonsle's probable[70] succession to the Satara throne.

Besides, Raghuji Bhonsle was keeping himself closely interested in the affairs of Satara. As such, there were some possibilities of Mudhoji Bhonsle being placed on the Satara throne, firstly, because Raghuji Bhonsle had kept himself associated with the affairs of Satara, and, secondly, because there existed now cordial relations between the Peshwa and Raghuji Bhonsle, as Shahu had marked[71] the jurisdiction of both of them as early as 1743 A.D.

At the same time, the Peshwa's visit towards Karnatak from Vaduth was not liked by Sakwarbai. She wrote[72] a letter to the Peshwa and asked to return immediately and to finish the incomplete task of the "Wadas" (queens' residences) and the Jadhavas. She added[73] that he should have obtained the permission of the king before he marched towards Karnatak. This shows that she was annoyed. But she left the matter to be decided by the king.

The financial condition of the State had not yet improved in spite of the agreement of the queens. Shahu got alarmed at the intolerable situation regarding the financial position of the State. He ousted[74] the Peshwa, for which Sakwarbai has again been held responsible.

It is alleged that Sakwarbai manoeuvred[75] the Peshwa's dismissal. According to this allegation, "Let the king turn Balaji out of his office," whispered the insiduous queen, "and confiscate his property and the royal treasury will be filled to overflowing." Sardesai writes[76], "The Peshwa's opponents poured into the king's ear all sort of bitter complaints against the Peshwa and attributed mischievous motives to him." The sweeping assertions made by above writers needs to be examined.

Sakwarbai and Sagunabai were interested in the different affairs of the State. This is apparent from their communications to Brahmendraswami and other Sardars from time to time. They also drew the king's attention to the events in the palace and the State. However, this was not an unusual routine, with which the queens were acquainted. But Sakwarbai's letters to Brahmendraswami and the Peshwa also reveal that she was not always very anxious to probe into the matters bearing political importance. At times, she had written to Brahmendraswami to deal[77] directly with the king instead of writing to her. She had also asked[78] the Peshwa to take previous sanction of the king before he moved towards Karnatak. The king had not given[79] the fort of Payagad to Bande as she had desired. Therefore, it is difficult to say definitely how far Shahu was influenced by her in ousting the Peshwa. Further, the accounts show that he had again and again asked the Peshwa to improve the financial condition of the State. The desired improvement had remained unachieved.

Besides, it is obvious that the king had to take the unavoidable step to oust the Peshwa after sustained consideration and with much inconvenience to himself. Shahu had to choose the said course of action, as it was for the sovereign to decide and act. Hence it is doubtful that Sakwarbai could have influenced the king to the extent of getting the Peshwa ousted.

The Peshwa took[80] the dismissal order in February, 1747 A.D. calmly. Shahu did not appoint anyone as Peshwa. However, the king desired[81] Raghuji Bhonsle, Rayaji and Santaji to reach Satara immediately; but they did not reach there. It is said that the king wanted that Raghuji Bhonsle should take up the

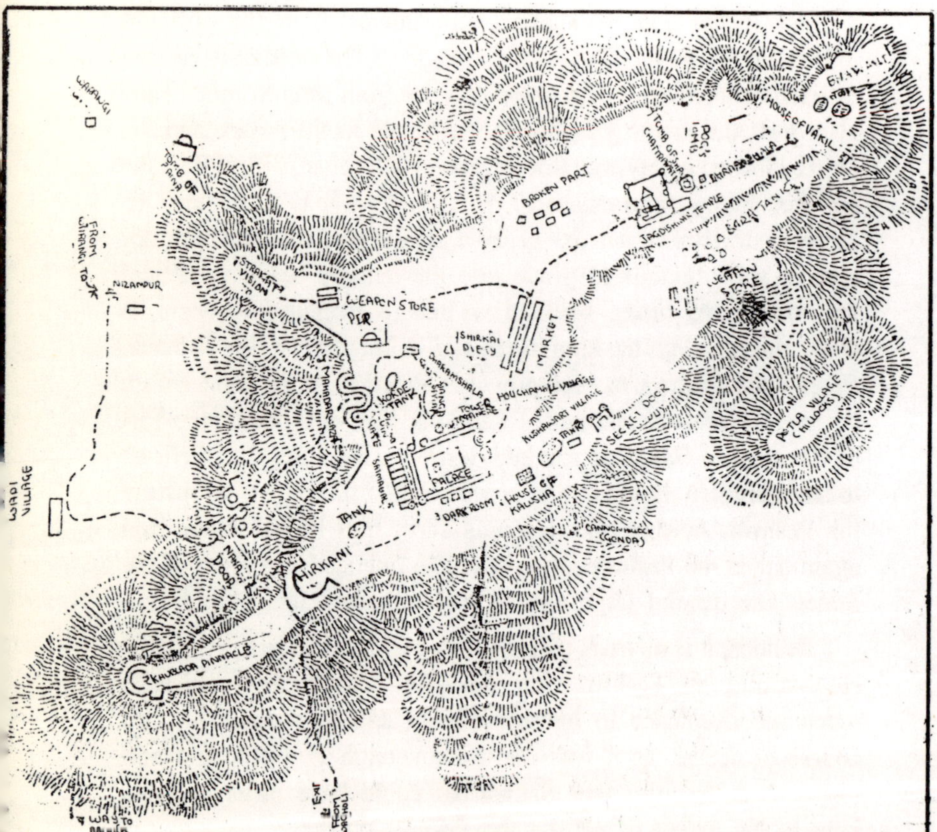

Raigarh Fort (Conceptual Thinking)

responsibility of managing the State affairs. Sardesai mentions[82] that the Peshwa had entered into a "secret understanding" with Raghuji Bhonsle. Possibly, Raghuji Bhonsle did not like to offend the Peshwa or to take up the difficult responsibility. Another candidate, who had once aspired to be the Peshwa, was Babuji Naik. Shahu was not well disposed towards him, because of his defeat at Trichinopally at the hands of Nizam-ul-Mulk in 1743 A.D.

Meanwhile, the Nizam-ul-Mulk and the Angre started fresh troubles in Konkan. Jijabai II, the queen of Sambhaji II of Kolhapur, had invited Morarrao Ghorpade. They had planned[83] an attack on Shahu's territory to take revenge of Sadashivraobhau's intervention in Karnatak. The Peshwa waited for some time, but could not remain unconcerned for long. He communicated to the king, and clarified his position that he had already settled the demands of the queens through Chitnis Govindrao. He said that he did not hope that the queens would put forth new claims. As regards the personal debt of the king, he was prepared to pay[84] back the amount to the creditors, if he was once allowed to march on an expedition. He added[85], "To say that I should first pay off the debt and then move from here, is an impossible proposition beyond my power to execute. I would at least require a couple of months to move about and arrange the matter." He also promised to give up his encroaching[86] activities at Karnatak.

The Peshwa also communicated to the king that the Nizam-ul-Mulk had proceeded towards Karnatak and had opposed Sadashivbhau's army there. He advised the king that Pilaji Jadhav should immediately be sent with an army towards Karnatak. He also requested Shahu to let him leave the place and promised to act as the king desired after his return. Shahu was also anxious due to recent developments. He reinstated[87] Balaji Bajirao as the Peshwa on 6th April, 1747 A.D. Later events show that the king's authority had begun to decline for all practical purposes.

The king had reinstated the Peshwa, but it appears that he

was not[88] satisfied with him as his debts were not yet paid. Yashwantrao Potnis and Chitnis Govindrao approached queen Sagunabai to pacify the king to favour Balaji. The king blamed Chitnis Govindrao for the trouble regarding the debts. Sagunabai agreed to pacify the king on the condition that Balaji would pay off the king's debts. But when Sagunabai approached the king, he was annoyed.[89] Meanwhile, the Peshwa had taken the fort of Manikgad which belonged to Manaji Angre. Sagunabai did not like that the Peshwa should harass him. She desired that he should deliver the fort to Manaji Angre. The Peshwa did not do so for nearly an year.[90]

Further, the accounts show that the queens were not satisfied[91] with the Peshwa. The Peshwa did not like that the queens should be familiar with Sardars, specially Raghuji Bhonsle. Sagunabai was also annoyed with the Peshwa. The Peshwa was also aware of it. He approached Narayanbaba to mediate between them and thus to bring in favourable atmosphere for him.

Narayanbaba was a saint. He lived at Yavateshwar hill. Sagunabai was his devotees. As such, it was possible for the Peshwa to be acquainted with the events taking place in the palace and the State. This is indicated by the two letters[92] of Nana Purandare to the Peshwa. The Peshwa was quick to understand the situation. He sent a letter[93] to Sagunabai through Mahadji Salokhi. She was in no mood to receive it because of the condition that prevailed at Nimbgaon. She did not take the letter and asked the Chitnis to return it to the Peshwa. However, the Chitnis did not take it from her. The queen had sadly expressed, "I am very angry with the Peshwa because, though he is known to be on cordial terms with me, he creates trouble to my people and drives them out probably from Nimbgaon."

The reaction of Sagunabai was soon visible. Narayanbaba communicated[94] to her, regretting that she (Sagunabai) was giving ear to the gossips about the Peshwa just like the elder queen Sakwarbai. However, he desired that Sagunabai should write a consolatory letter to the Peshwa, otherwise there was no use of her being a devotee to him. He awaited the reply from her to be sent to the Peshwa's messenger. This also indicates that the queens were not satisfied with the activities of the Peshwa. At the same time, Sagunabai fell[95] ill. After some time, her condition was serious. Purandare communicated the news to the Peshwa. Further he added that, according to the physicians, the malady was not[96] curable.

Shahu had no time or energy to look after the other affairs of the State. He took Sagunabai to Jejuri,[97] more for divine blessings than for treatment. He became more indifferent to the affairs taking place at Satara or in the kingdom. Sakwarbai continued to live in the palace but visited the king often. Shahu visited the palace only once when Sakwarbai's father visited Satara.

In spite of all the care and treatment, Sagunabai died[98] on 25th August, 1748 A.D. at Jejuri. Shahu returned[99] at Mahuli. He was afflicted mentally and physically. He came to Satara. Soon he developed peevish nature. As mentioned, the king had given assent to the succession of Ramraja. This was still not favoured by Sakwarbai. She doubted the validity of the statement of Tarabai regarding Ramraja's birth. Further, she declared that the whole affair was a hoax, concocted[100] by the wicked Tarabai in order to satisfy her vanity and ambition to secure power in her own hands.

It is also said that she had written[101] to Sambhaji of Kolhapur to adopt Mudhoji Bhonsle and claim the whole of the Maratha kingdom to himself and his adopted son. Thus, he would be able to save the Maratha kingdom from being given to other. How far the above statement is authentic cannot be said in absence of more reliable evidence. However, Sambhaji visited[102] Satara and stayed there for six months, might be on some business. This provided an opportunity[103] to others to think him the prospective rival to the Maratha throne. Moreover, the letter[104] of queen

Jijabai II to the Peshwa shows that there was possibility of Sambhaji's accession to the Satara throne which could not be materialised as the king did not favour his accession.

The king had approved[105] of the claim of Ramraja to succeed him after his death. As known, this was not liked by Sakwarbai. She apprehended further trouble. She relied[106] more on Pratinidhi Jagjiwan, Mutalik Yamaji Shivdev and a few others. It is said that she contemplated to murder the Peshwa, which needs to be examined.

Kincaid and Parasnis write[107], "She meditated the murder of the Peshwa. She entrusted the task to her confidant agent Yamaji Shivdev and for a moment Peshwa's life was in danger." However, the facts are that Yamaji Shivdev plotted to kill Govindrao Chitnis instead of Peshwa, for which the reasons have not been mentioned, nor known. It is also to be borne in mind that Sakwarbai had no reason to be dissatisfied with the Chitnis. No account mentions that Sakwarbai showed any concern when the plot failed. Besides, there is no evidence to show that Sakwarbai closely confided in him. Further, the allegation has not been supported by any other piece of reliable account. Hence it is very difficult to associate Sakwarbai with Yamaji Shivdev in his plot. But it is certain that her name in the heinous act provided a very good cause to those who wanted to let Ramraja succeed Shahu in spite of Sakwarbai's opposition to his succession.

Sakwarbai apprehended troubles from those who supported[108] Ramraja's accession. She prepared herself to meet any situation and informed Shahu of her army preparations to meet any emergency. Shahu was quite ill. The financial condition had not[109] improved. He was disgusted. He asked the Peshwa to come to Satara immediately with an army of trusted soldiers. It was quite sufficient for the Peshwa to be alert.

Further, Sakwarbai asked the killedar of the Satara fort to prolong the confinement of Tarabai under strict vigilance.[110] She also kept a vigil on the visitors of Shahu. It is given that none was to see him unless permission was obtained from her previously. Shahu was lonely and spent his time in brooding. Different accounts show that he considered only the Peshwa would be able to save the situation from further deterioration.

Immediately after the death[111] of Shahu on 15th December, 1749 A.D., the Peshwa took up the control of the entire city of Satara. He flooded[112] the township with his troops. He asked his men to round up the active collaborators of Sakwarbai, Pratinidhi Jagjiwan and Yamaji Shivdev. He sent them to distant[113] places.

Tarabai came down from the fort to the palace. She had a discussion with others on the future course of action to be taken. She expressed[114] to Govindrao Chitnis, "If Sakwarbai remained, she would create confusion in the State and will thus ruin it. She will never allow security to anyone... It will be alright if she remained with me. With regard to her being a 'Sati', she should act according to her own choice and next we proceed on as we decide." But no account is available to show that the proposal was ever communicated to Sakwarbai. Kincaid and Parasnis mention,[115] "All agreed that she was a turbulent, unmanageable woman. If she were allowed her liberty, she would certainly denounce Ramraja as an impostor, and adopting a son to her dead husband, would with the aid of Sambhaji of Kolhapur, embroil the Maratha nation in civil war. On the other hand, the imprisonment of Shahu's queens would deeply offend Maratha sentiments and would give Damaji Gaekwad and other Maratha leaders an excellent excuse for rebellion."

Chitnis writes,[116] "If she does not commit Sati, she should be forced to do so. If she remained behind, she would cause ignominy and strife. It will not be of any use to repent afterwards. We must now put an end to it." According to Sardesai[117], it was decided that she should ascend the funeral pier, for if she lived she would create problems for Raja and Sambhaji II was not to be called to Satara. Finally, Kuwarji Shirkey, Sakwarbai's brother, was sent for to persuade her to commit Sati according to the prevalent custom. Sakwarbai ascended the funeral pier, though it is still difficult to say that she did so on her own accord. Kincaid and Parasnis further[118] write, "To hide her intrigue, she meant to immolate herself and the council waiting on her brother won him over to the view that if she now shrank from the ordeal, she would stain the honour of her house." The sources leading to such an assumption are not mentioned. However, the account of Govindrao corroborates other accounts with slight difference in the form of narration. But again these writers have not referred to any source regarding their remarks and the role of different persons in the episode. Further, no account mentions that she had publicly uttered her desire to immolate herself, though "Sati" was an honourable practice followed by women in those days. She had only addressed herself to her brother, Kuwarji Shirkey. As mentioned, he was asked by the council to influence[119] the course of action. Sardesai writes[120], "She resolved it in her mind and concluded that if she refused and lived after her husband, she would have to suffer untold miseries at the hands of her opponents." This opinion is also supported by Dr. H.N.Sinha. He writes[121], "Sakwarbai was given the alternative to live under the protection of the Peshwa and that was not an unusual step and therefore there was choice for her whether she should live or commit sati." It is not difficult to imagine whether Sakwarbai would agree to live under the protection of the Peshwa, specially when she had differences with him. It can be shown from different accounts that even during the lifetime of Shahu, and Peshwa in office, she was not happy. During her years of struggle, she had the Peshwa as an obstacle while Shahu had to play between extremely opposite views.

The Peshwa apprehended trouble after the death of Shahu from her supporters. He instantly applied himself to crush the only adversary he had. He imprisoned her supporters without whom she had the least prospects of success, but even this could not deter her from opposing the succession of Ramraja.

Naturally, under such circumstances, one likes to get rid of one's own life. Such examples are found in the history of Rajputana and the Marathas in numbers. She preferred to commit 'Sati' rather than depend either on the Peshwa or on Tarabai. Soon arrangements were made for her to commit 'Sati', but even from the funeral pier, she declared that Ramraja was a pretender and that Sambhaji of Kolhapur was alone the rightful claimant to the Satara throne. Later events showed that she was not wrong in her observation which was also supported by Tarabai when the power of Chhatrapati had already declined by 1752-53 A.D.

REFERENCES

1. Rajwade, V.K., Khand VI, L.N. 57.
2. Kincaid, C.A., and Parasnis, D.B. – *A History of the Maratha People*, Vol. II, p. 122
   Marathi Daftar, Roomal 1, p. 124.
3. *Itihas Sangraha* – Pustak 2, May 1910, Ank 10, pp. 38-39.
4. Riyasat, Vol. IV, *Sthir Budhi Rajaram*, pp. 134-135.
5. Forrest – *Selection from Letters Despatches and Other State Papers* – (Maratha Series), Vol. 1, p. 77.
6. Kincaid, C.A., and Parasnis, D.B. – *A History of the Maratha People*, Vol. II, p. 150.
7. *Ibid.*
8. Kincaid, C.A., and Parasnis, D.B. – *A History of the Maratha People*, Vol. II, p. 150.
9. *Ibid.*
10. *Ibid.*
11. Paranis, D.B. – *Life of Brahmendra Swami*, L.No.14, 112 and others.
12. Unpublished Paper – Peshwa Daftar – (not numbered); Through the courtesy of Shri S.V. Avalaskar.
13. Vaidya, C.V. – *Vaidya Daftar*, L.N. 37 (1743) :
    The letter indicates the direct dealings of the queens in the trade. Keso Trimal writes to Vaidya brothers how Antaji Ghatge had become troublesome to the people at Chinchghen near Palgad. He looted villages and robbed even the store-keeper of queen

Sagunabai who had come to take salt. The writer requests them to ask queen Sagunabai to check the troublesome pranks of Ghatge and Mahad people.

14. Paranis, D.B. – *Life of Brahmendra Swami*, L.No.93, 94, 95, 99, 100, 101, 102, 262, 263.
15. *S.P.D.* Vol. VIII, L.Nos. 42, 43.
16. *Madhya Yugeen Charitra Kosh*, pp. 216, 574.
17. *S.P.D.* Vol. III, L.No. 4, 16.
18. Unpublished Paper – Chitra Daftar, Poladpur :
    Aurangzeb's general Zulphikar Khan had captured the fort of Raigad in 1689 A.D. and named it Islamabad. It was in the possession of the Moghuls till the death of Aurangzeb in 1707 A.D. Two Rajputs, named Sursingh and Shivsingh, were the killedars in succession. After Aurangzeb's death, when the Moghuls marched to Delhi, the killedar left Raigad, came to Poona and joined the Moghul army. Thus, the fort remained unoccupied and was later taken by Siddis of Janjira.
    — (Through the countesy of Shri S.V. Avalaskar).
19. *S.P.D.* Vol. III, L.No. 16.
20. *S.P.D.* Vol. III, L.No. 3.
    P.D. Vol. I, L.No. 104.
    S.P.D. Vol. XXX, L.No. 322, p. 327.
21. Parasnis, D.B. – *Life of Brahmendraswami*, L.No. 7.
22. *S.P.D.* Vol. III, L.No. 5, 5-a.
23. Parasnis, D.B. – *Life of Brahmendraswami*, L.No. 9.
24. *Ibid*, L.No. 12 :
    It is also indicated that the queens were asked to perform "Vrat Vaikalp", which they did.
25. Parasnis, D.B. – *Life of Brahmendraswami*, L.No. 90.
26. *Ibid*, L.No. 112.
27. Parasnis, D.B. – *Life of Brahmendraswami*, L.No. 255 :
    Brahmendraswami's language had always been ornamental and flowery. Historians are of opinion that there were few who could write like him, and he was the best among them. He mentioned Sakwarbai as "Yogbhrishta" or "Yogmata".
28. Parasnis, D.B. – *Life of Brahmendraswami*, L.No. 257.
29. Dhabu, D.G. – *Kulabkar Angre Sarkhel*, p. 61
    Rajwade, V.K., Khand III, pp. 513, 522.

30. *S.P.D.* Vol. XXXIII, L.Nos. 388, 397, 401, 409 :
"Manaji Angre and Tulaji Angre were illegitimate sons of Kanhoji Angre. Sambhaji was the legitimate son and therefore he was to get Sarkhelship. But the Peshwa favoured Manaji Angre. Hence a dispute took place between them."
31. *S.P.D.* Vol. III, L.Nos. 177, 181, 192.
32. *S.P.D.* Vol. III, L.Nos. 184, 187, 196, 199.
33. Riyasat, Vol. V, *Punya Shlok Shahu, Peshwa Bajirao*, p. 435, *S.P.D.* Vol. XVIII, L.No. 6.
34. Daftar – Shri Bhaushastri of Pratapgad :
Accounts show that Virubai was concerned more with comforts of Shahu. She was devoted to him so much that when he once fell ill in 1730 A.D. and his condition became quite serious, she journeyed to Pratapgad. She mortgaged her bangles to evoke divine blessings for Shahu's quick recovery.
— (Through the courtesy of Shri S.V. Avalaskar).
35. Rajwade, V.K., Khand III, L.No. 18.
Shahu Roznishi, No. 90.
S.P.D. Vol. VIII, L.N. 48.
36. Sardesai, G.S. – *New History of the Marathas*, Vol. II, p. 263.
37. *Ibid.*
38. Parasnis, D.B. – *Life of Brahmendraswami*, L.No. 100.
39. *Ibid.*, L.No. 102.
40. *Ibid.*, L.No. 102.
41. Rajwade, V.K., Khand II, L.No. 69, 71.
42. Parasnis, D.B. – *Life of Brahmendraswami*, L.No. 11.
43. *Ibid.*, L.No. 94, 95.
44. *Aitihasik Patra-Vyawahar*, L.No. 41 :
The letter is a long one. It gives information about the Sardars in whom the Peshwa confided and who were stationed in different places. The Peshwa was facing more than one problem at the time. The letter also shows the cause of the financial stringency at Satara Court.
45. *Aitihasik Patra-Vyawahar*, L.No. 41.
46. *S.P.D.* Vol. XVIII, L.No. 85.
Aitihasik Patra-Vyawahar, L.No. 44 :
Shahu says, "I have no power. This has been taken by the queens. They are quarrelling with everybody. Today, grocers had come, but they left without giving anything ... Now, I am bankrupt."

47. *Aitihasik Patra-Vyawahar,* L.No. 59.
48. *Ibid.*, L.No. 38.
49. Sardesai, G.S. – New History of The Marathas, Vo. II, p. 265.
50. *Aitihasik Patra-Vyawahar*, L.No. 39.
51. Parasnis Papers :

    Rules, drawn up for the guidance of the queens by the Peshwa at Shahu's request :-

    (1) Neither Rani should quarrel with the other.

    (2) The Raja should grant to each Rani similar cash allowance and land.

    (3) All Jagirs in the occupation of the Ranis without Sanads should be surrendered.

    (4) The Ranis should not requisition supply of money from towns or districts alienated to Zilledars (cavalry, soldiers or Mukasdars).

    (5) The Ranis should not seize other persons' Jagirs or other persons' Saranjams.

    (6) The Ranis should not confiscate the Deshmukhiship or village officers or Watans or hereditary village grants of lands.

    (7) Whosoever gives one Rani a present of land should make a similar present to the other.

    (8) The Ranis should not take sides in disputes arising in the Capital.

    (9) The Ranis should not hear suits brought by creditors against debtors.

    (10) The Ranis should not levy taxes or tolls.

    Both the Ranis have accepted these terms. This should continue for ever.

    Aitihasik Patra-Vyawahar, L.No. 39.
52. Sardesai, G.S. – *Currents of Maratha History*, p. 87.
53. Sen, S.N. – *Military System of the Marathas*, pp. 70, 71.
54. Rajwade, V.K., Khand III, pp. 20, 27.
55. Sinha – *Rise of the Peshwas*, pp. 188, 189.
56. Grant Duff – *History of the Marathas*, Vol. I, p. 489.
57. Riyasat, Vol. V, *Punya Shlok Shahu, Peshwa Balajirao*, p. 53.
58. *S.P.D.* Vol. XL, L.No. 28 :

    This was the king's personal estate. However, the annual payment was to be made in Government treasury.

59. Sen, S.N. – *Military System of the Marathas*, pp. 258.
60. Sen, S.N. – *Administrative System of the Marathas*, pp. 112.
61. Vaidya Daftar, L.N. 1, p. 41, 1745 A.D.
    L.N. 28, pp. 27-28, July, 1745 A.D.
    L.N. 34, p. 30, 24th August, 1746 A.D.
62. Vaidya Daftar, L.N. 42, pp. 38, 39, 22nd Nov., 1746 A.D.
63. Vaidya Daftar, L.N. 23, p. 26, 16th August, 1747 A.D.
    L.N. 25, p. 27, 2nd September, 1747 A.D.
    L.N. 26, p. 28, 29; Sept., 1747 A.D.
64. Sen, S.N. – *Military System of the Marathas*, p. 71.
    Rajwade, V.K. – *Lekh Sangraha*, Khand I, pp. 138, 139.
65 *Aitihasik Patra-Vyawahar*, L.N. 59.
66. *Ibid.*.
67. Kincaid, C.A., and Parasnis, D.B. – *A History of the Maratha People*, Vol. II, p. 296.
    Grant Gazetteer, p. 304.
68. *Ibid.*
69. Vaidya Daftar, L.N. 24, p. 21, 14th July, 1748 A.D.
    (Date corrected at B.I.S.M., Poona)
    From queen Sagunabai to Raghuji Bhonsle, to bring with him Burhanji Mohite who was her brother. Raghuji's wife, Sou. Salubai, was Sagunabai's step-sister. This explains the possibility of Mudhoji being a prospective claimant to the Satara throne.
70. Vaidya Daftar, L.N. 26 (1747).
71. Vaidya Daftar, L.N. 24, p. 25, 7th July, 1743 A.D.
    S.P.D. Vol. XX, L.N. 31.
72. *S.P.D.* Vol. VIII, L.N. 38.
73. *Ibid.*
74. Riyasat, Vol. V – *Punya Shlok Shahu, Peshwa Balajirao*, p. 156.
75. Kincaid, C.A., and Parasnis, D.B. – *A History of the Maratha People*, Vol. II, p. 296.
    It is also mentioned that Shahu sent a few messengers to Poona to find out correct information about the Peshwa's conduct. It should be borne in mind that Sakwarbai and a few persons had reported to the king about the looseness of the Peshwa's private life which was not blameless.
76. Riyasat, Vol. V – *Punya Shlok Shahu, Peshwa Balajirao*, p. 155.
77. Parasnis, D.B. – *Life of Brahmendraswami*, L.No. 102.

78. *S.P.D.* Vol. VIII, L.N. 38.
79. *Aitihasik Patra-Vyawahar*, L.No. 59.
80. Riyasat, Vol. V – *Punya Shlok Shahu, Peshwa Balajirao*, p. 157.
81. Vaidya Daftar, L.N. 13, p. 13, Ist May, 1747 A.D.
82. Sardesai, G.S. – *New History of The Marathas*, Vo. II, p. 267.
83. *S.P.D.* Vol. XXVI, L.Nos. 15, 18.
    Besides, many letters in *S.P.D.* Vol. XXVIII give full account of Karnatak affair.
84. Sardesai, G.S. – *New History of The Marathas*, Vol. II, p. 266.
85. *Ibid.*
86. *Aitihasik Patra-Vyawahar*, L.Nos. 59, 65.
87. *S.P.D.* Vol. XXVI, L.N. 137.
    Purandare Daftar, Vol. I, p. 159.
88. *Aitihasik Patra-Vyawahar*, L.No. 76.
89. *Ibid.*
90. *S.P.D.* Vol. XXIV, L.N. 16:
    The Peshwa had taken the fort of Manikgad on 28th May, 1747 A.D. According to Angrekaleen Ashtagar Extract No. 164, the fort was in the hands of the Peshwa on 28th April, 1748 A.D.
91. *S.P.D.* Vol. VIII, L.N. 42.
92. *S.P.D.* Vol. VIII, L.Nos. 42, 43.
93. *S.P.D.* Vol. VIII, L.N. 39.
94. *S.P.D.* Vol. VIII, L.N. 42.
95. *S.P.D.* Vol. XVIII, L.N. 7 :
    One of the queens of Shahu is ill. She must be Sagunabai as found in other accounts also.
    S.P.D. Vol. XVIII, L.N. 88 :
    The letter mentions about the illness of Sagunabai as well as the financial condition of the king during his last days.
96. *S.P.D.* Vol. XVIII, L.N. 153.
97. *S.P.D.* Vol. VIII, L.N. 8, 9.
98. Vaidya Daftar, L.N. 31 (1748)
    S.P.D. Vol. XVIII, L.N. 90.
99. *Shahu Roznishi* – No. 95 (p. 39).
100. Kincaid, C.A., and Parasnis, D.B. – *A History of the Maratha People*, Vol. II, p. 299.
101. *Ibid.*
102. *S.P.D.* Vol. XI, L.Nos. 19, 21, 29, 31.
    S.P.D. Vol. XXVI, L.Nos. 13, 14.

103. *S.P.D.* Vol. VI, L.N. 1.
104. *S.P.D.* Vol. VI, L.N. 2 :
The letter indicates that Jijabai had hoped that Sambhaji II would succeed Satara Gadi through the efforts of the Peshwa and his supporters. The letter is written in 1748, nearly a year before Shahu's death.
105. Kincaid, C.A., Parasnis, D.B., *A History of the Maratha People* – Vol. II, p. 296.
106. *Ibid.,* p. 299.
107. *Ibid.*
108. Riyasat, Vol. V – *Punya Shlok Shahu, Peshwa Balajirao*, p. 172.
109. *Aitihasik Patra-Vyawahar*, L.No. 44.
110. Riyasat, Vol. V – *Punya Shlok Shahu, Peshwa Balajirao*, p. 172.
111. Rajwade, V.K., Khand II, p. 111.
112. Kincaid, C.A., and Parasnis, D.B. – *A History of the Maratha People*, Vol. II, p. 301. (Troops 45,000)
In other accounts, the number of troops is 34,000.
113. Kincaid, C.A., and Parasnis, D.B. – *A History of the Maratha People*, Vol. II, p. 301.
114. Chitnis, K. – *Shahu Maharaj Yanchi Bakhar*, p. 86.
Sinha, H.N. – *Rise of the Peshwas*, p. 229.
115. Kincaid, C.A., and Parasnis, D.B. – *A History of the Maratha People*, Vol. II, p. 301.
116. Chitnis, K. – *Shahu Maharaj Yanchi Bakhar*, p. 86.
117. Riyasat, Vol. V – *Punya Shlok Shahu, Peshwa Balajirao*, p. 178.
118. Kincaid, C.A., and Parasnis, D.B. – *A History of the Maratha People*, Vol. II, p. 302.
119. Chitnis, K. – *Shahu Maharaj Yanchi Bakhar*, p. 86.
120. Riyasat, Vol. V – *Punya Shlok Shahu, Peshwa Balajirao*, p. 180.
Sardesai, G.S. – *New History of the Marathas*, Vol. II, p. 274.
121. Sinha, H.N. – *Rise of the Peshwas*, p. 233.

CHAPTER 6

RADHABAI

A Woman of the House of Peshwa in Maratha Politics (1730-1740)

Jijabai and women of the House of Shivaji, if played a vital role in Maratha politics, the women of the House of Peshwas also did not lag behind, the foremost being Radhabai. In some aspects her role was broadly in line with Yesubai. Her service to the cause of Maratha state and her family are noteworthy.

Radhabai hailed[1] from the Barve family of Newre or Newas. She was the daughter of Duberkar Antaji Malhar Barve of Nasik. Little is known about early life but as per existing custom, she must have been married with Balaji Vishwanath at an early age. With the result, she had an opportunity to be with him during his career as the Peshwa. This provided her a chance to be close to the Maratha centre of power.

During these days, the western coast of India was mostly under the shadow of the sea power of the Siddis of Janjira who were Muslims of Abyssinia settled in this coastal part during Malik Ambar's days. They oppressed those who did not follow their dictates. Balaji's father, Vishwanath Bhatt, was the Deshmukh[2] of the village of Shrivardhan in the service of Siddis for a long time, but when differences cropped up between Balaji [illegible] and political oppression, Balaji had to invoke divine blessings.[5] The saint had a good hold on the family.

Balaji Vishwanath purchased the patilship of Garade near Saswad and came in contact[6] with Purandare and later on with Balaji who acquired the position of Deshmukh of Dandarajpuri and Sabhasad of Dabhol[7] under Balaji Vishwanath. Balaji was mostly engaged in the realisation of the revenues which also required the maintenance of a few soldiers. However, Balaji Vishwanath became a revenue collector and Sar-Subedar[8] of Daultabad between the year 1699 and 1708 A.D., he came in close contact with the Muslim officers of the State as well. During this period, Radhabai also came to know Balaji Vishwanath as her father Duberkar Antaji Malhar Barve enjoyed the confidence of Balaji Vishwanath. This close contact between the family of Barve with Balaji Vishwanath, helped Radhabai to have first-hand training to understand political conditions prevailing in the State and other neighbouring areas during this period.

It may be noted that by 1700 A.D. the Deccan presented a picture of confusion and strife. According to Dr. S.R.Sharma, "this was a period of trial of endurance and resources between the Moghul Emperor and the indigenous people of Deccan[9]" which provided an opportunity to Balaji Vishwanath to understand the administrative and political problems facing the Deccan. He was not concerned merely with the revenue collection[10] but he was now a soldier on his own. He was undertaking various campaigns which required money because his soldiers were mostly mercenary. These problems faced by him were tough and rather difficult to deal with.

During these difficult days, resourceful attitude was shown by Radhabai who firmly stood by her husband Balaji Vishwanath. They got their sons and daughters married[11] in the families of influential Sardars. Their eldest son, Bajirao, born in 1700 A.D., was married to Kashibai[12], daughter of Mahadji Krishna of Chas, a rich banker who advanced loans to Balaji Vishwanath whenever needed. Their second son, Chimnaji Appa, born in 1710 A.D., played a distinguished role in the Maratha politics till his death in 1740 A.D. and was married to Rakhmabai, daughter of Visaji Krishna Pethe of Nasik. Pethe[13] Sardars became the strong supporters of Balaji Vishwanath and served Shahu's[14] cause along with him. They accompanied him on his campaigns. Radhabai's daughter, Anubai[15], was married to Venkatrao Ghorpade of Ichchalkaranji. They were valiant and courageous Sardars of the times. Till recently, they held their fief of Ichchalkaranji under the Kolhapur Raja. Her second daughter, Bhiubai,[16] was married to Abaji Naik Joshi of Baramati. They were rich bankers who had gained the confidence of Radhabai. They enjoyed the previlege to be with Radhabai in her visits to different places during the years 1733-35 A.D. Thus, it is evident that the matrimonial alliances brought substantial succour and social esteem to Balaji Vishwanath and Radhabai. Moreover, the Chaskars, Pethes, Ghorpades and Joshis also marched to the battlefields with Balaji Vishwanath whenever such an occasion arose.

However, it was not always that easy for Radhabai who had to face odd situations many a times. An account of this was the marriage of her second daughter Anubai[17]. During this marriage ceremony the women of Venkatrao Ghorpade's family in which the marriage was being performed insisted that Radhabai should appear in veil at the time of Anubai's marriage. Radhabai refused to accept this condition because she had never worn it and she was afraid that she would be made a subject of ridicule. However, she communicated to the women of Ghorpade family that any other condition was acceptable to her, but the latter refused to agree. There was a stage when it was feared that the marriage might not take place at all. Balaji Vishwanath appeared to be ... Radhabai. She and finally the Peshwa of the Maratha kingdom which must have elated Radhabai. Another meritorious service of the Peshwa was the treaty[19] between himself and Sayyid Hussain Ali. Balaji Vishwanath could bring practically everything which Shahu desired to have from the Moghul Emperor, Farrukhsiyar, but it was a tragedy for the Marathas that during his return journey to the South, Balaji Vishwanath died on the 2nd April, 1719 A.D.

Radhabai was greatly afflicted by the sudden tragic shock. However, she had the consolation to see her son, Bajirao receiving[20] robes of Peshwaship on 17th April, 1720 A.D., despite the opposition from some senior Sardars. Radhabai soon proved to be a good asset to her son, the new Peshwa Bajirao as she often manoeuvred to get the support of her brother, Malharrao Barve, who was serving as Maratha Agent[21] at the Moghul court. Through him it became possible for Bajirao to squeeze out valuable information regarding the Moghul court politics and this helped the Peshwa to plan his political strategy to deal with Delhi. Thus, it is evident that Radhabai had proved herself to be an asset to her family though remaining behind curtain.

Bajirao soon realised that Nizam-ul-Mulk was a formidable opponent of the Marathas in Deccan and his political game was to create problems for Shahu by extending his support to Sambhaji -II of Kolhapur. Nizam-ul-Mulk supported the claim of Sambhaji to realize Chouth and Sardeshmukhi of six Subas of the Moghul Deccan and thus he attempted to block the implementation of treaty concluded between Sayyid Hussain Ali and Balaji Vishwanath in 1719 A.D.

For the new Peshwa, Bajirao, a difficult political situation arose when Sayyid Hussain Ali was imprisoned[22] on the 14th October, 1720 A.D. as a result of major changes at the Moghul court and thus the Marathas lost a friend in Sayyid Hussain Ali. It was soon apparent that the Maratha interest would suffer as a result of his imprisonment. Meanwhile, Malharrao Barve informed[23] Ambaji Pant Purandare at Satara on the 15th October,

1720 A.D., "Sayyid Hussain Ali has been murdered by Aminkhan, the field is now open and you must not allow your enemies to capture it". This hint helped Bajirao to follow a set[24] and determined plan against the Nizam-ul-Mulk who was still undecided to make a move vis-a-vis the Peshwa and the Moghul Court politics. Bajirao immediately decided to take advantage of the inactions and the policy of wait and watch of Nizam-ul-Mulk.

The hostility between the Peshwa and the Nizam errupted when Shahu directed his Sarlashkar, Sultanji Nimbalkar to collect[25] Chouth from the region on the bank of Godavari. The Nizam-ul-Mulk dispatched Chandrasen Jadhav, Raorambha Nimbalkar and Mukhamsingh to meet the Senalashkar. A battle took place near Godavari on 15th December, 1720 A.D. Nizam-ul-Mulk was defeated.[26] This defeat of the Nizam now made the Peshwa to plan his course of actions in the north and Bajirao confidently advised[27] Shahu, "Let us strike at the trunk of the withering tree (The Moghul Empire) the branches will fall off themselves. Thus should the Maratha flag fly from the Krishna to the Indus." Thereupon, the Raja exclaimed, "You shall plant it upon the Himalayas."

The Nizam had thus been defeated and humiliated and when Anandrao Sumant, the foreign Secretary, arranged for a meeting between Bajirao and Nizam-ul-Mulk, the meeting[28] naturally passed off cordially on 5th January, 1721 A.D. amid great pomp and rejoicing. This meeting between Bajirao and the Nizam-ul-Mulk was an extra feather in the cap of Bajirao who was now free to follow his own course of action in the north.

Meanwhile Radhabai passed anxious moments when Bajirao was busy dealing with the Nizam-ul-Mulk. This denotes her keen [illegible] affairs of the family and her son Bajirao

Bajirao has been also writing to her often not only about his welfare but also about the state matters.

Moreover, Bajirao availed of the opportunity of prevailing chaotic conditions at Gujrat to plunder Gujrat, though opposed by Raja Girdhar Bahadur. At last, Girdhar Bahadur granted authority[29] to Udaji Pawar, Malharrao Holkar and Panoji Sindhia to levy Chouth and to retain half the Mokasa in payment of their troops.

Radhabai could not remain a passive spectator during the above enterprises of Bajirao. She was in communication with different Sardars and Chimnaji[30] Appa. This reveals that she kept herself acquainted with the events taking place at different fronts. Her letters[31] to Brahmendraswami appeared to be more significant as she could rely more on him after Balaji Vishwanath. How far she could win his co-operation is not difficult to assess from the very fact that he advised her from time to time. She also sent him the copies of the letters written to her by Bajirao, and added, "The copies[32] of which are being sent to you." Thus, the letters though vague were often apt expression of the events that corroborated historical facts of political importance.

At the same time, the letters reveal that Radhabai tried to fulfil the demands of Brahmendraswami from time to time. Once he had asked her to get necessary passport issued to him to carry on trade on western coast and a Sanad[33] to take salt free of taxes to his store room.

Meanwhile, the conditions in south changed to a considerable extent and the Nizam-ul-Mulk became more overbearing. He resumed[34] his hostilities against Shahu's feudatories. In this effort, he was being helped by his lieutenants Turktaz Khan, Raorambha Nimbalkar and Udaji Chouhan.

Shahu had the uninflinching support of Shambhusingh, Vyasrao and others. As mentioned,[35] Nizam-ul-Mulk got Sambhaji II of Kolhapur declared Chhatrapati of the Marathas. But Bajirao defeated him at Palkhed on 6th May, 1728 A.D., and Shahu secured[36] practically all that he desired by the treaty of Mungi-Sheogaon.

The northern victory of Bajirao over Nizam-ul-Mulk was well celebrated by Radhabai. She asked Chimnaji Appa to send her an elephant to be presented[37] to the Siddis of Janjira as a gift promised to him for the grand triumph of Bajirao as was suggested by Gangadhar. Thus, it is apparent that Radhabai tried to maintain good relations with Siddis of Janjira.

Bajirao also defeated Mohd. Khan Bangash, Subedar of Prayag, who had marched against Raja Chhatrasal of Bundelkhand. Next, he defeated Sambhaji of Kolhapur and Trimbakrao Dabhade of Gujarat in 1730 and 1731 A.D. respectively.

While Bajirao was busy in his campaigns, Radhabai had to face a terrible situation at home. Bajirao's relations with Mastani,[38] a Muslim mistress, could not be liked well by the people and the inmates of the Peshwa's house. The matter would not have become so conspicuous, had she not been included[39] in the paraphernalia of the Peshwa about 1730 A.D. However, no account mentions that Radhabai attached any importance to the matter at all, as was being done by orthodox class of people. In spite of this, accounts show that Radhabai could maintain the prestige of the house tactfully against such criticism, though Bajirao and Mastani were made an easy pawn for discussion.

As known, Bajirao had defeated the Nizam-ul-Mulk at Palkhed in 1728 A.D. Yet the latter approached Shahu and desired to meet Bajirao. Shahu asked[40] Bajirao to meet the Nizam-ul-Mulk. Radhabai was perturbed to hear about the new development. She [illegible] faith in the professions of Nizam-ul-Mulk, more so also shows that she doubted whether Bajirao would be able to avoid the meeting. She also advised him that if there was no alternative but to meet Nizam-ul-Mulk, he should first meet Rambhaji Nimbalkar and Turktazkhan and see that all arrangements for his safety and security had been perfectly made. It also shows that she had more faith in Turktazkhan and Rambhaji Nimbalkar than in the Nizam-ul-Mulk.

Bajirao also received numerous letters from his relations to avoid the meeting. His sister Shiubai entreated[42] Radhabai not to allow Bajirao to meet the Nizam-ul-Mulk until Chimnaji Appa was with him.

Bajirao's next move shows that he paid due to consideration to the above suggestions. He met Rambhaji Nimbalkar and Turktazkhan. They escorted him to the Nizam-ul-Mulk. He welcomed[43] Bajirao on 27th December, 1732 A.D. at Rohe-Rameshwar in the neighbourhood of Ausa, eight miles north of Latur, and honoured him by presenting dresses, pearls, horses and elephants. It is also stated that they entered into a secret understanding.[44] The Maratha government promised to leave Deccan unmolested and levy nothing beyond Chouth and Sardeshmukhi from them. In return, the Nizam-ul-Mulk promised to remain neutral during the projected Maratha invasion of Hindustan. Thus the meeting ended to the great relief of Radhabai, Bajirao and Shahu. Bajirao was now free to follow his own course of action for northward expansion.

The Moghul Emperor naturally suspected the purpose of the meeting between the Marathas and Nizam-ul-Mulk. He appointed[45] Sawai Raja Jaisingh as the Governor of Malwa in 1732 A.D. to counteract the Maratha ravages in the province. But he had to face a difficult situation against Vithoji Bule, Holkar's lieutenant, and Anandrao Powar. Sawai Raja Jaisingh paid six lakhs of rupees to the Maratha Sardars and saved himself from dire consequences. To counteract the Maratha ravages, he formed[46] a league of Rajput princes in 1734 A.D. and prepared himself to drive the Marathas out of Malwa. In 1735 A.D., the imperial army proceeded against the Marathas from two routes. One section was headed by Mir Bakshi Khan Dauran and the other was by Qamaruddin Khan. They marched into Rajputana from western and eastern routes respectively. The imperial army and the Marathas met[47] at the field of Rampura. A severe battle was fought between them, followed by many battles in different places. The imperial army was badly defeated. Through the mediation of Sawai Raja Jaisingh, Mir Bakshi Khan Dauran agreed[48] to pay 22 lakhs of rupees to the Marathas as Chouth from Malwa, and went back to Delhi in April, 1735 A.D.

After this victory, Bajirao aspired to be the Viceroy[49] (Deputy) of Malwa. But he found it rather difficult to attain his aim in spite of Sawai Raja Jaisingh's mild attitude towards him.

At this juncture Radhabai expressed her desire to start on a pilgrimage, particularly to Udaipur and Jaipur. This indicates that she was thinking in an entirely different way. Rajput-Maratha cordiality was the need of the hour. Chimnaji Appa at once arranged for her visit to the northern places. A few of the noted Sardars, such as Babuji Naik, Sadashiv Ballal, Krishnarao Mahadeo and Vasudeo Joshi accompanied her during her pilgrimage.

Radhabai crossed Burhanpur on the 8th February, 1735 A.D. She reached Udaipur on the 6th May. The letter of Babuji Naik, written to Bajirao on behalf of Radhabai, indicates that she was accorded a grand reception at Udaipur, equal to that offered to a State guest. In that letter, Radhabai also asked Bajirao to get a letter written to Ranaji by Shahu. She added,[50] "I have therefore to suggest that Swamiji (Shahu) should now write letters to Beharidass, Diwan of Udaipur Rana, and Ranaji, stating that it the Peshwa's family. Thus, it can be said that Radhabai was trying to get something more for the Peshwa. She continued to stay at Udaipur for eight to ten days and the time was well spent in rejoicings.

Radhabai left[51] Udaipur on the 8th May, 1735 A.D. and reached[52] Jaipur on the 21st June. Sawāi Raja Jaisingh received her cordially. Henceforth, Maratha-Rajput friendship appears to have taken a definite shape. Besides, Radhabai is held[53] to have been struck with the idea of having Jaisingh's son, Nathaji, as the successor to the Satara throne after Shahu. How far this opinion is reliable cannot be said in absence of other evidence. However, it should be borne in mind that at the time of the hunt for a successor to the Satara throne in about 1745-46 A.D., the name of Nathaji could draw the attention of a few persons at Satara. Radhabai stayed at Jaipur for three months, the maximum period of her stay but how for this affected Maratha-Rajput or Maratha-Moghul cordiality cannot be said in absence of evidence. Yet, it can be said that the visit was quite favourable[54] to the Marathas, particularly to the Peshwa. This is indicated by later events. Bajirao soon received a call[55] from Sawai Raja Jaisingh to visit him with Sardars Sindhia, Holkar and Jadhav. He also agreed to pay four lakhs of rupees as well as the charges of the troops moving with him northwards. Moreover, he made it clear that after his (Bajirao's) arrival, he would be able to confer with Mir Bakshi Khan Dauran to arrange for the Peshwa's visit to the Moghul Emperor.

While Radhabai had left Jaipur in September, the Peshwa started[56] for the north on the 9th October, 1735 A.D. with Sindhia, Holkar, Tukoji, Anandrao Powar, Kanthaji Kadam Bande and Baji Bhivrao. With 8000 forces, he reached Udaipur in February, 1736 A.D. He was received well at Jaipur. He received the grant of one and a half lakhs of rupees. But he could not receive the Pargana of Manora[57] as he had desired. The Peshwa was again invited[58] to visit Jainagar. Meanwhile, the Peshwa's Vakil, Mahadeo

Bhatt Hingne, had already proceeded with the terms Sawai Raja Jaisingh would propose to the Moghul Emperor to win Maratha friendship.

It should be remembered that Sawai Raja Jaisingh had attempted to form a league of Rajput Princes to defeat and oust the Marathas from his province. However, he had failed in his attempt. He had become indifferent[59] to the imperialists' policy. It was obvious that the fall of the Moghul Empire had begun. Hence there is little doubt that Bajirao would not use this opportunity to benefit himself by the weakness of his opponents, the Rajputs and the Moghuls.

Bajirao was moving towards Udaipur. His agent, Mahadeo Bhatt Hingne, met Sawai Raja Jaisingh at Jaipur in January, 1736 A.D. He put forth his demands which consisted[60] of a cash subsidy of twenty lakhs of rupees in Malwa and a Tankha on the territory of Dost Mohammad Rohilla, along with other facilities.[61] The imperial Government appeared to have come to terms with Bajirao, but the Moghul Emperor thought that the demands[62] were quite exhorbitant. As such, these could not be fulfilled by him. The Maratha forces entered Bundelkhand with Sardars Sindhia, Holkar, Bande and Anandrao Powar. They started devastations in the territory of Mewar. Bajirao marched towards Doab and carried on plunder, ravages and hostilities against the Moghuls.

While Bajirao was busy in his northern campaigns, Radhabai continued to win the goodwill of the other Sardars. She appears to have kept herself acquainted with the events taking place at different places. She was greatly respected by Kanhoji Angre wrote[63] to her from time to time. Similarly, she was in problem at home. It was obvious that the people had become more vehement in their critcism of Bajirao and Mastani. This was felt[64] more at the time of the thread ceremony of Raghunathrao and the marriage of Sadashivrao in 1739 A.D. The priests refused to perform the ceremonies. However, the opposition of the priestly class appears to have subsided, may be because of the absence of Bajirao from home. As known, he was busy fighting against Nasirjung, son of Nizam-ul-Mulk, in 1739 A.D.

As mentioned, Mastani was considered to be the cause of all the trouble and the disturbances in the Peshwa's family[65] from time to time. It is also known that Chimnaji Appa was not[66] disinterested in her, as he is said to have obtained[67] her from the Gujarat Camp in 1730 A.D. Mastani was, however, interested in Bajirao. Chimnaji Appa got her imprisoned at Parwati[68] gardens. This drastic action of Chimnaji Appa was not appreciated by Radhabai. She apprehended that something unusually serious would take place in the family. She asked Chimnaji Appa to "remonstrate[69] with Bajirao about his ways and arrange matters, presumably as regards Mastani."

Even the imprisonment of Mastani could not stop the criticism of the people. They entreated[70] the king to let Mastani be separated from Bajirao. But the king did not approve of it. He made them understand that it was for Bajirao to decide as to what he should do about it. Bajirao had encamped at Pattas. Mastani escaped[71] and reached there. Ultimately, Radhabai, Nana Purandare, Chimnaji Appa and Kaka Morshet met Bajirao and talked over the matter. Mastani was brought back.

Bajirao heard about the march of Nasirjung near Aurangabad. He closely pursued[72] him. But, as Bajirao wanted to move towards north and Nasirjung towards south, they came to terms.[73]

The Peshwa was not keeping good health. However, he marched towards Rawerkheda on the banks of river Narmada. But he could not bear the exigencies of frequent actions. His health deteriorated. He fell ill on 23rd April, and expired[74] on 28th

April, 1740 A.D. At the time of his death, his wife Kashibai[75] was with him. His son, Balaji, was at Kolaba.[76] He hurried towards Rawerkheda with Chimnaji Appa. According to a few writers, Mastani also reached Rawerkheda and passed[77] through flames.

Radhabai had the greatest shock of her life. Her zeal and enthusiasm appears to have subsided to a considerable extent, even though her grandson received[78] the robes of Peshwaship. Besides, Radhabai had to suffer more because of the death[79] of her second son, Chimnaji Appa, in October, 1740 A.D., hardly five months after Bajirao's death.

Still Radhabai could not keep herself unconcerned with the passing events. This is indicated by the letter she wrote[80] to Brahmendraswami. She sadly expressed her inability to send emeralds or jewels or horses to him. She asked him to wait, and added, "We do not know what Appa had promised to you..." She entreated him to bless them all and requested that the "tree he had planted should be preserved." Thereby, she gave credit to Brahmendraswami for all that the family had achieved till then.

Nizam-ul-Mulk took Trichinapally in 1743 A.D. Shahu was distressed[81] to hear of the loss of Trichinapally. He asked Babuji Naik, who was in charge[82] of Karnatak, to proceed against Nizam-ul-Mulk and take back Trichinapally. But Muzzafar Jung and his supporters defeated Babuji Naik near Baswapattan on 15th February, 1745 A.D. Babuji Naik held the king and the Peshwa responsible for his defeat, because they had shown no interest in the expedition. He returned to Baramati, and threatened[83] to starve himself to death. All attempts to make him give up his decision to go on fast failed. It was in this awkward situation that ... She wrote[84] to the

Babuji Naik, it can be deduced that either because of her efforts or, may be, due to other reasons, he did not carry out his previous decision to fast unto death. Chitnis states, "Shahu supplied him with necessary funds to meet his expenses, though Yashwantrao Potnis was asked to take charge of Karnatak."

Radhabai once more had to use all her wits to save Poona from Damaji Gaekwad's attack. As known, Damaji Gaekwad, the Senapati of Umabai Dhabade, marched[85] with all fury towards Poona to support Tarabai in her fight against the Peshwa, Balaji Bajirao, in 1750 and 1751 A.D. Balaji had already proceeded to south. Under the circumstances, Radhabai had no other alternative but to take shelter[86] at Sinhgad along with Kashibai and others.

Kincaid and Parasnis mention[87], "She at once wrote a letter to Damaji Gaekwad to desist from aggression upon the innocent city." The letter received no regard from Damaji Gaekwad. He was sarcastic in his remarks, and expressed his determination to take Poona. He retorted,[88] "The revered mother has fled to Sinhgad? Where was the need for her to write to me? I know, you have come to get the news. Take away what you have seen. Tell the mother we erected the arch...... your troops must pull it down."

Purandare handled[89] the situation rather tactfully. Damaji Gaekwad changed his route without giving a concentrated battle which might have harmed Balaji's interests. Thus, though the credit of averting a disaster was given to Purandare by the Peshwa, it is difficult to deny that Radhabai had a hand in it. The Peshwa was finally victorious.

Radhabai had now no cause of anxiety about the stability and the progress of her family. She had the fortune to witness the rise of her family from a mere revenue collector's status to that of the head of the Maratha state in her own life time. She had equally shared in the trials and the tribulations of the family. She had to undergo inconveniences and troubles along with her husband, Balaji Vishwanath, her son, Bajirao and grandson Balaji Bajirao.

Facts and documents prove that she was an ideal wife and mother, tactful and courageously resourcesful. It was only of her that we know that she could read and write. This is evident from a few lines she sometimes added[90] in the letters. As such, it was within her reach to write letters of political importance to the Sardars for necessary actions. Besides, the vagueness of her letters and the guarded languge used therein give her the credit of being a shrewed diplomat who always avoided coming to the forefront. The present of an elephant to the Siddis of Janjira can be counted as the way she tried to pacify her opponents and win their goodwill. This was more desirable at the time, as it provided favourable atmosphere to Bajirao to move northwards. Moreover, there is nothing to presume that she had ill feeling towards any one, much less towards the women of Chhatrapati's house, from whom she appears to have kept at a respectable distance. She was greatly respected by the people and served the cause of her family for thirty years by active participation in the state affairs till her death on 20th March, 1753 A.D.

REFERENCES

1. *Itihas Sangraha* – Aitihasik Sphut Lekh, Pustak-2, November, 1909, Article-4, p. 43.
2. *Peshwayanchi Bakhar*, p. 1
   Khare, W.W. – *Ichchalkaranji Sansthan Ch Itihas*, p. 26.
3. *Peshwyanchi Bakhar*, p. 9.
4. Parasnis, D.B. – *Life of Brahmendraswami*, p. 9.
5. *Ibid.*
6. *Patre Yadi Vagere*, L.N. 495, p. 489.
7. *Varshik Itivrutta Shak* 1834, pp. 200, 209.
8. S.P.D. Vol. VII L.N. 1, 6.

14. B.I.S.M. – Pethe Daftar, L.Ns. 1, 2, 10.
15. *Patre Yadi Vagere*, L.N. 494, p. 486.
16. *Ibid.*
17. Khare, W.W. – *Ichchalkaranji Sansthan ch Itihas*, p. 28.
18. *S.P.D.* Vol. XXXI, L.N. 112.
19. Khafi Khan – Muntakhabu-L-Lubab, *H.I.H.*, Vol. VII, p. 468.
    Rajwade, V.K., Khand IV, p. 36.
20. Rajwade, V.K., Khand IV, pp. 37-38.
    Shahu Roznishi, No. 8 (pp. 42, 43).
21. Khafi Khan – Muntakhabu-L-Lubab, *H.I.H.*, Vol. VII, p. 468.
    Patre Yadi Vagere, L.N. 494, p. 486.
22. Khafi Khan – Muntakhabu-L-Lubab, *H.I.H.*, Vol. VII, p. 515.
23. *S.P.D.* Vol. XXX, L.N. 24.
    Muhammad Kasim – "Ibratnama", *H.I.H.*, Vol. VII, p. 573.
24. *S.P.D.* Vol. XXX, L.N. 265.
25. Chitnis, K. – *Life of Shahu Maharaj*, p. 71.
    Grant Duff – *History of Marathas*, Vol. I, p. 373.
26. Riyasat, Vol. V – *Punya Shlok Shahu, Peshwa Bajirao*, p. 35.
27. Irvine, W.W. – *Later Moghuls*, Vol. II, p. 165.
28. *S.P.D.* Vol. X, L.Nos. 5, 6, 7, 11.
29. Grant Duff – *History of Marathas*, Vol. I, p. 419.
30. *S.P.D.* Vol. IX, L.No. 5.
31. Paranis, D.B. – *Life of Brahmendraswami*, p. 38.
32. *Ibid.*, p.22
33. *Ibid.*, p. 20.
34. *Balaji Bajirao Roznishi*, pp. 226-228.
35. *Maathir-Ul-Umara*, Vol. II, p. 961.
36. *S.P.D.* Vol. XV, L.N. 86.
37. *S.P.D.* Vol. XXX, L.N. 70.
38. Mastani's whereabouts are shrouded in mystery. The opinions of the historians differ on this point. The available accounts show that she belonged to a class of professional Muslim dancers. A few writers are of view that she was presented to the Peshwa by Shujatkhan.

    Peshwyanchi Bakhar mentions that she was a mistress of Shujatkhan who was in command of the imperial forces in Central India about [illegible] A.D. Chimnaji Appa surprised Shujatkhan in a battle at Kapadwanj. Along with other things, he also found

Mastani. Later, he presented her to Bajirao. She became his mistress

Itihas Sangraha mentions that she was the daughter of Raja Chhatrasal of Bundelkhand by a Muslim mistress. As known, Bajirao had helped him against Mohd. Khan Bangash in 1730 A.D. As a return for his help, he presented her to Bajirao.

Still others state that she was the daughter of Champatrai, father of Chhatrasal. She preferred to be with the Peshwa Bajirao.

S.P.D. Vol. IX, L.No. 36 :

The letter states about one Miskin Mastan Kalawant (मिसकींणा मस्ताना कलावत). According to Dr. M.M. D.V. Potdar, "it leads one very strongly to identify this person with the famous Mastani," – *Bajirao in the famous land of Bundelas*, p. 8. However, it is yet very difficult to establish that she was in any way related to him. *Tarikh-i-Muhammadshahi*, Vol. I, p. 413 :
"She was a Kanchani (a dancing girl), possessing fine horsemanship and skill in handling the sword and the spear. She always accompanied Bajirao in his campaigns and rode stirrup to stirrup with him".

39. Kincaid, C.A., & Parasnis, D.B. – *A History of the Maratha People*, Vol. II, p. 176.
40. *S.P.D.* Vol. XXX, L.N. 90.
    Sardesai, G.S. – *New History of the Marathas*, Vol. II, p. 143.
41. *S.P.D.* Vol. IX, L.N. 7.
42. *S.P.D.* Vol. XXX, L.N. 90.
43. *S.P.D.* Vol. XXX, L.Nos. 32, 104.
44. Riyasat, Vol. V, *Punya Shlok Shahu, Peshwa Bajirao*, pp. 261, 264.
45. Irvine, W.W. – *Later Moghuls*, Vol. II, p. 275.
    Raghubirsingh – *Malwa in Transition*, p. 222.
46. *Ibid.*, p. 231.
47. *Ibid.*, p. 231.

In this connection, it is worthwhile to note that during the scuffle for power between the Peshwa Balaji Bajirao and Tarabai in 1750-51 A.D., there was rumour that the Peshwa had brought a boy and kept him at Avaji Kavdey's Wada to enthrone him as a King. Sambhaji of Kolhapur also came to know about him, as he was interested in Satara politics. He got the news verified. According to the messenger, the boy, who was at Avaji Kavdey's Wada, was about 22 years old (*S.P.D.* Vol. VI, L.N. 200). It should be remembered that, when Radhabai had visited Jaisingh in 1735 A.D., she had fondly caressed one of the sons of Jaisingh, who was five years old or so; that is to say that if he was five years old then, he should not be less than 20 and more than 23 years of age in the year 1750 A.D. As such, the age of the boy corroborates the information verified by the messenger. But whether he was the same boy is difficult to ascertain in absence of suitable evidence.

54. Raghuvirsingh – *Malwa in Transition*, Vol. 1, p. 235.
55. *Ibid.*
56. *Ibid.*, p. 237.
57. Sarkar, J. – *Fall of the Moghul Empire*, pp. 260, 262.
   Annals and Antiquities of Rajasthan, Vol. I, p. 440.
58. *S.P.D.* Vol. XIV, L.N. 50.
59. Refer p. 282, F.N. No. 2.
60. Raghuvirsingh – *Malwa in Transition*, Vol. I, p. 240.
61. Irvine, W.W. – *Later Moghuls*, Vol. II, p. 285
62. *S.P.D.* Vol. XV, pp. 92, 93, 95, 96 :
   The demands were :
   (1) Hereditary estate under the crown.
   (2) Grants of Mansab for himself and his chiefs.
   Cessation of hostilities against his armies.
   (3) The office of Sar-deshpande of the Deccan.
   (4) An indemnity to meet the war expenses.
   (5) He desired to see the Emperor in the Court.
   (6) To levy tribute in Orchha, Datia, Narwar, Chanderi, Bhadawar, Kota, Bundi, [illegible].
63. *S.P.D.* Vol. IX, L.N. 32.
64. Riyasat, Vol. V – *Punya Shlok Shahu, Peshwa Bajirao*, p. 409.
65. *S.P.D.* Vol. XXX, L.N. 334.
   S.P.D. Vol. [illegible], Nos. 30, 31, 32, 33.

66. *Itihas Sangraha*, Aitihasik Charcha, Lekhank 1, 2, pp. 9, 10.
67. *Peshwyanchi Bakhar*, pp. 29, 30.
68. *Itihas Sangraha*, Aitihasik Charcha, Lekhank 4, p. 12.
69. *S.P.D.* Vol. IX, L.N. 34.
70. *S.P.D.* Vol. IX, L.N. 32.
71. *Itihas Sangraha*, Aitihasik Charcha, Lekhank 3 (F.N.), p. 11.
72. *P.D.* Vol. I, L.Nos. 138, 139.
73. *S.P.D.* Vol. XV, L.N. 84.
74. *P.D.* Vol. I, L.N. 426.
    Patre Yadi Vagere, L.N. 489, p. 458.
75. Kincaid, C.A., & Parasnis, D.B. – *A History of the Maratha People*, Vol. II, p. 266.
76. *Ibid.*, p. 266.
77. *Itihas Sangraha*, Aitihasik Charcha, Lekhank 4, p. 12 :
    Mastani died at the Shanwar Palace. One of the gates of this place is still called after her. She was buried at Pabal. The neighbouring villages of Kendur and Loni had been granted to her. — (*Poona Gazetteer*).
78. *Patre Yadi Vagere*, L.N. 489, p. 458.
79. *P.D.* Vol. I, L.N. 426.
80. Parasnis, D.B. – *Life of Brahmendraswami*, L.N. 23.
81. Sardesai, G.S. – *New History of the Marathas*, Vol. II, p. 258.
82. *Patre Yadi Vagere*, L.N. 47.
83. *S.P.D.* Vol. IX, L.N. 40.
    S.P.D. Vol. XXVIII, L.N. 22.
84. *S.P.D.* Vol. IX, L.N. 40.
85. Refer p. 213, F.N. No. 3.
86. *Baroda State Records*, Vol. I, L.No. 40 (7-3-1751).
87. Kincaid, C.A., & Parasnis, D.B. – *A History of the Maratha People*, Vol. III, p. 9.
88. *S.P.D.* Vol. VI, L.N. 163, p. 146 :
    - मातोश्री तोरणा चा पदर तुमची फाषि तोरणार
    Kincaid, C.A., & Parasnis, D.B. – *A History of the Maratha People*,

CHAPTER 7

UMABAI DABHADE

Centrifugal Power Politics (1728-1752 A.D.)

An important adjunct of the Maratha politics had been the clash between the most outstanding Peshwa of the Maratha history, Bajirao I, and Umabai Dabhade, wife of Senapati. This clash was the recrystalization of the struggle for power between Senapati and the Peshwa Bajirao-I, and later on with his son Balaji Bajirao with the House of Senapati.

While Tarabai and Radhabai were participating in the affairs of their respective families and the state, Umabai Dabhade played an eventful role at Gujarat and influenced the political trends of the period between 1728 and 1752 A.D. She hailed[1] from a renowned Maratha family of Thoke Sardars of Abhone. She was the daughter of Ambhorkar, and was married to Khanderao Dabhade who had served Sambhaji and followed Rajaram[2] in his flight from Raigad to Jinji in 1689 A.D. During Khanderao's sojourn at Jinji his mother had received[3] the Mouza of Dhamne at the time of the birth of a son to Rajaram. Rajaram was also grateful to him for his creditable services and granted[4] to him the Taluka of Induri, Chakan and Junnar in Talegaon as his hereditary possession. Since the days of Shivaji, the finances of the Maratha state mainly depended[5] on Chouth and Sardeshmukhi and money collected through military campaigns. In 1705 A.D., on the instruction of Ramchandrapant who was looking after Maratha [illegible] Maharashtra when Rajaram was in far

Later on Khanderao Dabhade, by his valour and sincerity gained the confidence of Raja Shahu. He and his son Trimbakrao Dabhade, were made[6] Senapati and Sena-Khas-khel respectively in 1717 A.D. Umabai received[7] the villages of Bahje and Kurle. Khanderao Dabhade maintained good terms with Peshwa Balaji Vishwanath and each had regard for the other. Khanderao Dabhade had actively participated in military campaigns with Balaji Vishwanath. Hence, after the death of Peshwa Balaji Vishwanath, Khanderao aspired for the Peshwaship but this position was given[8] to Balaji's son, Bajirao, who was only 20 years of age and other senior Sardars resented the preferential treatment of Shahu to Bajirao but they remained quiet for the time being as they did not possess the strength and power to challenge the decision of Shahu. Although Khanderao Dhabade remained silent, Umabai could not remain quiet and expressed[9] her dissatisfaction on the decision of Shahu to appoint Bajirao as Peshwa fearlessly whenever she got a chance to do so. Moreover, at this juncture a feud was coming up between old nobility and the Peshwa. This old nobility and the Sardars considered[10] themselves equal to Peshwa and demanded the same respect from him as he expected from them. Among such Sardars Kanhoji Angre and Dabhades were prominent.

Bajirao was not slow to perceive the disgruntled feeling in the senapati Khanderao Dabhade. He considered Khanderao as a danger for his safety and well being and hence, he adopted a definite policy to ignore the Senapati whenever he was undertaking any important campaign. This attitude of Peshwa Bajirao made Senapati Dhabade cautious in his relations with Peshwas and since he was not in a position to challenge him openly, he reconciled[11] himself with indifference to the new situation, more due to his approaching old age. He began to concern himself more in his own sphere of influence at Gujarat and Baglan.

At this time, Nizam-ul-Mulk had proceeded[12] to south, much against[13] the desire of the Moghul Emperor, to establish his sway in the Deccan. He wanted to be away from the gay court life of the Moghuls. He sought the help of Hamidkhan, Deputy of Gujarat and the Marathas and promised to the Marathas the grant of Chouth and Sardeshmukhi in lieu of their support. At this juncture Chimnaji Appa used to receive the half share of Gujarat revenue on behalf of the Peshwa. But Shahu issued[14] an order by which Senapati Khanderao Dabhade was now to receive the full revenue of Gujarat but despite this arrangement, Gujarat proved[15] to be a happy hunting ground for ravages and plunders, of various Marathas Sardars. The Maratha revenue officials were seen everywhere, demanding[16] their claims.

Khanderao Dabhade was quite advanced in age and hence died on 27th September, 1729 A.D. His eldest son, Trimbakrao Dabhade, got the robes[17] of Senapati on 8th January, 1730 A.D. He was a sturdy soldier, but was an inexperienced man. Umabai, though afflicted, had to take an active part in the administration of Gujarat and Maratha politics in order to safeguard the interests of her family.

This was the time when Peshwa Bajirao decided his northward penetration[18] for the annexation of more territory. For this it was necessary to have his sway over Malwa due to its strategical position. He asked[19] Trimbakrao Dabhade to give him half share in Gujarat revenue. In lieu, he promised to give Dabhade half share of Malwa revenue when he would get control over that territory. However, Trimbakrao disagreed to this proposal and said that he would not ask for any share in Malwa revenue. Bajirao and Chimnaji were totally dissatisfied with this reply of Dabhade and formed[20] a plan to enter Malwa through Gujarat. It was decided that Chimnaji Appa would follow the western route through Baglan and Khandesh while Bajirao was to march from the eastern side through Ahmadnagar, Berar, Chanda and Devagad via Bundelkhand.

which her family possessed. She added that she would also be sending the dues of the year to Shahu. At the same time, she took precautions[23] not to allow anybody's army to march through her territory without her permission. Looking at this political crisis between Dabhades and the Peshwa, Shahu called Krishnaji Dabhade to see him personally.

However, Chimnaji Appa marched through Baglan to defeat[24] Raja Girdhar Bahadur, the Moghul Deputy at Malwa, and his confidant, Darya Bahadur. In the battle of Amjhra[25], fought between them on Nov., 1728 A.D. Raja Girdhar Bahadur lost[26] his life. Chimnaji Appa sent the news of his victory to Bajirao, who congratulated him and asked him to march on to realize money from Ujjain and Malwa. Many Sardars sent their good wishes to Chimnaji Appa on his victory.

Umabai Dabhade was aggrieved at the attitude of the Peshwa and Chimnaji Appa and continued to communicate with the king directly.

Whether the Peshwa had really the authority to pass through the territory of Dabhade is difficult to conclude because of serious political conditions. Yet the consequences were not favourable to the Dabhades. This is further apparent from the Peshwa's action, who exercised his will in spite of the repeated protests from Umabai. Besides, Shahu's quiet attitude gives rise to the presumption that either he was not informed of the situation or did not like to meddle in the activities of the Peshwa.

However, the feelings between the Peshwa and the Dabhades were further strained after the death of Khanderao Dabhade on 27th September, 1729 A.D. At such a critical time for the Dabhades, Chimnaji Appa entered Gujarat in 1730 A.D. forcibly. He claimed[27] a half share in Gujarat revenues from Sarbulandkhan, the governor of Gujarat, on the plea that he had a right to the same from 1728 A.D. Senapati Trimbakrao Dabhade and his mother, Umabai, did not agree to his claim. During this time, Malharji Holkar, Ranoji Shinde and Anandrao Powar carried on their ravages in the Pargana of Sultanpur.

Chimnaji Appa informed[28] Bajirao that he apprehended a conflict with the Dabhades. Bajirao also came to know about the complaints[29] that had been lodged against him to the king. Umabai was worried because of the activities of Chimnaji Appa at Nevasa, Gandapur and Valumy. He was also collecting sums from the areas. After some time, he was successful in having his claim for Chouth accepted[30] by Sarbulandkhan.

The Moghul Emperor viewed these events in the Deccan with concern and anxiety. He appears to have realized the failure of Sarbulandkhan in checking the Maratha ravages and to have come to feel the expansionist[31] move of the Marathas. He called Sarbulandkhan back, and appointed[32] Maharaja Abaisingh Rathor of Jodhpur in his place in October, 1730 A.D.

The repeated efforts of Umabai and Trimbakrao Dabhade to bring the action of the Peshwa and his brother Chimnaji Appa to the notice of the king failed to attract his attention. The Dabhades felt that Shahu, because of his deteriorating financial position, did not like to interefere with the Peshwa's activities or wanted to reign with least resistance. Meanwhile, Bajirao had concluded[33] a pact with Abhaisingh and had established his authority to collect Chouth from Gujarat.

Obviously, this was not expected by the Dabhades. Accounts show that they were anxious to safeguard their own interest. Therefore, they got themselves prepared to meet any situation. This is apparent from their efforts to reconcile[34] different Maratha Sardars. Umabai had also been to Ranola and met Kanthaji Kadam to evoke his support. Thereafter, she had returned to Navapur.

Meanwhile, Avaji Kavdev took her Thanas[35] as well as two hundred and fifty horses. She was greatly annoyed. She wanted [illegible] the Peshwa. She left Songad, where

He informed[36] the Peshwa that he had met the Dabhades and the Gaekwad also. From them, he had come to know that Umabai was anxious to go on 'Mohim' or 'Swari' with Chimnaji Appa. She also wanted to have the title of Sena Khas-Khel. She was also prepared to bear the expenses that would be incurred by Chimnaji Appa and Naro Gangadhar in the campaigns. But the accounts show that even then the situation for Umabai and her sons had not changed.

At this time, the only contenders for power in the Deccan were Bajirao and the Nizam-ul-Mulk. The Nizam-ul-Mulk had won[37] over the support of Sambhaji of Kolhapur. Meanwhile, the Sardars who supported Dabhades tried to negotiate with the Nizam-ul-Mulk. It would not have been at all difficult for him to secure Dabhades' support, as they were already an aggrieved party. But Umabai had not[38] yet joined him. Besides, the Nizam-ul-Mulk informed Umabai that unless she directly dealt with him, he was not going to believe her Sardars, either Pilaji Gaekwad or Kanthaji Kadam Bande.

Shahu did not like that bitterness should crop up between the Senapati and the Peshwa. He tried to effect a reconciliation[39] between them. He sent Naro Ram (Mantri) and Ambaji Purandare to Talegoan. He met the Dabhades, and informed[40] the Peshwa that the women of the Dabhade family were adamant not to visit the king, more because of the fate of the village Lohaner where Bajirao had carried on his ravages. Communicating other details, he asked the Peshwa to be careful lest any unpleasantness should crop up among the Maratha Sardars which might be harmful to his interests. He warned him, and said that the territory under him extended as far as Khandesh, Baglan and Surat. If any more territory is taken, it would result in a great turmoil. The Sardars would join hands with the enemies. He also advised him not to rely on the Dabhades as they were rather untrustworthy.

Shahu still hoped that the Peshwa and the Senapati would soon come to an understanding. But Chimnaji Appa said,[41] "If

Dabhade creates trouble for us, we are quite equal to stopping him from doing mischief, but if he goes over and joins the Nizam, Your Highness must not hesitate to deprive him of the office of the Senapati." As known, Shahu had tried for reconciliation, but the Dabhades had not come to Satara. Thus, much time was wasted in correspondence, etc.

Accounts indicate that Nizam-ul-Mulk intended to restore[42] Sambhaji of Kolhapur on the Satara throne and to give the position of Senapati to Umabai. The Moghul Emperor was aware[43] of the constant ravages by the Marathas in Gujarat and other parts of northern Deccan. He appointed[44] Mohd. Khan Bangash as Subedar of Malwa in December, 1730 A.D. to oust the Marathas from the region and to weaken the Nizam-ul-Mulk. As known, Mohd. Khan Bangash was one of the most determined enemies of the Peshwas. He met[45] Nizam-ul-Mulk at Akbarpur. The Moghul Emperor suspected his sincerity, and apprehended more trouble from them if they both co-operated. Taking into consideration all facts together, it can be said that while the Moghul Emperor was looking to his own stability and the welfare of the Empire, Bajirao was anxious for Maratha expansion. Meanwhile, Nizam-ul-Mulk and Dabhades were keen to further their own interests. They were also supported by Sambhaji of Kolhapur.

Bajirao apprehended trouble from the Dabhades and their supporters, but waited till the position of the Dabhades was quite awkward because of differences among their ownselves.

However, Shahu still hoped to pacify them. He had sent[46] Naro Ram and Naro Gangadhar to bring the Dabhades to Satara, but the mission was not successful. Meanwhile, Bajirao made his position secure with the king as well as with the Moghul Em[illegible] who never desired a strong opponent in Ni[illegible] Marathas were now more tolerabl[illegible] also won over Abhaisin[illegible]

Nex[illegible]

Dabhades one after the other. Notable among them were Bhausinh Thoke of Mandawe, Dalpatrao Thoke of Abhone and Kuwar Bahadur Deshmukh of Sinnar. The Thoke Sardars were the family members of Umabai. As such, they had been staunch supporters of the Dabhades. Therefore, their having been won over by the Peshwa, disgusted Umabai and Trimbakrao Dabhade. They were enraged and could not keep quiet.

The Dabhades had already prepared themselves to meet the Peshwa. Later on, he was joined by the contingents of Nizam-ul-Mulk, Gaekwad and Bande with an army of Kolis and Bhils. His army marched[48] towards Dabhoi. Shahu was alarmed. He never desired to harm either the Peshwa or the Senapati. As such he cancelled[49] the grant of share of Gujarat revenues to the Peshwa, which Umabai had all along demanded but it was too late. It is mentioned that "the Peshwa did not at once give effect to this order and waited for the course of action." That such an important message was not communicated to Umabai is rather strange and speaks of the resolute action of Bajirao. He did not delay the battle, and marched towards Gujarat. He was supported by veterans like Pilaji Jadhav, Ranoji Sindhia, Holkar, Sardar Dhamdhere and others. It is said that the Dabhades had 50,000 soldiers while the Peshwa had only 25,000.

The armies of the Peshwa and the Dabhades met[50] at the field of Thawai near Dabhoi on 1st April, 1731 A.D. The Senapati fought valiantly. It appeared that Bajirao would not be able to win the battle easily. Most of the Sardars lost[51] their lives on both sides. Meanwhile, Bhausingh Thoke who had gone over to Bajirao reached[52] near Trimbakrao Dabhade on some pretext. While both of them were engaged in a talk, a musket from Bhausingh Thoke hit[53] Trimbakrao Dabhade. He died instantly. His death decided the battle in favour[54] of the Peshwa. Later, Shahu defined[55] the boundaries of Malwa and Gujarat. He passed orders that half the revenue of each province should be paid direct to the royal treasury by the Peshwa.

Bajirao, though successful, fled[56] to Shahu. He was closely pursued by Dabhade brothers, Yashwantrao and Baban, who were determined to kill him. Bajirao begged[57] mercy from Shahu. He mediated and pacified the Dabhades. They returned, but warned the Peshwa to face the consequences.

The news of the death of Trimbakrao Dabhade shocked Umabai Dabhade and Shahu alike. Dr. H.N. Sinha writes[58], "Shahu was smitten with remorse and did all that he could to effect a reconciliation" between the Dabhades and the Peshwa. While Shahu could reconcile himself because of his magnanimity of heart, Umabai could not forget and forgive. Bakhars state that the sad plight of the lady attracted the attention of the king. He proceeded[59] towards Talegoan and brought Umabai to Satara. But a more reliable account mentions[60] that Umabai and Yashwantrao visited Shahu after the death of Trimbakrao Dabhade. It is mentioned[61] that the king handed over a sword to Umabai and, presenting Bajirao before her, asked her to avenge the death of her son if she so desired. Bajirao begged her to excuse him on a promise of any compensation. The grief stricken lady did nothing, and excused him. But the later events and accounts show that she could not keep her word for long.

Yashwantrao, younger son of Umabai, received the robes[62] of Senapati from the king. Different accounts mention that he was incompetent to handle different situations tactfully. Hence Umabai had to continue her hold in the different activities of the Senapati. Henceforth, she had to rely more on Sardar Pilaji Gaekwad and later on his son, Damaji Gaekwad. Shahu never pressed Umabai to pay the half share of Gujarat revenues to him as had been laid down in the Dabhoi treaty.

Further, accounts show that Pilaji Gaekwad wanted to join Nizam-ul-Mulk along with other Sardars. But Umabai was not prepared to join him. She ordered them to return[63] immediately to their respective places. Nizam-ul-Mulk was not prepared to enter into any understanding unless Umabai communicated to him.

Meanwhile, differences[64] had cropped up in Umabai's camp. Baburao Dabhade had differences with his brothers. Damaji Gaekwad was not keen to pay the dues of the king. Umabai was rather serious for the payment. Dissatisfied, Baburao had gone to Haldwani and Umabai had proceeded to Warsaw. Umabai managed to borrow money which was to be paid to the king and sent the dues to the Pratinidhi through Udoji Pant for payment to Shahu.

As known, the Peshwa had also made arrangements to realise revenues from Gujarat, Malwa and Khandesh. To attain this, he had effected[65] a division between the Sardars, Sindhia, Holkar and Pawar. Similarly, Kanthaji Kadam, Santaji, Raghuji, Pilaji Jadhav and others were to realize[66] revenue from Khandesh. The Peshwa's agent, Dhondoram, in Khandesh and Naroshanker in Malwa were relied upon to send the same to the Peshwa.

Meanwhile, Umabai, as if in remorse and being desperate, carried on her ravages in Gujarat. She harassed[67] the officials and realized the revenues not only from the above areas but also from the "Moglai Prant". The Peshwa's Sardar, Dhondoram, informed Bajirao that he could not realize amount from Kanthaji Kadam, Santaji, Raghuji, Pilaji Gaekwad and others. Similarly, Malharrao Holkar had not been able to check her predatory activities. He asked[68] the Peshwa to persuade Umabai to return at once the horses and all that she had plundered and taken away from the village Ozar, Tehsil Dindori. It is mentioned that she had rebuked Naroshanker and had retorted, "I was able to take revenge but could not, so even if you write to Bajirao, it will be of no use."[69]

Thus the respective areas experienced confusion and chaos. Meanwhile, Abhaisingh thought to enter Gujarat by swoop in Dawda and Dabhoi. He invited Pilaji Gaekwad on some pretext and assassinated[70] him. He also attacked his forces all of a sudden on 23rd March, 1732 A.D. The Marathas were routed and defeated.

from campaigns). Further, Baburao set[80] fire to the 'Peth' of Songad and the country was devastated. Meanwhile, Damaji Gaekwad had quarrelled with Dabhades and captured the fort (probably of Songad). Krishnaji Dabhade apprehended some trouble, because of the shortage of finances. He had taken shelter at Songad fort. Krishnaji Dabhade requested Chimnaji Appa to save the 'Mokasa' from destruction in his northward journey through Khandesh.[81]

Shahu did not like the rebellious attitude of Baburao Dabhade. He asked the Peshwa to take action[82] against him. However, Yashwantrao Dabhade requested the Peshwa to excuse his brother and see that he did not indulge in harmful activities again[83]. Afterwards, Umabai was more amiable[84] to Chimnaji Appa. She had not sent the dues of the king, as is indicated[85] by Visaji Bhikaji's letter to Chimnaji Appa. He had also informed that Umabai had not been able to collect the revenue, though she wanted to pay the full amount. She wanted two months' time to pay the full amount. The money was kept at Songad, and could not be got over unless orders were given for the same. He added, "It is heard that Damaji Gaekwad has returned and is coming towards Wadnagar and Vishalnagar. If he goes towards Ahmadnagar, I will go with him along with Umabai's clerk to get the work done." He further added that the financial condition in Umabai's camp was not at all satisfactory. She was handicapped badly, so much so that even a day's meal in her army (Lashkar) was difficult to arrange. Such was the state to which she was reduced.[86] However, she had issued stern orders[87] to Damaji Gaekwad to pay the king's dues. She also informed Chimnaji Appa that as he had been overwhelmed with orders, he was finding it difficult to carry out the same. However, she promised that the money would be sent to him on his (Damaji Gaekwad's) return.

As if to meet the expenses, Umabai took[88] the possession of the Thana of Nasik from Abdul Aziz Khan. She took 10,000 rupees from Sadashiv and gave him the possession of the Thana.

Further she collected ten khandis of grain from Vani tract and 4,000 rupees. She sent out 1000 horsemen towards Khandesh. They created disturbances in many places. Bhagres and Dighes lived[89] near Avada and Patta forts. Umabai called a few of them, presented robes and golden bangles to them and sent them to the forts for secret services. She had also moved towards Khandesh to capture a few places.

It was also apparent that Umabai did not like to annoy the Peshwa. She was prepared to act to his satisfaction, provided her difficulties regarding finances (revenues) were solved. Kacheshwarbaba had come from Satara to take her to the court. Umabai had also written a letter to the Peshwa and awaited his reply.

As known, Visaji Bhikaji's main object was to realize the revenue dues from Umabai. He also informed the Peshwa about the events taking place at Dabhades'. Besides, the above accounts show that the Peshwa was anxious to know the relations that existed among Umabai, her sons and Damaji Gaekwad. Meanwhile, Baburao Dabhade laid siege[90] to Haldani. Umabai was in a difficult situation. The writer advised the Peshwa to help Umabai Dabhade, which alone will enable her to maintain her position (sardari). People at the Dabhades' were anxious to know whether the Peshwa would help and chastise the unruly servant (Damaji Gaekwad).

However, Umabai Dabhade was also anxious to know about the intentions of the Peshwa. She was anxious to know why Govindpant was with Damaji Gaekwad. Umabai received the information that he was there to know only the intention of Damaji Gaekwad. Henceforth, she was satisfied and remained quiet.

Umabai Dabhade was at Navapur[91] with her lashkar. Krishnaji Dabhade and Kaloji Bhonsle had gone to Damaji Gaekwad. She had received a letter from the Peshwa. It appears that he had put certain terms[92] to Umabai which she had not accepted. At the same time, Damaji Gaekwad and the Dabhades wanted to meet each other. The writer informed the Peshwa that he would communicate to him other details of the probable meeting between Damaji Gaekwad and Umabai Dabhade. However, they did not[93] come to terms easily, though they reconciled[94] after some time and thought over the situation that existed. Damaji Gaekwad agreed to pay her 50 lakhs of rupees and paid 5 lakhs immediately. It was decided that the king's dues would be sent within a week, positively. The dues amounted to eleven lakhs of rupees. Damaji Gaekwad presented two elephants and other gifts to her. Umabai Dabhade also honoured him by giving him robes and an elephant.

The reconciliation between Damaji Gaekwad and Umabai Dabhade shows that she had successfully handled the difficult situation in order to maintain the welfare of her family. Once again, Umabai and Damaji Gaekwad had their own plans to further their interest. However, she had not sent the remaining[95] dues. Meanwhile, the financial condition went on deteriorating in Umabai's camp. The Shilledars of Baburao's forces had not received any amount. Great disturbances followed in his camp as they had become quite unruly. It was now difficult for Baburao Dabhade, to escape from the fort Haldani. Umabai and Devji could only bring him to Songad tactfully. Umabai had become quite desperate. She sent her soldiers towards Khandesh.

Baburao Dabhade proceeded[96] to Dahevalli. Umabai Dabhade and Senapati were also there. Accounts show that the local creditors as well as the army of Baburao Dabhade wanted to have the amount paid to them. However, Umabai adjusted the debts by part payments. She paid to Antoba Naik, Dado Hari and Krishnarao Mahadeo, one third of the amount to each of them. While she had to pay Rs.47,500, she paid only Rs.21,000, and issued a Hundi to Damaji Gaekwd to pay the rest of the amount. The writer said that if Damaji Gaekwad accepted the Hundi, he would accept it. She had similarly paid off to other creditors. The writer demanded[97] from her the arrears also. She sternly replied that he should accept what she had given and she would pay more if it was possible for her to do so.

Umabai Dabhade had to bear another shock, as Baburao Dabhade, Sena Khas Khel, died[98] on 5th December, 1736 A.D. It was decided that Yashwantrao Dabhade's son would receive his position, for which arrangemnts were soon made.

As mentioned, Radhabai had returned[99] from her northern tours in 1736 A.D. Bajirao had started[100] for north, and, because his demands were not fulfilled by the Moghul Emperor, he had started devastating Moghul territory at Agra and Doab. Next, he proceeded towards north-east. Chimnaji Appa inquired of Umabai about the position of different Sardars at Ahmadabad. Umabai cordially[101] replied that Renkoji Annaji had marched with 5,000 and 10,000 forces and had laid siege to Ahmadabad. Damaji Gaekwad had also gone to collect money from Surat to meet the expenses.

Meanwhile, Umabai was anxious to know where Bajirao was at the time. Once more the situation for Umabai was favourable. She started her ravages and captured territories. She came near the fort of Patta and compelled[102] the Patel of many villages to pay her hundred rupees as revenue. She had taken[103] Adagad and besieged Songad. She continued to say that the Peshwa had seized her thirty-two Parganas and Baglan. She replied[104] that she had not taken any Thana except the three which belonged to her. She gave out that she was prepared to leave these Thanas if the Peshwa left her Thanas in Khandesh. She also said that she had not stationed her army anywhere permanently and was prepared to withdraw if the Peshwa removed his forces from such areas.

. Bajirao moved towards Khandesh. He thought of befriending[105] Nasirjung. He wanted that Umabai Dabhade should vacate the Thanas of Ankola and Vani and let the Moglai be collected by the Peshwa. Umabai insisted that it was really surprising that he (Chimnaji Appa) should be anxious for two or three thanas that she possessed. Thus, she tried to keep her Thanas.

After Bajirao's death in 1740 A.D., there was apparent change in Umabai's attitude towards the Peshwa Balaji Bajirao. She did not indulge in carrying out the ravages so resolutely as she had done till then. The Dabhades apprehended an attack by the Nizam-ul-Mulk on Surat in 1748 A.D. She sought the support of the Peshwa to face him. Balaji agreed[106] to help her if she would give half of Gujarat to him. Umabai did not accept the proposal, and retorted that the Peshwa should not speak anything about Gujarat. If money was required, it would be sent. However, the death of Nizam-ul-Mulk in 1748 A.D. subsided the tension, and she was now relieved from her anxieties.

As known, the king had not taken any strong measure against her, even though her ravages and plunder had disturbed the peace of the State sometimes. However, after the death of Shahu, Balaji, being in need of finances, asked Umabai to pay the revenue of Gujarat.

Umabai refused to pay it on the plea that she had never paid half share of Gujarat revenues. She maintained that the Mokasa of Gujarat was given to the Dabhades by the king. She tried that the Peshwa should accept her point of view. She sent her Agent, Yado Mahadeo Nirgude, to the Peshwa, who pleaded[107] her claim. The Peshwa was not prepared to accept it. Moreover, Balaji wanted his Kamavisdars to collect revenue with him from Gujarat. Yado Mahadeo Nirgude did not like this, and he returned without taking dresses from the Peshwa. Still Umabai had not lost hopes of pacifying the Peshwa. It is mentioned,[108] "Unwilling to rebel if she could attain her ends by other means, she demanded and obtained an interview with the Peshwa."

Umabai met[109] the Peshwa before 22nd November, 1750 A.D., at Alandi. "She pleaded her sons' rights and repudiated the terms imposed on them after Dabhoi." On the other hand, the Peshwa was adamant[110] in his demands to realize the revenue from Gujarat. Greatly disappointed, she returned.

It was evident that Umabai had only two courses to adopt in

the circumstances. One was to accept the demands of the Peshwa, and the other was to fight against him in a battle. With her discomfiture, she resolved to take a decisive action to uphold her cause in conjunction with Tarabai. As mentioned, Umabai and Tarabai prepared themselves to defeat the Peshwa. The Gujarat army, under the command of Damaji Gaekwad, marched towards Poona and Satara in March, 1751 A.D. Open battles were fought and reverses were taken. The decisive phase of the battle was reached on the 30th April, 1751 A.D. The Peshwa, in spite of the armistic, swooped[111] on Gujarat forces. The Gujarat army was taken by surprise. Damaji Gaekwad and his son, Khanderao, as well as Umabai, her son, Yashwantrao Dabhade, and Ramchandra Baswant were captured. On 16th May, 1751 A.D., Umabai and others were taken to Holkarvada[112] and kept there under strict surveillance. But on no account did Damaji Gaekwad accept to cede half of Gujarat to the Peshwa.

At last, the Peshwa approached Khanderao Gaekwad. He abandoned the cause of the Dabhades, and consented[113] to accept the conditions laid down by the Peshwa. However, he asked the Peshwa to give a sufficient amount to the Dabhades to enable them to maintain their dignity.

In return, Damaji Gaekwad received the title of Sena-Khas-Khel. The Peshwa managed to get the claim of fifteen lakhs of rupees, besides half of Gujarat with all future conquests from the Dabhades.

Umabai saw, with disgust, the eclipsed power of her house. Needless to say that she and her family had to face poverty and disappointment. But no account mentions that she ever complained about it either to the Gaekwad or to the Peshwa.

Thus, Umabai's career was a strange conglomeration of climaxes and anti-climaxes. She played her role first alone and then with Tarabai. Her activities showed that she was resolute, scheming and arduous in her behaviour. Fearlessly, she carried on her ravages and plunders. She had proceeded on "Mulukgiri", realized revenues and established Thanas with much inconvenience to the Sardars, the Peshwa and the king. At the same time, she had to face a critical situation at home. On occasions, Umabai, Damaji Gaekwad and her sons disagreed among themselves. Damaji Gaekwad also pushed his own interest in Shahu's court. The Peshwa tried to win both Umabai and Damaji Gaekwad separately. This was a serious and immediate danger to the maintenance of solidarity and stability of her house. However, Umabai succeeded in pacifying Damaji Gaekwad and also her sons. Once more, they united in spite of personal differences. This shows that she possessed a wonderful pliancy for manipulation when it was the need of the hour.

She provided courage and a will to fight amongst odds, and commanded her supporters in the face of perilous dangers. But even these qualities could not further the cause of the Marathas and the Maratha state, as she was not prepared to part with half of Gujarat. Finally, she was defeated. She died in 1753 A.D., after seeing her house fade into insignificance.

REFERENCES

1. Sardesai, G.S. – *New History of The Marathas*, Vo. II, p. 128.
2. B.I.S.M. – *Senapati Dabhade Daftar*, Bhag I, L.N. 13.
3. *Ibid.*, L.N. 8.
   Dighe, V.G. – *Peshwa Bajirao and Maratha Expansion*, p. 24.
   Family tradition says that Shivaji Dabhade collapsed while carrying the royal fugitivies back to Maharashtra. His father escorted the ladies but was unable to rescue his own family from the doomed place. On his arrival in Maharashtra in 1699 A.D., Rajaram honoured his faithful servant with the command of a Paga and the dignity of Sena Khas Khel.
4. B.I.S.M. – *Senapati Dabhade Daftar*, Bhag I, L.N. 4.
5. Sen. S.N. – *Administrative system of the Maratha* pp. 205, 206.
6. Hakikat, P. 6. *Shahu Roznishi*, p. 150.
7. B.I.S.M. – *Senapati Dabhade Daftar*, Bhag I, L.N. 27.
8. *Patre Yadi Vagere*, L.N. 491, p. 474.

9. *S.P.D.* Vol. XII, L.No. 26.
10. Sen. S.N. – *Administrative system of the Marathas* p. 205.
11. *S.P.D.* Vol. XII, L.N. 5, 8.
12. Irvine, W.W. – *Later Moghuls*, Vol. II, p. 143.
    Indian Historical Records Commission Proceedings, Vol. XIV, p. 108.
13. Ferishta – *History of Dekkan*, Vol. II, p. 187.
14. *Shahu Roznish*, No. 159; *Hakikat*, p. 8.
15. *S.P.D.* Vol. XXX, L.N. 312.
16. Irvine, W.W., *Later Moghuls*, Vol. II, p. 199.
17. B.I.S.M. – *Senapati Dabhade Daftar*, Bhag I, L.N. 71.
18. *S.P.D.* Vol. XIII, L.N. 3.
19. *Hakkikat*, p. 8.
20. *S.P.D.* Vol. XIII, L.N. 22.
    Sardesai, G.S. – *New History of The Marathas*, Vo. II, p. 102.
21. *S.P.D.* Vol. XII, L.N. 16.
22. *Ibid.*, L.N. 18.
23. *Ibid.*
24. *S.P.D.* Vol. XIII, L.N. 5, 7.
25. *Ibid.*, L.N. 27.
26. Ali Ibrahim Khan – Tarikh-I-Ibrahimkhan, *H.I.H.*, Vol.VIII, p. 261.
27. Riyasat, Vol. V – *Punya Shlok Shahu, Peshwa Bajirao*, p. 185.
28. *S.P.D.* Vol. XII, L.N. 39.
29. *Ibid.* 116.
30. Riyasat, Vol. V – *Punya Shlok Shahu, Peshwa Bajirao*, p. 185.
31. *Annals and Antiquities of Rajasthan*, Vol. I, p.324.
32. Irvine, W.W., *Later Moghuls*, Vol. II, p. 203.
33. Dighe, V.G., *Peshwa Bajirao and Maratha Expansion*, pp. 36, 37.
34. *S.P.D.* Vol. XII, L.N. 37.
35. *Ibid.*, L.N. 41.
36. *Ibid.*, L.N. 41.
37. *Indian Historical Records Commission, Proceedings*, Vol. XIV, p. 111.
38. *S.P.D.* Vol. XII, L.N. 44.
39. *S.P.D.* Vol. XII, L.N. 42
40. *Ibid.*
41. Sardesai, G.S. – *New History of The Marathas*, Vol. II, p. 124.
42. *S.P.D.* Vol. X, L.N. 61

43. Khafi Khan – Muntakhabu-L-Lubab, *H.I.H.*, Vol. VII, pp. 525, 529.
44. Irvine, W.W. – *Later Moghuls*, Vol. II, p. 249.
45. *Ibid.*, p. 251.
46. *S.P.D.* Vol. XII, L.Ns. 41, 42.
47. Sardesai, G.S. – *New History of The Marathas*, Vo. II, p. 123.
48. *S.P.D.* Vol. XII, L.N. 46.
49. *Ibid.*, L.N. 299.
50. *Baroda State Records*, L.Ns. 12, 13.
    Hakikat, p. 9.
51. Parasnis, D.B., *Life of Brahmendraswami*, L.No. 26.
52. *Hakikat*, p. 9, 10.
53. B.I.S.M., *Senapati Dabhade Daftar*, Bhag I, p. 74 (F.N.)
54. *S.P.D.* Vol. XII, L.N. 46.
55. Kincaid, C.A., & Parasnis, D.B. – *A History of the Maratha People*, Vol. II, p. 194.
56. *Hakikat*, p. 10.
57. *Ibid.*
58. Sinha, H.N. – *Rise of the Peshwas*, p. 101.
59. Sardesai, G.S. – *New History of The Marathas*, Vo. II, p. 129.
60. *S.P.D.* Vol. XII, L.N. 49.
61. *Hakikat*, p. 9.
62. *Shahu Roznishi*, No. 155 (14).
    B.I.S.M. – *Senapati Dabhade Daftar*, Bhag I, L.N. 73.
63. *S.P.D.* Vol. XII, L.N. 47.
64. *Ibid.*, 52.
65, *S.P.D.* Vol. XXX, L.N. 320, pp. 319, 320.
66. *S.P.D.* Vol. XVII, L.N. 29.
67. *S.P.D.* Vol. XII, L.N. 58 :
    Letters addressed both to Bajirao and Chimnaji Appa by Naroshanker in service of Malharrao Holkar: "Umabai has plundered the area and wanted to come to village 'Amba', Pargana Dindori, but I took care to save it." He also said that she should not act as she did, because she was also in the service of the king.
68. *S.P.D.* Vol. XII, L.N. 58.
69. *Ibid.*
70. *Shahu Roznishi*, No. 161; Watson, J.W. – *History of Guzerat*, p. 110.

71. Watson, J.W. – *History of Guzerat*, p. 111.
72. Dighe, V.G. – *Peshwa Bajirao and Maratha Expansion*, p. 41.
73. *S.P.D.* Vol. XII, L.N. 57.
74. *Ibid.*, L.N. 65.
75. *Ibid.*, L.N. 67.
76. *Ibid.*, L.N. 68.
77. *Ibid.*
78. *Ibid.*, L.N. 72.
79. *Ibid.*, L.N. 72.
80. *Ibid.*
81. *Ibid.*. 73.
82. *Ibid.*, L.N. 75.
83. *Ibid.*, L.N. 78.
84. *Ibid.*, L.N. 80.
85. *Ibid.*, L.N. 81.
86. *Ibid.*
87. *Ibid.*, L.N. 82.
88. *Ibid.*, L.N. 84.
89. *Ibid.*
90. *Ibid.*, L.N. 85.
91. *Ibid.*, L.N. 86.
92. *Ibid.*
93. *Ibid.*, L.N. 86.
94. *Ibid.*, L.N. 87.
95. *Ibid.*, L.N. 89.
96. *Ibid.*, L.N. 90.
97. *Ibid.*
98. *S.P.D.* Vol. XII, L.N. 93.
    Ibid., L.N. 95.
99. Refer, p. 199.
100. Refer. p. 199, F.N. No. 3.
101. *S.P.D.* Vol. XII, L.N. 98.
102. *Ibid.*, L.N. 103.
103. *Ibid.*, L.N. 104.
104. *Ibid.*, L.N. 105.
105. *Ibid.*
106. *Patre Yadi Vagere*, L.Nos. 65, 68.
107. Kincaid, C.A., & Parasnis, D.B. – *A History of the Maratha People*, Vol. III, p. 3.

108. Kincaid, C.A., & Parasnis, D.B. – *A History of the Maratha People*, Vol. III, p. 3.
109. *P.D.* Vol. I, L.N. 239.
110. *Ibid.*, L.N. 265 :
     "Umabai is always talking about money matters. She is not ready to deliver part of Gujarat. We have come to decision that Umabai's case is to be decided on the strength of sword."
111. *Baroda State Records*, L.N. 40.
     Watson, J.W. – *History of Guzerat*, p. 138.
112. Riyasat – *Peshwa Bajirao*, p. 80.
113. Watson, J.W. – *History of Guzerat*, p. 138.

Conclusion

This study reveals that the Maratha women actively participated in the affairs of the state during the period 1620-1752 A.D. They distinguished themselves in administration, especially in the field of revenue supervision. In times of crises, for the state or the family they provided leadership. However, sometimes their participation in the affairs of the state, especially with regard to succession issues, created complications as is evident from the career of Tarabai.

Jijabai who played foremost role in the foundation of the Maratha state despite being a traditional woman, boldly faced the mental tormentation by the blood dispute between her parental and husband's family as a result of the "Elephant Episode". Although, afflicted by the treacherous murder of her father Lukhji Jaduavrao, she marched with her husband Shahji from fort to fort during his struggle with Moghuls in 1633 A.D., with her three year old son Shivaji. This reflected her dauntless character in face of grave adversity.

Jijabai was also a visionary and she always had the dream to see the foundation of a Maratha State in order to save the women and the temples from the onslaught of the oppressors. When she was asked by Shahji to manage the ancestral Jagir of Poona and while he was proceeding on campaigns in the south, she utilised the opportunity to sow the seed of Maratha State guided by the inspiration from the saints like Tukaram and Ramdass who by their devotional preachings caused a renaissance, "a pressage of a political revolution in the country." This had brought in an atmosphere of social and spiritual cohesion strengthened by "Pandharpur movement" in different Marathi speaking classes. Jijabai was not unaffected by it.

She devoted herself to nurture the ancestral Jagir entrusted to her for her son Shivaji who was to play a vital role in the realization of a vision of an Independent Maratha State. This Jagir was to be the foundation of future Maratha power, hence Jijabai began to play a notable role in revenue administration, specially in the field of land distribution and land tenure. She was keen to see that her orders were properly executed. Once she asked Dadaji to revise his decision in the light of her suggestions.

She issued 'Kaulnama' (Ajynapatra) to remedy any injustice done to any one. Her participation in the administration was a boon to the people, as she paid due attention to their progress, encouraged cultivation, donated lands and established 'Peths' (Bazzar). They were not to suffer any inconvenience at the hands of the estate officers. Her benevolence was not limited to any community or religion as she continued the vatans of Masjids and Darghas. Her tolerant attitude also influenced Shivaji. The confidence of the people which she enjoyed for her capacity to manage the state efficiently, is also explicitly indicated from the fact that the people did not allow her to commit 'Sati' after the death of Shahji in 1664 A.D., and pleaded, "What would become of the kingdom? 'Raje' cannot manage it."

As for the role of women as military leaders during the crises, facing the state or the family, Jijabai again acquires prominence. She accompanied Shivaji on Purandar Siege. During Panhalla Siege, she sent reinforcement from Rajgad to Panhalla as the Marathas were fighting on two fronts, Panhalla, where Shivaji was carrying on defence, and was besieged by the combined armies of the Bijapur king, the Moghuls, the English and the Siddis of Janjira. Jijabai had stationed herself at Rajgad and was looking to its defence. At one stage, the crucial state of defence at Panhalla, made the Senapati Netaji Palkar and Siddi Hillal to rush to Jijabai and inform her about the dangerous situation in which Shivaji was cornered by the combined forces of the enemy.

Jiiabai, on being informed not only snubbed them for leaving

Shivaji in the precarious condition and declared that she would personally march to Panhalla and see that Siddi Jauhar, the arch enemy of the Marathas is not only killed but would bring his chopped off head with her, while they (Siddi Hillal and Netaji Palkar) were to remain at Rajgad to defend it. The determined effort and courage at the age of about sixty years, was well replied by them, as they promised to do the needful and marched toward Panhalla, with new zeal, courage and hope. Jijabai, however, was not required to proceed to Panhalla.

Shivaji's coronation in 1674 A.D.; indicates that Shivaji and Jijabai had carved out a sound, worthy, politico-geographical entity by their steadfast effort, her guidance, sharp grasping power and undaunted courage.

Soyarabai the queen of Shivaji, although gained prominence after Jijabai, yet the homogenity, that had prevailed in the house of Shivaji could not remains so.

To build a state and to consolidate it was a hard task because Shivaji found himself in a precarious condition socially, financially and politically among the clamouring sardars who were on the look out to gain power, no sooner an opportunity arose. During this predicament Soyarabai was the only person who shared his worries and anxieties. This has brought on her the charge of influencing Shivaji in "Succession-Issue", "Karnatak Expedition", and "Posion-Episode".

Despite, the charges, the available evidence does not warrant or justify the charges which have been brought by the writers against Soyarabai either in "Succession-Issue", which falls flat as Shivaji never declared his successor or "Karnatak-Expedition" which was olitical necessity or "Poison-Episode". At the most, the poison de was a figment of imagination and a blemish on Soyarabai's chara ter that died a natural death after exterminating its innocent victim. The charges seem to be merely excuses that were concocted by the sardars, a result of the "feudal game at play".

Yesubai, the queen of Sambhaji, son of Shivaji had to fa

rather a critical situation due to the terror created by Sambhaji, who got possession of Raigad on the 18th June, 1680 A.D., after a strenuous effort and a series of adjustments, whereby he had to put under arrest a few of the most influential Sardars. His fear complex compelled him to start his career with an ordeal of horror and cruelty the impact of which was felt vigorously which was only minimized by the "angelic part of Yesubai." That she was quite interested in the welfare of people and administration of the state is amply evident by her reaction after the execution of Balaji Abaji, the Sachiv of the Maratha state. So much was the repugnance felt by her that she questioned Sambhaji, "you have killed Balaji Prabhu. It is not well. Even Shivaji Maharaj had fully confided in him. Besides, he had done nothing wrong. How could you act like a child? All karkoons are dead more by your injustice. All have gone one by one. How will kingdom be managed?" Apprehending further trouble, she took the Sikka (The Royal Seal) from Sambhaji, which brought no objection from Sambhaji shows that she enjoyed the confidence of her husband.

The tradition laid by Jijabai in the field of administration was continued by Yesubai, though in a limited way because of the struggle of Sambhaji against the Moghuls, the Portuguese and the Siddis of Janjira. During the absence of Sambhaji on his campaigns, Yesubai ably looked after the "Mulki-Arrangements". She had a seal of her own with words, "Sakhi Ragjne Jayate", and also "Ajrakhta Sou. Yesubai," inscribed on it. She equally paid attention to the religious and social festivities is evident from her letter to Diwakari Gosavi of Chaphal. Even in her Moghul captivity, she appears to have been the Deshmukh of certain villages and had the seal with the words, "Yesubai Walida Raja Shah."

It is interesting to note that the Maratha state had been ably served by these two women administrators during its early days.

The role of Tarabai in Maratha politics after the death of Rajaram and till 1708 A.D. is an example of military leadership provided by women to the Maratha state during crises. She resisted the persistent attack of the Moghul Emperor Aurangzeb who wanted to take advantage of the atmosphere prevailing in the Maratha camp after the death of Rajaram, she fought against the Moghuls at Satara, Panhalla, Vishalgad and other forts, she was defeated, and had to leave the forts to renew the struggle at a more appropriate time. In this way she could maintain the independence of the Marathas from 1700 to 1707 A.D., that is for seven years continuously against Aurangzeb; the most astute of the Moghul Emperors. However, her role from 1744-45 A.D., onwards did not prove conclusive to the interest of the Marathas.

Another important aspect of the role of women, especially of Tarabai, in Maratha politics was their deep interest in "Succession issues". In this respect Yesubai holds a prominent place. Her role kept the Marathas united after the execution of Sambhaji in 1689 A.D. when the Moghuls tried to defeat them. She allowed Rajaram to come in forefront and as such, he was made the regent and Shahu was declared Chhatrapati. She refused to be a regent, as suggested by a few Sardars.

The role of Tarabai in succession issues, created many complications, and later, it was not to the interest of the Maratha State. She participated with an ambition to keep power with her. Her refusal to accept Shahu as an heir to the Maratha throne divided the Marathas in two different camps. Her swift opposition to Shahu finally led to the establishment of the Kolhapur branch which could not be united with the Satara House and thus remained a constant source of anxiety to Shahu and his successor. She again got an opportunity to participate in the succession issue about 1744-45 A.D. She suggested to Shahu to accept Ramraja as his successor he being a decendant of Maloji Bhonsle, but when Ramraja agreed to the "Sangola Pact", she declared him an imposter, because this acceptance of the fact was contrary to her ambition.

The roles of Sakwarbai and Sagunabai, queens of Shahu, in Maratha politics brings out an aspect of court politics under any method was considered to be fair for the sake of achieving political ambitions. It is in this context that Sakwarbai had been subject to severe charges like the "Succession issue" and "Financial stringency" at Satara Court and palace but at the same time it also appears that much against her was being fabricated to protect the interest of the appirants of Sakwarbai and Sagunabai.

Virubai, the mistress of Shahu was capable, intelligent and none had anything to say against her. She continued to have regard from Shahu and his queens Sakwarbai and Sagunabai, not only in the palace but in foreign court also as is evident by the letter of British agent Captain Gorden from Bombay. Shahu lost her valuable services after her death in 1740 A.D.

Radhabai, mother of Bajirao, also took a sober interest in the politics of the day, and did her best to enhance the power and the prestige of her family. It is noteworthy that she never participated in any active campaign like Tarabai, Umabai and others. She kept herself aware of the intricacies of the politics of the day, which is evident from her communications to various sardars and Brahmendraswami and also from her suggestions to Bajirao not to proceed and meet Nizam-ul-Mulk unless he was accompanied by trusted Sardars and arrangements for full security were made. She had the quality to win over the goodwill of others, which strengthened the cause of her family. She was farsighted and could realize the need of Rajput cooperation for which she made her own efforts in her modest way.

Another Maratha woman who took to active warfare to safeguard the interest of her family was Umabai Dabhade of Gujarat. She did not fight aganist any foreign power. She resorted to arms to settle her disputes with Peshwas Bajirao and Balaji Bajirao who were interested in Gujarat, and as such, the interest of the Peshwas clashed with her interest, she showed exemplary courage and astute military leadership on the battlefield. More than once, she compelled her opponents to retreat. She also maintained unity in her house when her sons quarrelled among themselves and Damaji Gaekwad pushed his own interest in Shahu's, Court.

As such, it can be concluded that the Maratha women were politically conscious, well-versed in administration and provided good leadership on the battlefield. They participated in the succession-issue with varying results. The role of Yesubai was congenial while that of Tarabai proved detrimental to the Maratha State.

Appendix I

Rajwade, V.K. Khand I, pp.232-233, L.N. 367 :

The letter begins with the words,

अब, रा, बाबाजी भोंसले - कारकून व मोकदम कसबें ग्रेड गोंऊ पा। पाडेपडे गोऊ..................।

They were the Watandars of Arvi, Dewilgoan, Hingne, Pedgaon, Wadgoan and Shivpur.

Bhimsen Burhanpuri – *The Journal of Bundela Officers*, (Persian Sources)

The episode and incidents corroborate Marathi texts.

B.I.S.M. – *Shiva Charitra Sahitya*, Khand II, L.N. 23.

दास मालोजी बाबाजी व दास विठोणी बाबाजी

This inscription is in the temple of Grishneshwar, and it appears that it must have been removed and put on the compound walls later when Ahilyabai reconstructed the same temple.

Prof. Hodiwala – *Studies in Indo-Muslim History*, Vol.I, p.61.

Sabhasad – *Life of Shivaji*, p.1.

Ferishta – *History of Dekkan*, Vol.II, p.4.

A New Account of East India and Persia, p.171 :

"Valentyne apparently derived his information about Shivaji's ancestry from John Fryer, who says Seva-GI, derived from an ancient line of Rajas of the cast of Bounceloes, a warlike and active offspring." (*F.B.S.* p.480).

Khafi Khan – Muntakhabu-l-Lubab, *H.I.H.*, Vol.VII, p.254:

"His (Shivaji's) ancestors owe their origin to the line of the Ranas of Chitor."

Maathir-ul-Umara, p.783:

"Dadaji Bhonsle, one of the Raja's ancestors, was the head of the villages of Hakmi, Burhi, Devalgoan and the lower area of the Pargana of Poona."

Kincaid, C.A. & Parasnis, D.B. – *A History of the Maratha People*, Vol.I, p.112:

"His family claims descent from Sajjansinh, the grandson of Laxmansinh, the ancestor of the house of Udaipur. One of the family, Devraji by name, is mentioned as Kakaji, a name not to be found in Kolhapur genealogical tree, after a quarrel with Rana of Udaipur, fled to Deccan. There his descendants assumed the name of Bhonsle, from the family of 'Bhosavat' of Udaipur."

(F.N., p.113)

We believe in the genealogy from Babaji and onwards, but we have got no evidence to say anything regarding Babaji's father or the origin of the family.

Bakhars believe that they are from Sisodia family. M.M. Gaurishankar Ojha, in the *History of Rajasthan*, says that Bhonsles and the Udaipur dynasty are the same, but he has not given any authentic source to prove it. Curiously enough, the instances of manners, customs, the observation of festivals, Shiv-Puja, war cry, marriage alliances in different Gotras, are found to be observed in the family of the Bhonsles.

There is also a village named Bhonsle or Bhonsa, near Verul, district Aurangabad. From it, the name 'Bhonsle' might have been derived. One Bhonsle family still resides there.

Shiv-Bharat, Adhyay I, Shloks 42-43:

दक्षिणस्यां दिशि श्रीमान मालवर्मा नरेश्वरः।
वमूण वंशे सूर्यस्य स्वयं सूर्य हवोज सा।।42।।
महाराष्ट्रं जनपद महाराष्ट्रस्ये भूमिपः।
प्रशशास प्रसन्नात्मा निजधर्मधुरन्धरः।।43।।

Thus, it is clear that Maloji had no reason to serve as guards at Lukhji Jadhavrao's, as mentioned in Bakhars and other secondary accounts like *Vividh Gyan Vistar*, Varsh 60, August 1929, Ank 8, 91 Kalami Bakhars, Kalam IV, pp.6, 7, 8; Forrest – *Letters, Despatches and other Papers*, Vol.I, and other compilations. Besides, the above accounts have not been supported either by original or other authentic sources.

Appendix II

लेखांक 67 1608 फाल्गुन वण 11 अस्सल मोडी

रघुनाथ

श्री सू

खी राज्ञो

जयती

ई कोलनामें सौभाग्यवती राणजी वाई साहेब दामदौलत वजामीव मुकाम स्थल चाफल क माणेघोल सु सबा सन हजार 1096 समानेन अलफ दिल्हे अभयेपत्र ऐसे श्री देवाजी यात्रा आसी आहे यावेस लोक यावयास अनमान करीताती की आपने लोक दांडी वरून यात्रेस तसवीस देतील ऐसीयास अमयेपत्र अलियाने +++++++ देवाचा मोहछाये करीतील लणोन हुजूर मालूम जाले त्यावरून यात्रेस अभयेपत्र दिले आहे आमचे तर्फेने कोणी वाटे जाणार नाहीं गावोगावी कागव पाठऊन यात्रा करी बोलाऊन श्री जा समारमं करणे आभचे अभये जसे व मौजे मजकुरीचे सीगणवाडी श्री जे इनाम स्थल आहे जैसे सालावाद चालिले आहे तेणे प्रमाणें आपले ही पत्र पाहिजे लणोन राजश्री माघव गोसवी यानिं सांगीतले तेरी आमचे ही अभयेपत्र आहे देवाचे हनाम स्थल तुमचे अध्येन आहे आमचे तर्फेने आजार लागणार नाहीं मार्तव सुद देवाचा प्रसाद पाठवीला तो आलास पावला म।

मोर्स

ब सुद

तेरीख 24 माहे रविलाखर

Appendix III

From Raja Shahu to his Peshwa

It is hereby ordered that you should command the whole forces. I gave orders to every one else to do this, but none was destined to hold the post. We are ill and are afraid that we shall not recover. The government of the empire must be carried on. Someone of our relatives must continue the dynasty. But bring no one from Kolhapur. We have told everything to the Chitnis. He will tell you our wishes. Act accordingly. Be loyal and obedient to the descendants of our house and maintain the court and the nobles. The Chitnis is our faithful servant. In consultations with him preserve our kingdom. Our descendants will not interfere with your office. Be prudent and wise.

From Raja Shahu to R.R. Balaji Pradhan Pandit

We hereby state that we hope and believe that you will ably conduct the administration of this kingdom. The Chitnis, as I have already told you, is of proven loyalty. Our blessings rest on you. Our successors will continue you in office. Should our successors act otherwise, we hereby bind him with a solemn oath, and command him not to do so. Be obedient and loyal to him and protect our kingdom. Nothing more need be said. Be prudent and wise.

– Parasnis Papers.

– (Kincaid, C.A., & Parasnis, D.B., Vol.II, p.319)

Bibliography

Documentary Sources

Selections from the Peshwa Daftar

1. *Shahu's Campaign against the Siddis of Janjira* (1733-1736), Vol. III.
2. *Ramraja's Struggle for Power*, Vol. VI.
3. *Early Activities of Shahu and Balaji Vishwanath* (1707-1720), Vol. VII.
4. *Shahu in his Private Life*, Vol. VIII.
5. *Bajirao and his Family*, (1720-1740), Vol. IX.
6. *Early Strife between Bajirao and Nizam*, Vol. X.
7. *Shahu's Relations with Sambhaji of Kolhapur*, Vol. XI.
8. *The Dabhades and the Conquest of Gujarat*, Vol. XII.
9. *Bajirao's Entry into Malwa and Bundelkhand*, Vol. XIII.
10. *Maratha Conquest in North*, Vol. XXV.
11. *Bajirao's Advance upon Delhi*, Vol. XV.
12. *Shahu and Bajirao – Administrative*, Vol. XVIII.
13. *Private Life of Shahu and the Peshwa*s, Vol. XVIII.
14. *Balajirao Peshwa and the Events in the North* (1741-1761), Vol. XXI.
15. *Extracts from the Peshwa's Diaries*, Vol. XXII.
16. *Balaji Bajirao – Administrative*, Vol. XXIII.
17. *The Peshwa's Commitments on the West Coast*, Vol. XXIV.
18. *Balaji Bajirao Peshwa and the Nizam* (1740-1761), Vol. XX.
19. *Tarabai and Sambhaji*, (1738-1761), Vol. XXVI.
20. *Balajirao Peshwa and Events in the North – Supplementary*, (1741-1761), Vol. XXVII.
21. *Peshwa Balaji Karnatak Affairs*, 1740-1761, Vol. XXVIII.

22. *Miscellaneous Papers of Shahu and His First Two Peshwas*, Vol. XXX.
23. *Papers Selected from the Jamav Section*, Vol. XXXI.
24. *Miscellaneous Papers of Peshwa Balajirao*, Vol. XL.
25. *Document Illustrating Maratha Administration*, Vol. XLV.
26. *Shahu Chhatrapati*, Vol. I, Selection from the Satara Rajas' and the Peshwas' Diaries – Prepared by Rao Bahadur Ganesh Chimnaji Vad, B.A. Printed & Published by D.B. Parasnis, Sahasraskar Press, Satara.
27. *Balaji Bajirao Peshwa*, Vol. I, Prepared by K.W. Late Rao R.B.S.Vad, (1907) (Copy at B.I.S. Mandal, Poona).
28. Purandare, K.W. – *Purandare Daftar*, Vols. I & II, Publisher : Shripad Raghunath Rajguru, Poona (1929).
29. Rajwade, V.K. – *Marathyancha Itihassanchi Sadhane* – Vols. II, III, IV, VI, VIII, XV, XVIII, XX Publishers va Mudraka : S.R. Shankar Narhar Joshi, Chitra Press, Sadashiv Peth, Poona, (1928), (Copies at B.I.S. Mandal, Poona).
30. Vaidya, C.V. – *Vaidya Daftaratoon Niwadlele Kagad*, Khand 4 (From 1742 to 1749). Editor & Publisher : Shankar Laxman Vaidya, Poona, Shak 1817.
31. B.I.S.M. – Swiya Granthmala, Kramank 72, Shrimant Babasaheb Ichchalkaranjikar Smarak Granthmala Pethe Daftar, Bhag I, Pub : R.B. C.G. Karve, Sadashiv Peth, Poona 2, (1945).
32. B.I.S.M. – Quarterly Vol. 69, No.1-4, July 1990, April, 1991.
33. B.I.S.M. – Swiya Granthmala, Kramank 81, Senapati Dabhade Daftar, Bhag I, Editor : S.N. Joshi, Published by Chitnis, B.I.S. Mandal, Poona 2, (1951).
34. B.I.S.M. – Swiya Granthmala, Kramank 47, Shiv Charitra Sahitya, Vol. VII, Editor : G.H. Khare, Curator, B.I.S.Mandal, Poona, (1937).
35. *Aitihasik Patravyawahar*, Patre Wa Yadi, Editor : G.S. Sardesai, K.P.Kulkarni, Y.M. Kale, Publisher : S.R. Sardesai, Samarth Bharat Press, Poona 2 (1933).

36. *Shiv-Kaleen Patra Sar Sangraha*, Vols. I & II, Shri Shiv Charitra Karyalaya, Poona, (1930).
37. *Sambhaji-Kaleen Patra Sar Sangraha*, Editor: S.N. Joshi, Published by B.I.S. Mandal, Poona 2 (1949).
38. *Shri Sampradayachi Kagad Patre* (Ramdas-Ramdasi), Vol. IX, Published by Sat Karyauttejak Sabha, Dhulia.
39. Sardesai, G.S. – *Marathi Riyasat, Aitihasik Patrabodh*, Publisher : Keshav Bhikaji Dhawale, Mumbai 4.
40. *Selected Documents of Shahjehan's Reign*, Published by Daftar-i-Diwani, Hyderabad (1950).
41. *Selected Documents of Aurangzeb's Reign*, Government of Andhra Pradesh, Deccan (1958).
42. *Historical Selection from Baroda State Records*, Vol. I, 1724-1768, Baroda State Press, (1934), (Marathi and English).
43. *Selections from Letters, Despatches and Other State Papers*, preserved in the Bombay Secretariat, Government Central Press, Bombay.
44. *A Preliminary Report of the Historical Records at Goa.*

Original Narratives, Bakhara, Powades & Persian Sources

45. B.I.S.M. – *Purashkrut Granthmala*, Kramank 4, Shiv Charitra Pradee, Editor : D.V. Apte & S.M. Diwekar, Poona, Shak 1847.
46. B.I.S.M. – *Aitihasik* June Lekh, Chitnis Grarayachi Sanshipta Mahiti wa Sanada Patre, Published by Balkrishna Sukharam Kulkarni, Mumbai (1915).
47. Bendre, V.S. – *Rajaram Charitam Athwa Jinji cha Pravas*, Published by D.V. Potdar, Sardar G.N. Majumdar, M.L.A., Poona, (1931).
48. Chitnis, M.R. – *Shrimant Chhatrapati Sambhaji Maharaj Ani Rajaram Yanche Charitra*, Edited by Sane, R.B.K.N. (1915).
49. Kavindra Parmanand – *Shiv Bharat*, Editor Sadashiv Mahadeo Diwakar, Ganeshwadi, Mumbai 2 (1927).

50. Parmanandkavyam – *Gaekwad's Oriental Series* **CXX**, Edited by G.S. Sardesai, Oriental Institute, Baroda, (1952).
51. Khare W.W. – *Ichchalkaranji Sansthan cha Itihas Wa Ichchalkaranji Daftarateel Niwadak Patre wa Yadi*, Published by N.A. Draird, Aryabhushan Press, Poona (1913).
52. Kelkar, Y.N. – *Aitihasik Powade, Marathyancha Kavyamaya Itihas*, Vol. I, Vijaya Press & Ganesh Printing Press (1928) (Copy at B.I.S.Mandal, Poona).
53. *Kavya Itihas Sangraha Patre wa Yadi* (31). Published by Sane, R.B.K.N., Deccan College, Poona, Shak 1811.
54. Malhar-Khanderao – *Shahu Maharaj Yanche Bakhar* (Copy at B.I.S.Mandal, Poona).
55. Tapikar Shrikant – *Maharashtra Kille*. Published by Makarand Deo 154, Sahjiwan, Poona - 1987.
56. Paranis, D.B. – *Shri Mahapurush Brahmendraswami Dhawadshikar, Charitre wa Patravyawahar*, Published by Babaji Sakharam Ani Company, Yusuf Building, Bombay (1867).
57. Sabhasad – *Shiv Chhatrapati che Charitre*. Edited by Sane, R.B.K.N., Printed by Dravid, N.A., Poona (1912).
58. *Senapati Dabhade va Gaekwad Yanche Hakikat* (Kavya Itihas Sangraha - 20), Gyanprakash Chapkhanyat Chaplele, Shalivahan Sha, 1809.
59. Sohoni, K.V. – *Peshwyanchi Bakhar*, Published by Sane, R.B.N.K., IV Edition (History of the Peshwa Family, 1713-1818).
60. Deshpande, R.B. Babasaheb – *The Deliverance or the Escape of Shivaji, the Great, from Agra*, Published by Rao-Saheb G.K. Deshpande.
61. Irvine, W.W. – *Later Moghuls*, Vols. I & II, Edited & Augmented, Published by M.C. Sarkar & Sons, Calcutta, 1922.
62. Patwardhan, P.P. and Rawlinson, M.G. : *Source Book of Maratha History*, Vol. I, obtainable from the Supdt. Govt. Printing Press and Stationery, Bombay (1929).

63. Sen, S. – *Shiv Chhatrapati* (Extracts and Documents relating to Maratha History), Calcutta University Press.

Sen. S.– *Studies in Indian History*, Calcutta University Press.

Todd, J. – *Annals and Antiquities of Rajasthan*, Published by Hari Mohan Mukherjee (1877), Calcutta.

Persian

64. *History of India as told by Its Own Historians*, Vols. VI, VII, VIII. The Posthumus Papers of the Sir H.M. Elliot, K.C.B., Edited and continued by J. Dowson, M.R.A.S. London, Trubner & Co., 57 & 59, Ludgate Hill (1877).

65, *History of Dekkan* by Ferishta. From the First Muhammadan Conquests, comprised in six parts by Jonathan Scott. Vols. I & II, Printed by the Asiatic Society, Calcutta, (1952).

66. Maasir-i-Alamgiri – *Bibliotheca Indica*. A Collection of Oriental Works. A History of the Emperor Aurangzeb Alamgir by Saqi Must'ad Khan. Translated into English by Jadunath Sarkar, Kt. C.I.E. Printed by Royal Asiatic Society of Bengal, 1 Park Street, Calcutta, (1947).

67. Maathir-ul-Umara – *Bibliothica Indica* Work No.202. By Nawab Samsam-ud-Dawla & his son Abdul Hayy, Tr. by H. Beveridge, B.C.S. Annotated by Dr. Baini Prasad, Vols. I & II, Printed by Calcutta Oriental Press, Pub : Asiatic Society Ltd., Calcutta (1952).

68. *British Museum Persian Manuscript Sangrah*, Vol. I.

Hindi

69. *Virvinod – Marathon Ki Tawarikh* No.1593 (Personal Copy).

Foreign Sources

70. *English Records on Shivaji*, Published by N.C. Kelkar & D.V. Apte, Shiv Charitra Karyalaya, House No.312, Sadashiv Peth, Poona, (1931).

71. *Foreign Biographies of Shivaji*, Edited by S.N. Sen., The Book Company, Calcutta (1927).

72. *Historical Miscellany Series* No.31, Editors and Publishers : D.V. Potdar & G.N. Majumdar, Madras, (1928).
73. Manucci Nicollae – *Storia-d-Mogor*, Indian Text Series, Vols. III & IV, Published by John Murray, London, Alke Marble Street (1908).
74. Ormes – *Historical Fragments of The Moratoes and of the English Concerns in Indostan from the Near M.D.C. LIX*? Printed for C. Nourge in the Strand, M.D.C. LXXXII.
75. *Travels of Thevenot & Careri* Edited by S.N. Sen, Director of Archieves, Govt. of India, Published by the National Archieves of India, Queen's Way, New Delhi (1949).

Modern Works or Compilations
Marathi

76. B.I.S.M. – *Shiv Charitra Vrutta Sangraha*, Kramank 53, Khand III (Parsi Bibhag)? G.H.Khare (1941).
77. B.I.S.M. – *Shiv Charitra Vrutta Sangraha*, Kramank 47, (Kannadi Bibhag), Tr. P.B. Desai, M.A. (1938).
78. B.I.S.M. – *Poona Nagar Sanshodhak Vrutta*, Quarterly, Years 1 & 2, Poona, C.C. Karve (1942).
79. B.I.S.M. – *Mandal VI Sammelan Vrutta*, No.4, R. Vol. XV, (1920), Poona.
80. B.I.S.M. – *Swiya Granthmala* Kramank 44 – Shiv Kaleen Shakawali, Editor S.N. Joshi, (1937), Publishers : D.V. Potdar & G.N. Majumdar, Poona.
81. B.I.S.M. – *Swiya Granthmala* Kramank 69. Aitihasik Sankeerna Nibandh, Part I, (1947).
82. Apte, D.V. – *Mudhol Gharanyacha Itihas* (Bakhar Printed in Mudhol Ghorpade Gharanyacha Itihas), Pub : A.V. Patwardhan, Arya Bhooshan Press, Poona, (1934).
83. Sadashiv Martland Gorge – *Go. Ya.* Rane Prakashan Pune 9, 1968.
84. *Arvacheen Maharashtretihas-Kalanteel Rajyakar-bharacha* Abhyas, Part I (1600-1680), by S.N. Joshi, Pub : Poone Vidyapeeth (1959).

85. Bendre, V.S. – *Chhatrapat Sambhaji Maharaj*, Published by Bendre, W.C. 1227/4, Shivaji Nagar, Pune 4 (26th Jan., 1969).
86. Dhabu, D.G. – *Kulabkar Angre Sarkhel*, Published by D.G. Dhabu, Alibag, Kolaba, Shak 1861.
87. *Kaifiyat*: Yadis C. Vad, Rao-Bahadur Ganesh, Published by Puroshottam Vishram Mawjee, Alienation Offices, Poone.
88. *Mahamahopadhyaya Prof. D.V. Potdar Commemoration Volume*, Editor Dr. S.N.Sen, Published by D.K. Sathe, Poona, (1957).
89. *Madhyayugeen Charitra Kosh* From 321 B.C. to 1818 A.D., Published by Cidheshwar Chitnis, Bharatvarshiya Charitra Kosh Mandal, 58, Shanwar Peth, Pune 2.
90. *Maharashtriya Dhyan Kosh*, Vols. 1 to 23, Prepared by Shridhar Vyanktesh Ketkar, with the help of Mandal, Published by Maharashtriya Dhyankosh Mandal Ltd., Nagpur, 841, Sadashiv Peth, Pune.
91. Sardesai, G.S. – *Marathi Riyasat*, Vol. I, Shahji Bhonsle; Vol. II, Shak-Karta Shivaji; Vol. III, Ugra Prakriti Sambhaji; Vol. IV, Sthirbudhi Rajaram, V.V. Khare – *Aitihasik Lekh Sangraha*; Vol. 1-14. *Jadhav Gharanyachi Kafiyat* (B.I.S.M. Pune); *Treaties, Engagements and Sanads* (B.I.S.M. Pune); Vol. IV – Punya Shlok Shahu (Peshwa Balaji Vishwanath, 1707-1720); Vol. V – Punya Shlok Shahu (Peshwa Bajirao, 1720-1740); Vol. V – Punya Shlok Shahu Peshwa Bajirao Nanasahib (1740-1749); Vol. V – Punya Shlok Shahu Peshwa Bajirao Nanasahib (1740-1753); Vol. IX - Aitihasik Patraboth, Published by Keshav Bhikaji Dhawale, Shree Samarth Sadan, Benam Hall Lane, Girgaon, Bombay (1953).
92. *Shivaji Nibandhawali*, Anukram II, Part I, Published by C.Kelkar & D.V.Apte, Chitnis, Shree Shiv Charitra Karyalaya, 312, Sadashiv, Poona No.2, Shak 1851.
93. *Shivaji Charitra, Nibandhawali*, Anukram 2, Published by N.C. Kelkar & D.V. Apte, Chitnis, Shree Shiv Charitra Karyalaya, 312, Sadashiv, Poona, Shak 1851.

English

94. Ranade, H.G., Telang, K.T. – *Rise of the Maratha People & Other Essays & Gleanings from Maratha Chronicles*, Published by T.V.Chidambaram, Registrar, University of Bombay (1961).

95. Raghubir Singh — *Malwa in Transition*, D.B. Taraporwala Sons & Co., Bombay (1936).

96. *Sardesai Commemoration Volume*, Editor : Shripad R. Tikekar Dhawale, Bombay (1938).

97. Sardesai, G.S. – *The Main Currents of the Maratha History*, M.C. Sarkar & Co., Calcutta (1928).

98. Sardesai, G.S. – *Historical Genealogies*, Publisher : Bombay Govt. (1957).

99. Sardesai, G.S. – *Shivaji Souvenir*, Publisher : Kesho Bhikaji Dhawale, Girgaon, Bombay (1927).

100. Sardesai, G.S. – *New History of the Marathas*, 3 Vols., Published by X.B.Dhawale for Phoenix Publication, Chira Bazzar.

101. Sarkar, J.N. – *History of Shivaji* (Studies and Documents of Maratha History), Royal Period, S.C. Sarkar & Sons, Ltd., (1948) (Source Book as well as Compilation).

102. Sarkar, J.N. – *M.S. Jadunath Sarpa Collection.*

103. Sen. S.N. – *Military System of the Marathas*, Book Co. Ltd., Calcutta (1928).

104. Sen. S.N. – *Administrative System of the Marathas* (From Original Sources), Published by University of Calcutta (1925).

105. Sharma, S.R. – *Maratha History Reexamined*, Karnatak Publishing House, Bombay (1944).

106. Shrinivasanchari – *A History of Ginjee and Its Rulers*, Publishers : University of Annamalai (1943).

107. Sarkar, J. *Shivaji & His Times*, M.C.Sarkar & Sons, Calcutta, 1948.

108. Sarkar, J. – *History of Aurangzeb*, Volume III, IV & V, M.C. Sarkar & Sons, Calcutta, 1924.

109. Sarkar, J. – *House of Shivaji* (Studies and Documents of Maratha History Royal Period), S.C.Sarkar & Sons Ltd., Calcutta, 1948.

110. Sarkar, J. – *Anecdotes of Aurangzeb & Historical Essays* (Akham-i-Alamgiri, Persian Text with and English Translation), C.Sarkar & Sons, Calcutta, 1917.

111. Field Marshal Montogomery of Almien – *History of Warfare*, 1968.

112. *The Maratha Supremacy*, Editors R.C. Majumdar & V.G.Dighe : 1991, Bhartiya Vidhya Bhawan.

113. Sinha, H.N. – *Rise of the Peshwas*, Indian Press Ltd., Allahabad (1931).

114. Vaidya, C.V. – *The Founder of Maratha Swarajya*, Publisher : C.V. Vaidya, Poona (1931).

115. Watson, J.W. – *History of Gujerat*, Printed in Government Central Press, Bombay.

116. T.S.Shejwalkar, T.S. – *Vijay Nagar Samrajya*, Gaurav Granth.

Dutch

117. Dagh Register, Volume 29-A/Folio – 636, 5th May, 1660 A.D. (Vingurla Office Letter, Baravia).

Other Unpublished Sources

118. Account from Shri Bhaushastri Hadap of Pratapgad, (Thorugh the Courtesy of S.V.Avalaskar).

119. Volume of Published and unpublished Record, by V.S.Bendre (Volume at B.I.S.Mandal, Poona, 1959-60).

English Periodicals

120. Indian Historical Records Commission Proceedings, Vol. III; Vol. VII; Vol. VIII; Vol. X; Vol. XII; Vol. XIV; Vol. XVI; Vol. XVII; Vol. XVIII; Vol. XXIII & Vol. XXIV.

121. *Journal of the Indian History*, Vol. IX.

112. Modern Review, Vol. XXII; Vol. XXIV; Vol. XXV; Vol. XXVI & Vol. XXIX.

123. *Gazetteer*, Vol. XVIII, Part II, Bombay, 1885.
124. *Gazetteer, Kolhapur*, 1884.
125. *Gazetteer, Madras*, 1885.
126. *Gazetteer, Satara*, 1885.
127. *Imperial Gazetteer*, W.W. Hunter, Vols. III, IV & V.

Marathi Periodicals

128. Itihas Sangraha – Pracheen Maratha Sardars, Aitihasik Sphut Lekh, Aitihasik Charitre, Aitihasik Tippane, Aitihasik Charcha.
129. Bharatvarsh – Pant-Pratinidhichi Bakhar, Junya Aitihasik Goshti, Yadi Vagereh, Karvirkar, Raje va Tyache Striyan.
130. Bharat Itihasik Sahshodhak Mandal Varshik Ahwal or Ittivrutta and Quarterlies.
131. Vividh Gyan Vistar, Pustak 16, Ank 6, 21-7-1884; Pustak 24, Ank 2, 1-9-1892; Pustak 26, Ank, 3, 4; 10-10-1891; Varsh 52, January 1921, Ank 1 (Shiv Digvijaya, Tr. by S.N. Sen.); Varsh 52, Feb., 1921, Ank 2; Varsh 56, March, 1925, Ank 3; Varsh 60, June, 1929, Ank 6 and Varsh 60, August 1929, Ank 8 (Shiv Chhatrapati che Kalami Bakhar – 91 Kalam, 4 to 35).
132. *Navbharat*, June 1961 issue (Copy at B.I.S.M., Poona).
133. *Shivneri-Che-Sahal*.
134. *Pratapgrad-Che-Sahal*.
135. *Poramdar-Che-Sahal*.
136. *Raigad-Che-Sahal*.

INDEX